1989

POETRY AND PHANTASY

POETRY
AND PHANTASY

ANTONY EASTHOPE

Senior Lecturer in English,
Manchester Polytechnic

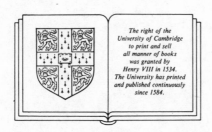

The right of the
University of Cambridge
to print and sell
all manner of books
was granted by
Henry VIII in 1534.
The University has printed
and published continuously
since 1584.

CAMBRIDGE UNIVERSITY PRESS

Cambridge
New York   New Rochelle
Melbourne   Sydney

Published by the Press Syndicate of the University of Cambridge
The Pitt Building, Trumpington Street, Cambridge CB2 1RP
32 East 57th Street, New York, NY 10022, USA
10 Stamford Road, Oakleigh, Melbourne 3166, Australia

First published 1989

Printed in Great Britain at
the University Press, Cambridge

British Library cataloguing in publication data
Easthope, Antony
Poetry and phantasy.
1. Poetry. Psychological aspects
1. Title
809.1′001′9

Library of Congress cataloguing in publication data
Easthope, Antony.
Poetry and phantasy / Antony Easthope.
p.   cm.
Bibliography.
Includes index.
ISBN 0 521 35598 2
1. English poetry – History and criticism. 2. Fantasy in
literature. 3. Psychoanalysis and literature. 4. Romance poetry –
History and criticism.   1. Title.   11. Title: Poetry and fantasy.
PR508.F36E27   1989
821′.009′15 – dc19   88-23437   CIP

ISBN 0 521 35598 2

CONTENTS

ACKNOWLEDGMENTS

A number of people have been good enough to comment on parts of this book as it was written. I am grateful to Andrew Collier, Stewart Crehan, Jonathan Dollimore, Elspeth Graham, Geoff Hodgson, Cora Kaplan, Alf Louvre, Toril Moi, Kate Scott, Alan Sinfield and John Storey for discussion from which I have learned a great deal. Terry Eagleton read an early version of the manuscript and his criticisms, equally frank and constructive, were a major encouragement.

Both Elizabeth Wright and John Drakakis were asked to read a completed manuscript and I would like to thank them for sympathetic, lucid and perceptive comments both in general and in detail.

As a main contribution I should like to acknowledge the work of those whose interest in psychoanalytic theory was fostered in different ways by their association with the film journal, *Screen*, and especially Catherine Belsey, Rob Lapsley, John O. Thompson and Michael Westlake. It remains the case that what goes into a book is one thing and what comes out is another.

Part of a draft of chapter 8 was printed in *English Studies*, 64, 4 (1983); a version of the analysis of *Paradise Lost* that appears in chapter 5 was published in *Southern Review*, 20, 1 (1987). The poem by J. V. Cunningham on p. 206 is reprinted with the kind permission of Ohio University Press.

Finally, I would like to thank the President and Fellows of Wolfson College, Oxford, for the award of a Charter Fellowship in 1985 which enabled me to continue my writing, and also my colleagues in the Department of English and History at Manchester Polytechnic for the support which allowed me to take that study leave.

POETRY AND PSYCHOANALYSIS

> Then as th'earths inward narrow crooked lanes
> Do purge sea waters fretfull salt away,
> I thought, if I could draw my paines,
> Through Rimes vexation, I should them allay.
> John Donne, 'The Triple Foole'

A strip of parchment, part of MS Rawlinson D.913 in the Bodleian Library, contains twelve medieval lyrics. One of these is now called 'The Maiden in the Moor'. It was a popular, secular song, and has been dated as between 1330 and 1360 (see list of texts). The text is very much a modern construction, the manuscript giving it in prose and without spelling out the repetitions after the second verse. 'Well' means good, 'mete' means food, the 'primerole' is the primrose; 'chelde' is not chilled but a Southern form for cold; 'welle spring' is 'not a "well" in the modern sense (which would suggest human habitation) but the source of a stream'; 'bour' does not imply a place closed with foliage but means simply a lady's chamber (Burrow 1977, p. 3):

> Maiden in the mor lay,
> In the mor lay,
> Sevenight fulle ant a –
> Sevenight fulle ant a –
> Maiden in the mor lay,
> In the mor lay,
> Sevenights fulle ant a day.
>
> Well was hir mete,
> What was hir mete?
> The primerole ant the –
> The primerole ant the –
> Well was hir mete,
> What was hir mete?
> The primerole ant the violet.

> Well was hir dring,
> What was hir dring?
> The chelde water of the –
> The chelde water of the –
> Well was hir dring,
> What was hir dring?
> The chelde water of the welle spring.

> Well was hir bour,
> What was hir bour?
> The rede rose ant the –
> The rede rose ant the –
> Well was hir bour,
> What was hir bour?
> The red rose ant the lilie flour.

The poem does not fit together. Why should a virgin live on a moor for a week? And why should the text, having told us three times that it was a week, suddenly add it was a week and a day? Why should she eat primroses and violets, and how can these be good food? We can understand drinking springwater as good (it is now marketed in expensive bottles, even in Britain) but it is disconcerting that her 'bour' or bedroom should turn out to be red roses and lilies. And what about the form of the poem, the questions and answers which stay alive now only in the oral tradition of schoolchildren? It begins with a statement in verse one but, after starting verse two with a statement, moves without anticipation into a question ('What was hir mete?'), half answers the question, repeats the statement and the question, and then completes the answer to the question. Even if this is simply an oral convention, incremental repetition,

> The chelde water of the –
> The chelde water of the –
> . . .
> The chelde water of the welle spring,

the uncompleted meaning or *aposiopesis* becomes a kind of innuendo which leaves other *words*, unspoken words, floating in the gap opened up before the closure of the last line. What words?

After remarking how open the text is, D. W. Robertson says it 'makes perfectly good sense' if it is given a patristic reading, in terms of the teaching and symbolism of the Church fathers ('the number seven indicates life on earth', 1950, p. 27). E. Talbot Donaldson cites Robertson's interpretation but says 'I cannot find that the poem, as a poem, makes any more "sense" after exegesis than it did before'

(1970, p. 151). A reading which drew on the psychoanalytic tradition would be able to suggest two lines for inquiry. One might propose that nature and landscape in the poem represent the maternal body (in dreams, 'landscapes . . . are invariably the genitals of the dreamer's mother', Freud *SE* v, p. 399) in which case the maiden appears to be narcissistically closed in on herself and the satisfaction of her own needs. Another might stress that the maiden is spoken *about* in the poem, either by a speaker who asks and answers their own questions or in a dialogue between two speakers. If this is a dialogue between two men (and it is not certain), then the text will take its place along with many others which envisage a woman as an object in exchange between two men ('Well was hir bour, / What was hir bour?'), an effect analysed by Freud in his account of dirty jokes (*SE* viii, pp. 97–100). Either psychoanalytic reading would supplement the location of the text in a traditional ideological context by which women are construed in relation to nature (eating flowers, sleeping in them) while men are seen to partake of culture (talking about women).

The problem of reductiveness

There is now no alternative to reading literature in some relation to psychoanalysis, a fact increasingly recognised among most of those concerned with literary study. To those who respond to any mention of psychoanalysis in application to literature with McEnroe-like cries of 'You cannot be serious', I can only reply by asking them to suspend their disbelief. This, initially, for two reasons. One is that conventional literary criticism already assumes a psychology for the human individual, and a questionable psychology at that, as I shall argue shortly. A second is that psychoanalysis, perhaps because it seems to be so threatening to received opinion, has often been misrepresented and misunderstood. Accordingly, the first two chapters here will be general and theoretical discussion, beginning with the issue of whether psychoanalysis as a framework for reading poetry is inevitably *reductive*.

Conventional literary criticism, for all its pluralism, generally retains the historical author as centre for its theoretical framework. In so doing it commits itself to a psychology and a view of 'Man'. When F. R. Leavis writes that someone 'is a poet because his interest in his experience is not separable from his interest in words' (1972, p. 17), a number of assumptions are being made. The poet stands outside language and outside his own experience able to take an interest in both from a point beyond them. This poet is conceived in terms of a self-consciousness fully present to itself and thus able to inspect its own experience, experience in which there is no hidden or unconscious quality. Proceeding on this basis literary criticism must see poetry in terms of what psychoanalysis describes as the levels of the conscious and the pre-conscious – in this psychology there is no room for the work of the unconscious. And, as source and author of his poetry, the poet is simply taken for granted. He is there and, one has to add, a man.

Psychoanalysis undeniably aims to put the human subject in question, to see 'Man' as a variable construct rather than something given. Yet often psychoanalytic writing came to the discussion of literature in a reductive way which did not challenge but rather confirmed inherited notions about 'Mankind'. Instead of referring to conscious and pre-conscious intentions it referred to the (supposed) unconscious intentions of a text's historical author, thus leaving conventional ideas about authorship untouched. One of the first critical texts to break with this is Roland Barthes's essay on 'Racinian Man'. Barthes's analysis refuses to compete with the 'excellent psychoanalytic study of Racine, by Charles Mauron' and avoids 'inferring from the work to the author and from the author to the work'. Instead its intention is to attempt from the texts themselves to reconstruct 'a kind of Racinian anthropology, both structural and psychoanalytic' (1964, p. vii). So the way is opened for a return to what – it is argued – is the main conception of aesthetic texts in psychoanalysis: not as expressions by an author but as occasions for phantasy to be shared by a reader.

Anne Clancier's *Psychanalyse et critique littéraire* lists seven kinds of psychoanalytic approach to literature (see 1973, p. 39):

1 the study of the author considered as individual to be psychoanalysed;
2 the study of the process of creation as a form of play, day-dream or night-dream or joke;
3 the study of literature treated as a form of interpretation to which psychoanalysis can supply its discovery of a deeper meaning beneath the apparent meaning;
4 the study of the reader, whose identifications and pleasure may be analysed;
5 the study of fundamental symbols;

6 the psychoanalysis of the hero or heroine in a narrative, novel, or play;
7 the study of genres in relation to wit, day-dream, the uncanny.

These seven kinds (see also Wright 1984) really amount to four, as Terry Eagleton has suggested:

> Psychoanalytical literary criticism can be broadly divided into four kinds, depending on what it takes as its object of attention. It can attend to the *author* of the work; to the work's *contents*; to its *formal construction*; or to the *reader*.   (1983, p. 179)

According to this categorisation, the present study attends to 'the work's *contents*' and its implied effect on 'the *reader*' rather than 'the *author*' or 'its *formal construction*'. Saussure's linguistics breaks down the common sense notion of words by distinguishing between the signifier and the signified, that is, between the level of the shaped sound and that of the concept or meaning, a distinction in effect between the means of representation and the represented. My earlier book on poetry, *Poetry as Discourse* (1983), was directed at the level of the signifier in poetry and argued that in the poetic tradition from the Renaissance on, the formal features of poetic language, especially rhyme and metre, were organised so as to draw attention from the poem to 'the poet', to give the effect of an individual voice 'really' speaking. Intended in many ways as a sequel to this previous work and relying frequently on its analysis of the formal properties of the tradition, *Poetry and Phantasy* will be directed mainly at the level of the signified in poetry and at the poetic text considered as a potential vehicle for phantasy. Although ultimately a conceptual distinction between signifier and signified must remain arbitrary in relation to the working of any particular text (the issue of the particularity of the text will be taken up again in the concluding chapter), it becomes less arbitrary and more justifiable when texts are grouped together, as they will be here. It will be argued that the poetic tradition's commitment to voice and individualism in its formal properties is carried through at the level of meaning.

A willingness to mobilise psychoanalysis in the study of literature is always felt to risk being reductive, and this is an issue that must be confronted at once. The charge of reductiveness presumes (not without some warrant in the past) that the psychoanalytic tradition sees its relation to literature as corresponding to that between reality and appearance so that the specific effect of literature is dismissed as a mere appearance beneath which psychoanalytic interpretation discovers the real meaning. This presumed relationship has had different consequences according to whether it has been understood in terms of truth or in terms of the nature of literature, and they will be discussed separately here.

On the question of truth, psychoanalysis has been considered reductive in so far as it has claimed to be an absolute metalanguage able to speak the truth denied to its object, literature, and against which literature can be 'read off' as symptom or illustration. However, to invoke psychoanalysis at present does not provide any guarantees of truth – far from it. Terry Eagleton (for example) says that 'What Freud produces, indeed, is nothing less than a materialist theory of the making of the human subject' (1983, p. 163). But such belief – one that goes no further than underwriting the theoretical possibility of psychoanalysis – must be measured against the scepticism of Karl Popper (for example), who writes:

And as for Freud's epic of the Ego, the Super-ego, and the Id, no substantially stronger claim to scientific status can be made for it than for Homer's collected stories from Olympus.   (1969, p. 38)

Psychoanalysis has not yet achieved the impersonal status of a scientific discourse, and this is signalled by the fact that it is still equated very much with the work of a single author, Sigmund Freud. For the purposes of this present study the scientific status of psychoanalysis has been bracketed.

Even if the truth (or otherwise) of psychoanalysis is put to one side, there is still the question of the 'strategic' effect of psychoanalysis on literature – what it enables or prevents literature from saying. It is felt that the nature of literature is betrayed when it appears within the purview of psychoanalysis. This sense of reductiveness is discussed forcefully and succinctly in Shoshana Felman's introduction to *Literature and Psychoanalysis* (1977, pp. 5–10), which will be taken here as a typical statement of the position.

Felman announces two possible views of the connection between psychoanalysis and literature. In the first, psychoanalysis regards itself as occupying 'the place of a *subject*, literature that of an *object*' (p. 5), a relation like that of Hegel's master and slave such that psychoanalysis claims authority as 'the sole window' (p. 8) through which we perceive reality. Accordingly, 'the psychoanalytic reading of literary texts precisely *misrecognizes* (overlooks, leaves out) their literary specificity' (p. 6). In the second view, that of the literary critic, 'literature is a subject, not an object'; and, since 'literature tells us that authority is a *language effect*' (p. 6), literature will tend to deconstruct the fantasy of authority borne by psychoanalysis, by showing that 'psychoanalysis itself is equally a body of language' (p. 6). From this basis Felman's project is not to reverse the supposed mastery of psychoanalysis over literature but to displace it, avoiding 'the very structure of the opposition, mastery/slavery' (p. 7).

There are, I believe, two related errors here that represent very well the widespread feeling that psychoanalytic readings are reductive. The first is the assumption that literature somehow exists 'in itself' as literature, as a subject, as something that tells us (for example) that 'authority is a *language effect*' (p. 8). But literature does not exist like that; it always exists as an object produced and reproduced in interpretations and contexts of reading (whether these are explicitly acknowledged or not) and is silent – cannot tell us anything – outside these. And since a text 'can always mean *some thing* to someone else' (Ray 1984, p. 142) and never loses the capacity to exceed any given reading, then *all* readings are reductive, all inevitably misrecognise the specificity of the literary text. As André Green points out in a defence of psychoanalytic readings, 'No interpretation can avoid constraining the work, in the sense that it necessarily forces it into the frame provided by a certain conceptual approach' (1979, pp. 19–20). The full text 'in itself', outside interpretation, is an impossible object.

A related error now appears. For if literature does not say anything apart from the power of the various discourses in which it is produced, then Felman's either/or cannot apply, that is, either the authority of psychoanalytic readings or literature 'in itself' which deconstructs that authority. Instead the choice is between the competing power and effects of the *different* discourses in which literature is produced at a given conjuncture (to affirm that a text is produced in the present is not to renounce the fact that the text so produced is always a historical text historically inscribed). In the prevailing circumstances of literary criticism the main option is between the institutionalised power of the conventional mode of interpretation and the challenge of various kinds of more radical criticism.

This argument does not exhaust the problems associated with the couple psychoanalysis/literature, starting with the reminder, 'But psychoanalytic theory is itself a text'. Thus, even if one explicitly brackets out the truth or falsity of psychoanalysis and even if it is conceded (as I think it must be) that all literary analysis constructs its object, the text, in terms of another discourse that inevitably stands apart from literature as a metalanguage, what are the limitations of psychoanalytic discourse in literary criticism? Rather than overload theoretical introductions at this point, I merely note these problems here to defer their discussion to the last chapter. We can still move forward on the basis that an application of psychoanalysis is better than the prevailing tradition.

Though under growing attack, conventional literary criticism continues to be deployed as the dominant discourse within which literature is constructed and where it takes on its meaning, force and consequence. Four features of this can be singled out. (1) Its method is impressionistic, self-contradictory and inexplicit (see Widdowson 1982, chapters 9 and 10). (2) It closes down the literary text by ascribing the work/play of meaning in it to the 'complex experience' of a supposedly full human subject, the historical author. (3) In accepting the category of 'experience', both in relation to the author and to the content of literature, it repeats uncritically the everyday assumptions of 'common sense'. (4) And, finally, in doing this, conventional literary criticism practises a conservative politics since it treats gender relations as natural, given, unalterable. On these four grounds the reading of literature determined in conventional criticism is strongly reductive and so, it can be argued, a psychoanalytic reading is both preferable and perhaps less reductive:

(1) Because it takes scientific discourse as its model, the psychoanalytic tradition offers a consistent, systematic and precise conceptual organisation. Although the rigour of this coherence entails the risk of premature closure, it carries by the same token the advantage of being unmistakably *explicit*, and consequently is a discourse that puts itself in question rather than presumes itself as given, along with 'common sense'. In the conventional account, literature is already seen as pre-eminently fictive, as fantasy. For example, as a first move in defining literature Helen Gardner's *In Defence of the Imagination* cites with approval C. S. Lewis's view that 'In reading great literature I become a thousand men [*sic*] and yet remain myself' (1982, p. 35). If in its way the prevailing account is correct to approach literature with the common sense notion of fantasy as fictional escapism, there may be at present no alternative to trying to deconstruct this by rethinking it systematically in terms of what psychoanalysis promises to analyse as phantasy.

(2) In denying the full and unified subject, in asserting that the subject and 'experience' are not given but constructed as an effect of the process of the unconscious, psychoanalysis conceives the subject as layered in an interaction multiply determined or overdetermined between different levels and mechanisms in the psyche (the 'stages' of oral, anal and genital; the Oedipal transition; the dynamic of ego, super-ego and id; the economy of the pleasure principle and the death drive). Correspondingly, an analysis of literature in terms of phantasy, far from being closed, is strictly interminable and cannot be brought to an end which is other than provisional. It should be recalled that in introducing a discussion of *Hamlet* in connection with the Oedipus complex in *The Interpretation of Dreams*, Freud states that 'all genuinely creative writings are the product of more than a single motive . . . and are open to more than a single interpretation' (*SE* IV, p. 266).

(3) Literature is concerned with the 'personal', to be sure, and psychoanalysis is at present uniquely capable of deconstructing 'personal experience', translating it into a different set of representations, other components, such that it may be exhibited at a distance as made up rather than ready made. No other discourse, for example, is so effectively available to defamiliarise the experience of 'being in love' (see below, chapter 4).

(4) Books, even books of criticism, are written at particular conjunctures, and at the present one literary study can no longer honestly discuss texts and ignore questions about gender. It would be hard to answer those who would deny this, who might complain, for example, that picking up Leavis earlier for writing unreflectingly of the poet as 'he' was tendentious and absurd. Psychoanalysis is particularly adapted to interrogate literary texts regarding questions of gender. The text which did most to put psychoanalysis back on to the agenda while introducing it into a field where one might least expect it, Juliet Mitchell's *Psychoanalysis and Feminism*, asserts that 'psychoanalysis is not a recommendation *for* a patriarchal society, but an analysis *of* one' (1975, p. xv). In concurring with this I would argue that a psychoanalytic reading can show literature sustaining and reinforcing traditional versions of identity and sexuality in areas and aspects of the text that remain invisible – and so beyond challenge – in any other mode of criticism.

Set out so far briefly and somewhat polemically, these positions need to be justified in detail. And already a new objection to psychoanalysis has been opened up, in the reference above to patriarchal society and so to the social meanings of literary texts: meanings which a concern with the unconscious appears to deny.

After the question of reductiveness, the next criticism made of any psychoanalytic literary study is that it must be unhistorical. The unconscious, so this familiar argument runs, is eternal, an unchanging feature of 'human nature', and so any fraternisation with Freud must lead to an anti-historical position, or one whose time scale is so hugely Darwinian, covering perhaps the whole history of the species, as to be effectively anti-historical. A main aim of *Poetry and Phantasy* is to counteract this presumption. In proposing to understand poetry as a form of phantasy it will seek to show that in poetry phantasy is made available to others in an intersubjective and social form. The project is to test the hypothesis that a poem may embody a historical form of phantasy, one that cannot be understood adequately either from the side of ideology alone or from that of phantasy alone.

The rest of this chapter and the whole of the next will go on to explore a theoretical basis for this assertion, firstly by approaching it from the side of psychoanalysis, secondly by reviewing work on the relations between psychoanalysis and historical materialism, the concept of ideology and that of the unconscious. And then the argument will be pursued through close examination in chronological order of a number of different texts from a series of widely contrasted historical conjunctures within a continuous poetic tradition: a poem from Ovid (as a point of contrast to the tradition) and an imitation of it from Donne, poems from the medieval period of courtly love, Augustan and Romantic poems, some representing Victorian poetry and Modernism. The basis for this revisionist history, the view that poetry needs to be understood as a form of *social phantasy*, could be summed up like this: a little psychoanalysis turns one away from history while a lot brings you back.

The interpretation of dreams and the interpretation of poems

We cannot avoid some recapitulation of fundamental concepts in psychoanalysis, material that may be new for some readers but not for others. There is no harm in retracing what may be familiar ground. Psychoanalysis as a theoretical system (for reasons it itself explains) is particularly susceptible to misrepresentation. There is for example the popular misrecognition which repeats the term 'subconscious' – one Freud had abandoned even before writing *The Interpretation of Dreams* – instead of 'unconscious'. Presumably the notion of a subconscious, with its associations of a submarine, implies material which lies submerged but which can easily be brought to the surface; and so the term resists the much more radical notion of an unconscious which is dynamically opposed to the consciousness in which it appears only as a symptom. Again, a distinction such as that between instinct and drive, central to psychoanalytic thought, is far too often ignored and can bear repetition even at the risk of an expositional tone. In addition, however, this review will try to define more clearly the particular way phantasy expresses itself in poetic texts as distinct from other forms in which it may operate.

For psychoanalysis the term *phantasy* (German: *Phantasie*) has a precise meaning that the ordinary usage 'fantasy' does not. It specifies: (1) an imaginary scene or narrative (2) in which the subject is present (3) but a scene altered or disguised (4) so that it may fulfil a wish for the subject. Phantasy turns ideas into narratives, for in dreams it has as its effect *'the transformation of a thought into an experience'* (*SE* xv, p. 129, italics original). But literature has always done this.

The concept of phantasy applies to both unconscious phantasies, such as occur in night-dreams, and waking phantasies as in day-dreams. Susan Isaacs proposed that two spellings should discriminate *fantasy* ('conscious daydreams, fictions and so on') from *phantasy* ('the primary content of unconscious mental processes', cited Laplanche and Pontalis 1980, p. 318) but the proposal has not succeeded because the unconscious is active in day-dreams as well as in night-dreams, and there is a clear continuity between them ('such phantasies' as day-dreams 'may be unconscious just as well as conscious', *SE* ix, p. 156). This means that as phantasy a poem has an unconscious effect for a reader as well as a conscious meaning. The necessary distinction between dream and poem lies not with the concept of phantasy but elsewhere.

The phenomenon, the object, which psychoanalysis seeks to analyse, occurs at a frontier between nature and culture where *Instinkt*, the organic functions of the body studied by biology, enters signification in the form of unconscious drive or *Trieb* (unfortunately the *Standard Edition* loses the distinction by translating both terms as 'instinct'):

an 'instinct' [*Trieb*] appears to us as a concept on the frontier between the mental and the somatic, as the psychical representative [*Repräsentant*] of the stimuli originating from within the organism and reaching the mind, as a measure of the demand made upon the mind for work in consequence of its connection with the body.   (*SE* xiv, pp. 121–2)

A similar assertion in different terminology is made in the paper on 'The unconscious':

An instinct [*Trieb*] can never become an object of consciousness – only the idea [*Vorstellung*] that represents the instinct can. Even in the unconscious, moreover, an instinct cannot be represented otherwise than by an idea. If the instinct did not attach itself to an idea or manifest itself as an affective state, we could know nothing about it.   (*SE* xiv, p. 177)

Psychoanalysis is about symbols rather than things, structures of representation rather than natural objects (hence, for example, when Freud refers to the penis he means a *symbolic* object, as can be readily understood from references to 'the mother's penis', an object for which there is no precedent in nature). It is because of Freud's insistence that drive has already taken on representation by becoming attached to a signifier that Lacan aims to turn 'the meaning of Freud's work away from the biological basis he would have wished for it towards the cultural references with which it is shot through' (1977a, p. 106).

So defined, a firm line is drawn between organic and psychic, biological determination and psychological determination, *Instinkt* and *Trieb*. On this basis a further distinction is made between a 'word-presentation' (*Wortvorstellung*), an auditory signifier, and a 'thing-presentation' (*Sachvorstellung*), a visual signifier. The distinction is integrated with that between conscious and unconscious:

the conscious presentation comprises the presentation of the thing plus the presentation of the word belonging to it, while the unconscious presentation is the presentation of the thing alone.   (*SE* xiv, p. 201)

Expression at the level of the conscious and the pre-conscious takes the form of both abstract, symbolic discourse and concrete, iconic discourse – roughly 'words' and 'images' – but the unconscious 'speaks' mainly in iconic discourse ('the dream-work makes a translation of the dream-thoughts into a primitive mode of expression similar to picture-writing', *SE* xv, p. 229). (This present study tries to resist the temptation of entering into a critical assessment of psychoanalytic theory but it must be added here that the word-presentation/thing-presentation distinction has been criticised; see Heath 1981, pp. 79–80, and Weber 1982, pp. 44–8.)

To the opposition between the extra-discursive (biological instinct) and representation, and the distinction within representation between conscious and unconscious in terms of word-presentation and thing-presentation, the work of L. S. Vygotsky would add a further antithesis between articulated, external discourse and inner speech, which is that discourse which goes on inside my head (and yours?) when I'm not talking to anyone, that which I speak for myself and not others (Molly Bloom's soliloquy at the end of *Ulysses* is an attempt to write down this mode of discourse). Rather than being simply external speech which has been silently internalised, inner speech in Vygotsky's hypothesis has 'a specific formation, with its own laws and complex relation to the other forms of speech activity' (1962, p. 131). Generalising from the egocentric speech observed in children Vygotsky describes inner speech as follows:

Its main distinguishing trait is its peculiar syntax. Compared with external speech, inner speech appears disconnected and incomplete . . . it shows a tendency towards an altogether specific form of abbreviation: namely, omitting the subject of a sentence and all words connected with it, while preserving the predicate.   (p. 139)

Characterised by a greater degree of condensation and abbreviation than external speech, inner speech works in a process rather like agglutination (that is, by combining terms) and by letting frequently repeated single terms stand for larger units of meaning, just as the title of a book can stand for the whole text.

Fragmentary, slipping without discomfort between many kinds and orders of discourse, working by paratactic juxtaposition rather than syntactic subordination, inner speech cannot be translated directly into speech or writing. These external or articulated discourses themselves must be discriminated into oral discourse – actual speech (both monologue and dialogue) – and textual discourse (textual rather than simply written because texts are uttered in photographs, tape, film, etc., as well as in writing). Textual discourse, relative even to its nearest kind, oral discourse, is syntagmatically more explicit and completed, calls for a more sustained homogeneity (see Easthope 1983, pp. 78–83).

Altogether, a general division can be made between four main registers or instances of discourse, each differentiated by some degree of specific effect due to their specific means of representation. Thus:

external discourse (textual and oral)	word-presentation
inner discourse (inner speech)	+ thing-presentation
discourse of the unconscious	thing-presentation
biological determination (extra-discursive)	the non-signifying

Of course each register occurs in continuity with the others, and they are sometimes mixed, as in drama when a written script is spoken on stage, textual discourse being presented as oral. The inter-relation between the registers is always historically variable, a topic on which work has begun in, for example, Marshall McLuhan's account of 'print-culture' and Derrida's analysis of the privileging of voice in the Western tradition. And the diagram really requires a third dimension to show the process of the unconscious as it acts across and under the other three. But the preceding argument and diagram lead to a simple conclusion: that the unconscious as phantasy 'insists' in poetry according to its specific means of representation as oral and textual discourse, external and public (in this book, only the tradition of written poetry will be considered). The operation of phantasy in a subject, typified in the example of a dream, has a quite different meaning and effect from its operation in aesthetic discourse, which includes poetry. In this respect, *phantasy in poetry is always already socialised* compared to the relatively private phantasies experienced in dreams.

A principle of psychoanalysis is that the repressed will return. Although the unconscious is mainly repressed, it tends to re-emerge into consciousness not directly but indirectly through its *derivatives*, that is, in an associated but displaced and distorted form. In a sardonic example Freud cites a monk who tried to get rid of erotic thoughts by gazing at an image of the Crucifixion and was rewarded with a vision of Christ in the form of a naked woman (*SE* IX, p. 35). In fact, if unconscious desire did not spill over into consciousness at the edges, it might remain unknowable. A dream admits such desire indirectly because it is composed of both a manifest content we may know about and latent dream thoughts that were present in the unconscious: 'the manifest dream, which you know from your memory when you wake up, can . . . be described as a *disguised* fulfilment of *repressed* wishes' (*SE* XI, pp. 35–6, italics original). Dreams are interpreted in two ways: by asking the person who has had the dream to associate ideas freely around an element remembered from the dream, and by drawing on a knowledge of the typical symbolism in which dreams express themselves. The unconscious meaning of a dream is both 'derived from the dreamer's mental life' (*SE* XV, p. 110) and conveyed in a shared system of representations:

the analysis of dreams has shown us that the unconscious makes use of a particular symbolism . . . this symbolism partly varies from individual to individual; but partly it is laid down in a typical form and seems to coincide with the symbolism which, as we suspect, underlies our myths and fairy tales.

(*SE* XI, p. 36)

Thus a dream is both individual ('the meaning of a dream depends on who the dreamer happens to be', *SE* XI, p. 174) *and* intersubjective – a claim Freud defends by saying a codifiable 'vocabulary' of dream symbols can be learned from many sources in oral and textual discourse,

from fairy tales and myths, from buffoonery and jokes, from folklore (that is, from knowledge about popular manners and customs, sayings and songs) and from poetic and colloquial linguistic usage. In all these directions we come upon the same symbolism.

(*SE* XV, pp. 158–9)

Because of the existence of these common grounds on which individuality takes up its position Lacan is able to affirm that 'the unconscious is structured like a language' (1977b, p. 20).

Even as it is dreamt, a dream is censored by consciousness, worked and re-worked to disguise latent in manifest content. This process of secondary revision is extended if the dream is reiterated – to use the terms introduced above – as inner discourse (your inwardly spoken recollection of it 'when you wake up'), as oral discourse (when you tell it to someone) and again as textual discourse (if it comes to be written down). But there is something even more important than levels of discourse and secondary revision in marking a line between dreams and poems: a dream has a dreamer, a poem does not. Discussing the 'ancient languages and scripts' he turned to in the

attempt to grasp the strange 'language' of dreams, Freud indicates
the characteristic present in such written texts but absent in dreams:

> A dream does not want to say anything to anyone. It is not a vehicle for
> communication; on the contrary, it is meant to remain ununderstood [*sic*].
>
> (*SE* xv, p. 231)

A dream has a meaning peculiar to the dreamer, and though it must
'speak' in a shared symbolism, the same dream would mean
something different if dreamt by someone else. It would not be the
same dream, in fact. A poem, having no dreamer, takes place 'in a
typical form' that is common for people without being the same for
everyone. The phantasy of an individual subject expresses itself
intersubjectively as a dream: a poem, uttered intersubjectively offers a
phantasy to a subject. Two consequences follow from this. One is that
while analysis of a dream is strictly interminable (its context is the
whole psychic life of an individual), discussion of a literary text as
phantasy may stop with greater confidence at the text, since there is
no way to reach behind the text to the mental life of the dreamer.
Another is that the phantasies made available in poetry are social, are
indeed historical.

The differences between dream and poem can be illustrated from
the following brief text:

> A whole crowd of children – all her brothers, sisters and cousins of both sexes
> – were romping in a field. Suddenly they all grew wings, flew away and
> disappeared.

This is recorded (in what is thus already textual discourse) as dreamt
by a woman first when she was four years old and the youngest of her
family, and repeatedly since then (*SE* iv, pp. 253–4). It is interpreted
as expressing her sibling rivalry, her desire that all her relations had
died so that, as Freud puts it, 'our little baby-killer was left alone . . .
the only survivor of the whole crowd'. Dreamt by someone else,
however, it could have another significance, one perhaps that would
call on the potential for 'dreams of flying . . . to be interpreted as
dreams of general sexual excitement' (*SE* xv, p. 155). Freud's
interpretation reads the text in the context of the life of the individual
dreamer.

The same two-sentence narrative could be transposed into lines,
introducing forms of parallelism that help to foreground the signifier:

> A whole crowd of children,
> all her brothers, sisters, and cousins of both sexes,

were romping in a field.
Suddenly they all grew wings,
flew away
and disappeared.

Separated from its author, the text now becomes a short, free-verse poem.

Immediately the text emerges within a quite new perspective. Its significance in the context of the dreamer's life falls away and what was previously to be regarded as manifest content, a rationalisation or disguise for the latent content, begins to exhibit the historical meanings that traverse the text, meanings that concern: the organisation of the family, the definition of sexual roles, the social categorisation of childhood, work versus leisure, class and the forces of production, as well as the more formulated ideological structures of religion and classical mythology. In the first place the constitution of a social group as 'brothers', 'sisters', 'cousins', implies a kinship relation specific to Western society, as well as a clear social discrimination of quite young children by sex ('both sexes'). That the children are 'romping', not working, further connotes a society in which childhood is marked off as an area protected for play. The 'field' presupposes an agrarian economy, and its use by children hints at their membership of a class that does not work, or not at least in this field they are at liberty to play in. That they 'grew wings' invokes the Christian image of angels and the Christian idea of the immortality of the soul. But the wings, as Freud notes, recall the way 'the peoples of antiquity' used 'to picture the soul as having a butterfly's wings' (*SE* xv, p. 155), so revealing the dependence of post-Renaissance Western culture on classical precedents.

None of this would tend to diminish the text's power as phantasy – rather, it is increased since potential phantasies cannot now be decided between by the context of the dreamer's life and so must be felt together. So the possibility of sibling rivalry must count along with the feeling about the brothers and sisters flying. In the absence of the dreamer, made outward in the mode of textual discourse, having become a poem, the text provides a form of aesthetic or social phantasy, one in which the phantasy *cannot be separated* from the ideologically determined meanings in which it is set. Desire for the death of the 'whole crowd of children', their disappearance by flying, remains imbricated with the historically determinate significance of images of the Christian angel and the pagan butterfly, the playing in the field, and (in English translation) the word 'romping'.

I believe that this example is strong enough to be taken as paradigmatic. It illustrates decisively the distinction between dream and poem, between the discourse of the unconscious as it speaks inwardly in dreams and again when it expresses itself externally according to the obligations of textual discourse as social phantasy. This possibility is not envisaged by psychoanalysis and it will be a main task of this present work to justify and provide evidence for it in relation to poetry.

It would seem tempting to claim that a dream is private, personal and asocial while a poem is social. But this cannot be the case since the dream is a human activity, taking place within the history of the human species, a history that is inescapably socialised, a matter of drive, representation and sign, not merely of instinct and signal (for sign versus signal, see Lacan 1977a, pp. 83–4). Again, it might seem enough to say that the wish concealed in the latent content of the dream is private yet its manifest content is social; but as will be pointed out shortly, that distinction itself is not an absolute one. In fact, exactly as with the opposition nature/culture, the distinction between asocial/social or personal/public can never have more than a relative force in relation to human phenomena, only applies as a moving point of difference. So the dream, while personal to the dreamer in the ways suggested, has a social basis as well. In the example, even this dream, made outward as textual discourse, by that ontological change itself acquires much more explicitly social meanings; an aesthetic text, designed for public presentation, is necessarily socialised to a much greater degree, as will be suggested. But social versus private is a relative distinction only.

Freud insists that the distinction between manifest and latent content in the dream should not be understood as that between appearance and reality: the essence of the dream lies not in the latent dream-thoughts but in the dream-work, the process that transforms and distorts the raw materials of the dream, including the latent content, to produce the manifest content. A note added to *The Interpretation of Dreams* in 1925 condemns those who

seek to find the essence of dreams in their latent content and in so doing they overlook the distinction between the latent dream-thoughts and the dream-work. At bottom, dreams are nothing other than a particular *form* of thinking, made possible by the conditions of the state of sleep. It is the *dream-work* which creates that form, and it alone is the essence of dreaming – the explanation of its peculiar nature.   (*SE* v, pp. 506–7, italics original)

Extended to textual discourse, the principle suggests that the 'particular form of thinking' represented by art has the effect of bringing phantasy and ideological meaning into intimate connection. In fact, when, in a series of writings, Freud does address the problem of aesthetic discourse, his theoretical account is directed especially at the formal properties of art, its specific means of representation, the pleasures it may bring. But his conclusion stresses the social meaning and effect of phantasy in art and literature. Discussion of Freud's theory of art has been reserved until here so it may act as a check and confirmation of what has been argued for. It, too, has often been simplified, bowdlerised and misrepresented by literary critics – sympathetic and unsympathetic – and I see no reason to apologise for rehearsing the main tenets.

Art and its pleasures

Freud's explanation of the aesthetic effect appears first in 1908 in the paper on 'Creative writers and day-dreaming', is repeated in the *Introductory Lectures* of 1916–17, and re-affirmed in *An Auto-biographical Study* of 1925. In the 1908 paper (*SE* IX, pp. 142–53) Freud begins by noting that the child, obedient to the pleasure principle rather than the reality principle, exercises to the full its freedom to play, even while knowing perfectly well that such play is a form of pretence. The adult, instead of playing, makes up phantasies in the form of day-dreams. There is a clear continuity between phantasy in dreams, day-dreams, day-dreams recounted to someone and phantasy in art: 'Every single phantasy is the fulfilment of a wish' (p. 146) and 'night-dreams are wish-fulfilments in just the same way as day-dreams' (p. 149). But there are differences between each level, differences that can be phrased in terms of the categories used above. Desires in night-dreams, a discourse of the unconscious, are more repressed and so must have a more distorted expression that those in day-dreams, inner discourse. Everyone has day-dreams, usually erotic or ambitious or both, but is ashamed to speak of them, to reproduce inner discourse as oral discourse. If you do tell your phantasies to other people, they generally find them boring and unpleasurable, because they are so obviously egotistical in character (so, one may note, personal diaries occupy a fraught and marginal space between discourse for the self and for the other). Working in textual discourse, however, the artist is able to transmute phantasies into a pleasurable form. How this is done remains art's 'innermost secret', though Freud suggests two methods by which the effect is brought about:

The writer softens the character of his [*sic*] egoistic day-dreams by altering and disguising it, and he bribes us by the purely formal – that is, aesthetic – yield of pleasure which he offers us in the presentation of his phantasies. We give the name of an *incentive bonus*, or a *fore-pleasure* [*Vorlust*] to a yield of pleasure such as this, which is offered to us so as to make possible the release of still greater pleasure arising from deeper psychical sources.   (p. 153)

Phantasy in art provides two distinct pleasures that day-dreams do not: that produced by 'the purely formal' and that made available by the phantasy itself now that its quality of self-concerned wish-fulfilment has been disguised. The distinction between pleasure in the formal and pleasure in the phantasy we would now understand as corresponding to the distinction between the signifier and the signified. It is *not* the case – as is often supposed – that the work/play of the signifier helps to disguise the phantasy; rather the signifier in art yields fore-pleasure that leads to a *separate* source of pleasure in the signified phantasy.

Two things should be noted. First, that Freud as always assumes that people experience pleasure in the work/play of the signifier. The main mechanism of the joke, for example, is to treat 'words as things' through puns and ambiguities, and this fore-pleasure, in the case of the tendentious joke (the adult joke with a point) enables the joke to function in 'getting rid of inhibitions' (*SE* VIII, p. 134), releasing meanings that could not otherwise be spoken. Ernest Jones recalls getting a letter from Freud in 1914 after he had spent an evening with a painter, a letter in which Freud wrote:

Meaning is but little to these men; all they care for is line, shape, agreement of contours. They are given up to the *Lustprinzip* [pleasure principle].
                                    (1957, III, p. 412; cited Derrida 1981a, p. 248)

Second, there is nothing opportunistic in the way Freud invokes the concept of fore-pleasure (*Vorlust*) to comprehend the formal properties of art and literature. A section of *Three Essays on Sexuality* is entitled 'The mechanism of fore-pleasure' and describes how some kinds of pleasure are satisfying in themselves but also that 'an experience of pleasure can give rise to a need for greater pleasure' (*SE* VII, p. 210) in which case it is necessary to distinguish between fore-pleasure and end-pleasure. Kissing, for example, is a version of fore-pleasure, not satisfying except as a condition for an end-pleasure, 'satisfaction derived from the sexual act' (*ibid.*). In the theory of jokes Freud also draws on the distinction, refers to the 'principle of fore-pleasure', using the equivalent term *incentive bonus* as in 'Creative writers and day-dreaming', and makes the claim, 'I have good reason to suspect that this principle corresponds with an arrangement that holds good in many widely separated departments of mental life' (*SE* VIII, p. 137). The distinction between fore-pleasure and end-pleasure in general is needed to explain why the raising of tension – fore-pleasure – can be consistent with the pleasure principle.

When the *Introductory Lectures* summarise the theory of aesthetic discourse, fresh emphasis is given to its effect on and for other people. The summary needs to be quoted at length:

a true artist . . . understands how to work over his [*sic*] day-dreams in such a way as to make them lose what is too personal about them and repels strangers, and to make it possible for others to share in the enjoyment of them. He understands, too, how to tone them down so that they do not easily betray their origin from proscribed sources. Furthermore, he possesses the mysterious power of shaping some particular material until it has become a faithful image of his phantasy; and he knows, moreover, how to link so large a yield of pleasure to this representation of his unconscious phantasy that, for the time being at least, repressions are outweighed and lifted by it. If he is able to accomplish all this, he makes it possible for other people once more to derive consolation and alleviation from their own sources of pleasure in their unconscious which have become inaccessible to them. (*SE* XVI, p. 376)

This distinguishes five aspects of aesthetic phantasy:

1   a working of the signifier provides fore-pleasure, the pleasure, that is, attached to the 'representation' of phantasy;
2   the signified phantasy has, by losing 'what is too personal' about day-dreams, become *impersonal*, available not just for the self but for others (it no longer 'repels strangers');
3   repressed desires have been reworked into a more effectively disguised and rationalised form ('proscribed sources' have not been eradicated but toned down) (in both respects – (2) and (3) – the reworking (secondary revision) can only take place if the phantasy is woven in with *ideological* content);
4   there is a relation of appropriateness between signifier and signified phantasy, for the 'particular material' has been shaped into a 'faithful image' of the phantasy;
5   art provides a vehicle or occasion for the phantasies of others, making it possible 'for others' to share enjoyment, 'to derive consolation and alleviation from their own sources of pleasure in their unconscious'.

In *An Autobiographical Study*, Freud reflects upon the point in the development of psychoanalysis at which his aesthetic theory was introduced via the recognition that works of art

> differed from the asocial, narcissistic products of dreaming in that they were calculated to arouse sympathetic interest in other people and were able to evoke and to satisfy the same unconscious wishful impulses in them too. Besides this, they made use of the perceptual pleasure of formal beauty as what I have called an 'incentive bonus'.   (*SE* xx, p. 65)

The 'perceptual pleasure of formal beauty' is fore-pleasure and needs no comment. Consistent with the increasingly social concern of his later work, Freud here stresses: (a) *the social function* of the aesthetic text for others (the creative writer is now omitted altogether); (b) *the social meaning* of aesthetic phantasy in contrast to the 'asocial, narcissistic products of dreaming'.

Freud's analysis of the aesthetic as phantasy has a recognisable concurrence with other theories of literariness (the specific feature that makes literature literature), for example, the Russian Formalist insistence on the role of the signifier in foregrounding artifice in the aesthetic text or Jakobson's discussion of repetitions in metre, intonation and rhyme as contributing to 'the poetic function' of poetry (1960, pp. 358–70). But the psychoanalytic theory yields a number of advantages denied to its competitors. It does not mark off the aesthetic from the non-aesthetic in two exclusive categories but rather poses a continuous incline from the scarcely disguised wish-fulfilments of everyday literature (stories in *Woman's Own*, the phallic phantasies of Ian Fleming) which provide immediate pleasure when they first appear through to instances of 'great art', that is, texts which seem able to survive and go on giving pleasure well after the moment of their first production. The theory breaks with all reflexive accounts of aesthetic texts as to be judged in terms of something (the personality of the author, class war) prior to their own productive and transformative work in and for the reader. Firmly denying that the aesthetic is an *essence*, a property inherent in the text, the theory as firmly asserts that the aesthetic is a *function* operating in the relation between the text and its reader in the present, a conception which pre-empts any account of the aesthetic effect as due to *either* the text 'in itself' *or* to readers 'in themselves'. Though not having Saussure's terms available, it does not privilege either signifier over signified or vice-versa, and nor does it collapse the two orders. Their autonomy is preserved while their relation is suggested: pleasure in the signifier (fore-pleasure) facilitates a separate pleasure in the signified (the social phantasy). Room is provided to think about the specificity of the individual aesthetic text: *this* particular fore-pleasure assists *that* end-pleasure, has become 'a faithful image' for it. Finally, the theory refers art to huge areas in the rest of human experience, from the play of the child to the secret day-dreams of the adult.

This analysis of the aesthetic text from the side of psychoanalysis arrives at the conclusion that phantasy in art necessarily takes on a social feature denied to it in dreams. Losing its 'asocial, narcissistic' quality, it becomes intersubjective, publicly available, phantasy for others. And thus – as the example of the dream transformed to poem ('A whole crowd of children . . .') demonstrated – phantasy changes its nature by being brought into intimate connection with ideological structures and meanings. The next chapter will approach the problem more from the side of historical materialism, by looking at some attempts to theorise a relation between ideology and the unconscious.

2

IDEOLOGY AND PHANTASY IN POETRY

Slogans will not fill the yawning absence of a worked out conceptual articulation between *ideology* and the *unconscious*. Michel Pêcheux

The question of the relation between ideology and the process of the unconscious brings into issue the possible relation between the two theoretical discourses of historical materialism and psychoanalysis. After revisiting briefly the account psychoanalysis proffers of how the subject is determined socially, this chapter will turn to some criticisms of that account from the position of Marxists and others, and then consider attempts made from the side of historical materialism to integrate the two problematics and the two topics of ideology and the unconscious. Concentrating on the relevant work of first Bakhtin and then Althusser means disregarding much else, including Wilhelm Reich's *The Mass Psychology of Fascism* (1972; first published 1933) as well as the Frankfurt School and Herbert Marcuse. Subsequent work from Pierre Macherey and Fredric Jameson will be assessed, but it should come as no surprise, nor necessarily a disappointment, that the review tends towards a conclusion very close to that advanced by Hirst and Woolley in *Social Relations and Human Attributes* (1982): no synthesis can be found able to integrate historical materialism and psychoanalysis within a single, theoretically coherent framework. Nevertheless, a concept of literature as social phantasy will be defined and its necessity for the analysis of poetry will be urged.

Psychoanalysis

While the concept of ideology envisages consciousness as historically determined in relations of power, psychoanalysis treats subjectivity

24

rather as universal and eternal, a process beyond history, or co-terminous with the history of the human species. Even on the basis of the clear distinction between *Instinkt* and *Trieb*, Freud's fundamental categories for the content of the unconscious correspond to the biological determinants described by Darwin: self-preservation and narcissism, reproduction and sexual drive, death and the death drive (see Sulloway 1980). 'All human beings, at all events in their early days, have approximately the same experiences' (*SE* XXIII, p. 98): the Oedipus complex in late-nineteenth-century Vienna shows no appreciable difference from that presented in the ancient Greek myth of Oedipus, the myth which helped Freud to theorise what he took to be a universal human experience associated with the universal taboo on incest. 'The respect paid to dreams in antiquity is . . . based upon correct psychological insight' (*SE* V, p. 614); and so, to go further back, one of the earliest recorded dreams is undoubtedly susceptible to psychoanalytic interpretation:

And he dreamed and behold a ladder set up on earth: and behold the angels of God ascending and descending on it. And, behold, the Lord stood above it . . .
(Genesis 28: 12–13)

By means of a written text Jacob's dream still makes available to the reader a phantasy of sexual intercourse ('staircases . . . are representations of the sexual act', *SE* V, p. 355) presided over but transcended by a supremely phallic, flying father who 'stood' above it.

We have learnt that unconscious mental processes are in themselves 'timeless'. This means in the first place that they are not ordered temporally, that time does not change them in any way and that the idea of time cannot be applied to them . . . Our abstract idea of time seems to be wholly derived from the method of working of the system *Pcpt.-Cs* [i.e. Perception-Consciousness] . . .
(*SE* XVIII, p. 22)

In contrast, as traditionally understood by historical materialism, ideology is entirely a product of time in the dimension of history.

Freud's conception of history abstracts it into two simple categories, the primitive and the civilised, the first typically considered as mythological, as in *Totem and Taboo* (1912–13), the second discussed mainly as imposing a necessary sublimation, as in *Civilisation and its Discontents* (1930). When Freud, in *Group Psychology and the Analysis of the Ego* (1921), tries to remedy the deficiency in the psychoanalytic approach to individuals in their social relations, he begins by recognising that individual psychology is always already social:

It is true that individual psychology is concerned with the individual man [*sic*] and explores the paths by which he seeks to find satisfaction for his instinctual impulses; but only rarely and under certain exceptional conditions is individual psychology in a position to disregard the relations of this individual to others. In the individual's mental life someone else is invariably involved, as a model, as an object, as a helper, as an opponent; and so from the very first, individual psychology is at the same time social psychology as well. (*SE* XVIII, p. 69)

Yet the account has the effect of evaporating the specific forms of the institutions mentioned, the army and the church, reducing their operation to forms of a flat, ahistorical structure.

It was, in fact, pressing political events – the Russian Revolution and the collapse of world trade after 1929 – which brought Freud's project into closest contact with historical materialism. The conclusion to the *New Introductory Lectures* (1933) gives what was at the time a brave and progressive endorsement to the Soviet Revolution on the grounds that it gave hope for a new order that would 'put an end to the material need of the masses' (*SE* XXII, p. 181). Freud has no difficulty whatever with the materialist assertion that social life is ultimately determined by the economic base, though his view is firmly that 'psychological factors cannot be overlooked', in particular the way the super-ego 'represents tradition and the ideals of the past'. This certainly accords with the view that 'the tradition of all the dead generations weighs like a nightmare on the brain of the living' (Marx and Engels 1950, I, p. 225), a sentence generally read without stress on 'all'.

Since the child's super-ego is modelled on the parents' super-ego each subject becomes 'the vehicle of tradition' (*SE* XXII, p. 167):

It seems likely that what are known as materialist views of history sin in under-estimating this factor. They brush it aside with the remark that human 'ideologies' are nothing other than the product and superstructure of their contemporary economic conditions. That is true, but very probably not the whole truth. Mankind [*sic*] never lives entirely in the present. The past, the tradition of the race and of the people, lives on in the ideologies of the super-ego, and yields only slowly to the influences of the present and to new changes; and so long as it operates through the super-ego it plays a powerful part in human life, independently of economic conditions. (*ibid.*)

The position is unequivocal and forms the basis for a wide range of conventional work locating the social essentially in the agency of the super-ego (see for example the chapter 'Psychoanalytic theory and cultural change' in Marcus 1984, pp. 165–90). Insofar as ideology is an effect of the unconscious it functions via the super-ego. And it is transmitted, so Freud speculates in a late work, because members of the species are able to 'inherit' (*SE* XXIII, p. 100) some 'memory traces of the experience of earlier generations' (p. 99). The conclusion is that 'if we assume the survival of these memory-traces we have bridged the gulf between individual and group psychology' (p. 100). These traces, as John Forrester argues (1980, pp. 70–83), constitute a medium for the universal 'language' of dream symbols (pp. 15–16). Such assertions once more rejoin Freud's own Darwinian inheritance in founding the human psyche on a basis of the phylogenetic, the biological determination of the species.

Historical materialism

The position of Raymond Williams well represents the kind of critique entered by Marxists and others on the Left against the whole system of psychoanalysis and its account of the subject and ideology. With a certain slippage between 'drive' and 'instinct', Williams in *Politics and Letters* (1979) both underwrites the view that 'fundamental human drives' are derived from 'biological, material conditions' and opposes it to what is termed 'Freudian instinct theory' on the grounds that such theory cannot provide for biological determination (p. 183). In denying that 'Freud and Marx could be combined', he says:

There can be no useful compromise between a description of basic realities as ahistorical and universal and a description of them . . . as modified by a changing human history.
(p.184)

Thus he refuses to refer human aggression displayed in war to 'a mythology of eternal drives' (p. 334). The kind of explanation this version of historical materialism would prefer is illustrated by Timpanaro's *The Freudian Slip* (1976). In a chapter on 'The good citizens of Vienna', Timpanaro argues that the verbal slips Freud collects and analyses have a cause in social repression and an archaic social structure (monarchic, clerical, anti-semitic, militarist) and so attention should be paid 'to the "social" rather than sexual character of very many of the "slips" (even where these have a sexual theme)' (p. 110).

While writers such as Williams and Timpanaro have aimed to

oppose psychoanalysis, others in the tradition of historical materialism have sought to incorporate it into an analysis of ideology. The work of Mikhail Bakhtin, published under the name of his colleague V. N. Voloshinov, still exemplifies one of the most throughgoing Marxist contentions with psychoanalysis. Bakhtin's first book, *Freudianism, A Marxist Critique* (1927), takes the hardline position that psychoanalysis universalises and dehistoricises the study of the subject:

That which in man is nonsocial and nonhistorical is abstracted and advanced to the position of the ultimate measure and criterion for all that is social and historical.   (1976, p. 11)

What psychoanalysis regards as the operation of the unconscious is in fact a form of 'inner speech', as theorised by Vygotsky (see above, pp. 13–14). There are thoughts, desires, dreams, but for Bakhtin

This 'content of the psyche' is *ideological through and through; from the vaguest of thoughts and dimmest and most uncertain of desires all the way to philosophical systems and complex political institutions, we have one continuous series of ideological and, hence also, sociological phenomena.*
                                                    (p. 24, italics original)

The view advocated here is reductive in that subjectivity is considered to be only another expression for ideology and no separate, autonomous activity is accorded to the unconscious.

Bakhtin's position is reworked in *Marxism and the Philosophy of Language* (1929, 2nd edition 1930). This draws on Saussure's account of the signifier to substantiate the argument that *'consciousness can arise and become a viable fact only in the material embodiment of signs'* (1973, p. 11: italics original); since signs 'can arise only on *interindividual territory'*, any sign, including the most subjective, is ideological. But the position is also significantly and perhaps inconsistently modified, for now a distinction is made between ideological signs and 'inner, subjective signs' (p. 39), a distinction which, crucially, attributes some degree of separate *autonomy* to the psyche as constituted through internalised signs. Though 'the ideological sign is the common territory for both the psyche and for ideology', yet 'the psyche need not be a duplicate of the rest of the world (the ideological world above all)' (p. 33). 'Common territory', a 'duplicate': Bakhtin's theoretical struggle is to find analogies and metaphors for the relation between the psyche and ideology:

The inner sign must free itself from its absorption by the psychic context (the biological-biographical context), must cease being a subjective experience in order to become an ideological sign. The ideological sign must immerse itself in the element of inner, subjective signs; it must ring with subjective tones in order to remain a living sign and not be relegated to the honorary status of an incomprehensible museum piece. (p. 39)

The problem is to grasp the definite and determined autonomy of subjectivity without severing it from its constitution within ideology, on that 'common territory' so that a change in one is always accompanied by a change in the other. Besides the metaphors which describe the ideological as swimming in subjectivity ('immerse itself') or being made to ring like a bell with 'subjective tones', the outcome in Bakhtin is a distinction between 'content' and 'context'. In 'content' the difference between the psyche and ideology 'is one of degree only' (p. 33) but – on common territory – subjective content occupies a separate region, 'the psychic context', glossed as 'the biological-biographical context'.

The content/context distinction aims to stay consistent with the classic Marxist principle that subject and object come into being simultaneously and in reciprocity, that production 'not only creates an object for the subject, but also a subject for the object (Marx 1973, p. 92). When Bakhtin describes the movement between inner speech and enunciated speech, this principle is explicit:

In each speech act, subjective experience perishes in the objective fact of the enunciated word-utterance, and the enunciated word is subjectified in the act of responsive understanding in order to generate, sooner or later, a counter statement. (pp. 40–1)

'Sooner or later' is the give-away. For the process of the unconscious has its own time and continues to operate beyond 'the enunciated word-utterance' and even beyond inner speech. The unconscious is denied autonomy in order to preserve subject and object as different aspects or regions or contexts of an essentially unified totality, one maintained as such by supposing that subjectivity expresses the same objective 'content' by moving it as though through a transparent medium into another 'context'.

Bakhtin's attempt to integrate psychoanalysis and historical materialism, to find a conceptual placing for the unconscious in relation to ideology, ends up with a *de facto* denial of the unconscious. The work of Freud on ideology and Bakhtin on the unconscious are the converse of each other; if Freud's account of the super-ego tends to reduce ideology into an effect of the unchanging human subject, Bakhtin's project reduces the unconscious to an effect of ideology.

More recently, the work of Althusser, especially in the section 'On ideology' in 'Ideology and ideological state apparatuses', has set out once again to think the relation between ideology and the process of the unconscious, this time through the concept of interpellation. Althusser's essay is well-known, and a shortened account of it can quickly lead on to criticisms of it. Of the Darwinian categories of self-preservation and reproduction, historical materialism has generally concentrated on the first, by theorising production and its social relation. Althusser's essay moves the other way by stressing the way a social formation seeks to reproduce itself and its relations of production by reproducing people. It does so, the essay argues, by ' *"constituting" concrete individuals as subjects*' (1977, p. 160; italics original). Althusser's account asks how people come to see themselves as free individuals, how a subject is formed contradictorily as: (1) a free subjectivity . . . responsible for its actions; (2) a subjected being, who submits to a higher authority' (p. 169). Its answer leans on Lacan's conception of self-identification in 'the mirror stage' (1977a, pp. 1–7).

Lacan proposes that the unity and identity of the ego is borrowed from the Other, from other people. Thus the infant is constituted as a primordial ego by the process of finding and loving its likeness in the Other (in the mother's smile, in other people's gestures of recognition). Once it is internalised, he or she treats this likeness as itself. Lacan defines a subject's ego as 'that which is reflected of his [*sic*] form in his objects' (1977a, p. 194) but this reflected likeness is appropriated as an obvious identity, the process of self-identification misrecognised as natural, as though when I look in the mirror awareness that my image is created by an optical effect – left for right, much smaller – were displaced by the simple response: 'it's me'. It is the very process of denial of this process which enables the ego to subsist, to identify itself as a unity.

Similarly, for Althusser, ideology functions through its self-effacement, its obviousness, by enabling the subject to treat what is produced, including crucially its own identity, as natural, unquestionable, self-evidently *there*. His model is someone who asks 'Who's there?' and I answer, 'It's me'. Through what Althusser names as a process of interpellation I come to recognise myself reflected in an 'Absolute, Other Subject, i.e. God' (Althusser 1977, p.

166) through a process of 'mutual recognition' (p. 168). I am hailed into position, interpellated as a unified subject, in a procedure like that through which someone calls out – 'Hey, you there!' – and I turn round recognising that this address means me. The subject-in-ideology is constituted to see itself as constitutive; it is an effect of a process by which it thinks of itself as source and origin.

Besides the fact that this sets aside a traditional sense of ideology as conscious meanings and also shuts the door on the way the 'I' is produced differently in different epochs and cultures, there are three main objections to this theoretical account. The first is that Althusser's essay follows Freud and the Marxist tradition closely in looking for a meeting ground between unconscious and ideology on the terrain of the super-ego, where social duty and individual conscience converge. Interpellation, as Colin MacCabe comments, 'has little to do with Lacan's concept of the subject but rather involves the construction of an ego completely dominated by a super-ego' (1981, p. 301). Second, in writing of recognition rather than fully co-opting Lacan's conception of misrecognition, the Althusserian account presupposes the subject as already *given* and 'with the attributes of a knowing subject' (Hirst 1979, p. 65) prior to the process of self-identification – given such that it can then, *subsequently*, recognise itself. But the essay must assume the subject as given once and for all because otherwise the subject is not there to be interpellated via the super-ego in the service of ideology (for Lacan the ego is produced – constituted – through the process Althusser names as interpellation).

Thirdly, Althusser's subject of ideology is understood as non-contradictory. If, as it must be, self-identification is conceived not in terms of a once and for all moment of recognition but as the consequence of an endless process of misrecognition, then the subject's positioning as ego can never be more than a temporary effect. As of course it is, since it is produced across the split between conscious and unconscious in an uneven operation that cannot fail to be contradictory and incomplete. Stephen Heath points out that in thus fixing the subject Althusser merely 'reproduces the subject as a kind of essence of ideology' (1981, p. 106), precisely as the subject-in-ideology. But the 'unconscious is not reducible to the ideological' (*ibid.*). Althusser's attempt to appropriate and incorporate the psychoanalysis of Lacan into historical materialism is ultimately no more successful than Bakhtin's and for the same reason: it fails to provide an autonomy for the operation of the unconscious. The subject of psychoanalysis is presumed as given; he or she is interpellated into an ideological formation essentially through the agency of the super-ego; and, crucially, ideology and the unconscious are subsumed to the same theoretical space, conceived as ultimately homogeneous.

There is, however, an important and suggestive dislocation between Althusser's account of ideology in this essay and his writing elsewhere. In *Reading Capital*, an argument concerning time is put forward whose effect is to deny the very possibility of an even and theoretically coherent articulation of ideology and the unconscious. Althusser affirms that the 'conception of historical time as continuous and homogeneous and contemporaneous with itself' must give way to recognition that *'there are* different times in history' (Althusser and Balibar 1975, p. 96, italics original). And so:

it is no longer possible to think the process of the development of the different levels of the whole *in the same historical time.* Each of these different 'levels' does not have the same type of historical existence. On the contrary, we have to assign to each level a *peculiar time,* relatively autonomous and hence relatively independent, even in its dependence, of the 'times' of the other levels. We can and must say: for each mode of production there is a peculiar time and history, punctuated in a specific way by the development of the productive forces; the relations of production have their peculiar time and history, punctuated in a specific way; the political superstructure has its own history . . .; philosophy has its own time and history . . .; aesthetic productions have their own time and history . . .; scientific formations have their own time and history, etc.   (p. 99, punctuation and italics original)

In *Positions* Derrida cites this view from Althusser and adds, 'I have always subscribed to this' (1981b, p. 58). Such an account changes the whole basis of the argument.

In the first place, if history is discontinuous and decentred in the way Althusser proposes, and no general principle governs all the levels and times, there is no need to suppose that the time of the unconscious coheres with the time of ideology; each must be recognised as acting transformatively in their own specific effectivity according to their own autonomy. Again, for the same reason, there need be no even or homogeneous assimilation of the three registers or instances discriminated in chapter 1: inner discourse; oral discourse; textual discourse. Each will act in its own time, and the discourse of the unconscious will manifest traces of its operation differently across each of these levels of process. And further, literature, as a form of 'aesthetic production', must be recognised as an autonomous formation, so that the issue of the relation between ideology and the unconscious must be re-considered in terms specific to literature, and indeed to written as against oral traditions within it. There can no longer be any guarantee the relation will be the same anywhere else. If analysis proceeds on this basis a different set of questions and answers about ideology and the unconscious emerges, and indeed has already begun to be written up. Following this line of development through will bring discussion back towards the imbrication of effects of ideology and phantasy in poetry.

Ideology and the unconscious in literature

A fresh attempt to theorise the unconscious within the terms of historical materialism can be marked as early as Althusser's 1964 essay on 'Freud and Lacan' (see 1977, pp. 181–202), an essay which encouraged a new departure in Marxist literary theory. Pierre Macherey's *A Theory of Literary Production* (1966) felt entitled to draw on psychoanalysis as a model for theorising the ideological effect of literature. Briefly, this proposes that 'what is important in the [literary] work is what it does not say' (1978, p. 87) and that in order to understand this we must have recourse to the notion of *'the unconscious of the work'* (p. 92, italics original):

we must show a sort of splitting within the work: this division is *its* unconscious, in so far as it possesses one – the unconscious which is history, the play of history beyond its edges, encroaching on those edges . . .

(p. 94)

Thus, in the popular novels of Jules Verne, the narrative is organised so as to make an explicit ideological assertion celebrating man's appropriation of nature while at the same time denying the imperialist project within which, in the late nineteenth century, that appropriation took place. But, to insist, all we have in Macherey's analysis is a metaphor or descriptive model: the text is seen not as a work of the unconscious but only as acting in a way *like* a work of the unconscious.

Deriving from the work of Althusser, Macherey's theoretical strategy effects an extraordinary and original transformation within the Marxist tradition of literary theory. For that has been dogged by

the 'reflexive problematic', by the determination to read and read off
literary texts as accurate or inaccurate reflections of social relations.
In the name of the Althusserian concept of practice, Macherey
cancels the tradition and proclaims that literary discourse must be
defined 'as a contestation of language rather than a representation of
reality' (p. 61). But if accordingly the literary text is conceived as an
intervention in the present, the difficulty is to retain an appropriate
account of the relation between text and history. By postulating this
as a negative relation according to a psychoanalytic paradigm, *A
Theory of Literary Production* aims to preserve the autonomy of the
literary text while retaining an account of its connection to history.
Just as conscious awareness is constituted by the repression of
unconscious so that the manifest meaning of a dream implies by
negation its latent significance, so the literary text reproduces history
by denying it. The work of Macherey forms a theoretical basis for
Terry Eagleton's *Criticism and Ideology* (1976) which gives
Macherey's account the status of an orthodoxy, though in so doing it
alters the argument by proposing that a text's contradictions are
brought about between 'the ideological' and 'the aesthetic' rather
than between 'conscious' and 'unconscious' levels. Fredric Jameson's
The Political Unconscious (1981) continues the Machereyan initiative
by pulling the critical perspective back towards psychoanalysis.

Densely suggestive yet strangely opaque, pluralistically comprehensive yet dogmatically committed to the Grand Narrative of
historical materialism, *The Political Unconscious* positions its reader
through postmodernist and deconstructive ironies in an undecidable
tension between reading it literally (for the truth it reveals) or reading
it rhetorically (for the persuasive force of the story it tells). It is a book
which could be easily discussed at booklength (and has been, see
Dowling 1984) but will be reviewed in outline here in so far as it
relates to the problems of the unconscious and ideology in literature.

Historical materialism traditionally has advanced itself as a
scientific discourse. As such it claimed not only to be able to discover
the truth about the functioning of the social formation (ultimately
determined by the economic base) but, in virtue of this, also to be
capable of explaining the operation of levels of the superstructure (including literature) – all this, while at the same time, by
acknowledging forms of knowledge as always socially determined,
historical materialism could defend itself not only as a knowledge but
as a version of radical political practice. Especially in the past decade

and – to a surprising extent in writing associated with aesthetic theory – this traditional comprehensiveness of Marxism has come under severe critique at its very centre: the account of economic determination by the mode of production. In Britain in the wake of Althusser's writing, this critique was put forward in the work of Barry Hindess and Paul Q. Hirst, which compelled recognition for the problem of theorising language and forms of discourse within the base/superstructure model. At the same time in the United States the claims of Marxism to scientificity came under attack from American deconstruction and its assertion that since knowledge was dependent on discourse, there could be no knowledge and no scientific truth (for a fuller account of recent events in the interaction between Marxism and post-structuralism, see Easthope 1988). Jameson's text can best be read as a brilliant and successful strategy to outflank both forms of critique by mobilising both the work of Pierre Macherey and Jean-François Lyotard's *The Postmodern Condition* (1984; French edition, 1979) while responding to the increasing reputation of psychoanalysis and renewed interest in the unconscious (hence the book's title).

Following Althusser, Lyotard distinguishes between science and ideology but reconceptualises these as scientific knowledge and narrative knowledge, arguing (1) that scientific knowledge was unable to legitimate itself while narrative knowledge always carried with it its own legitimation, and so (2) some version of the second in the form of a grand narrative has traditionally been introduced to support and legitimate scientific knowledge. He then goes on to describe two such great narratives legitimating knowledge in the post-feudal period: that of the emancipation of the people and that of the triumph of science (1984, pp. 31–7). He concludes with the suggestion that Marxism 'wavered between the two' (p. 36) and did not unite them as fully as it might by claiming that the emancipation of the proletariat could only be achieved via the knowledge made available only within the science of historical materialism (more will need to be said about Lyotard's own narrative of how Western Europe came to enter the postmodern condition in chapter 8, 'Modernism/Postmodernism').

Drawing on this, *The Political Unconscious* is willing and able to bracket history as the real and as an object of knowledge, asserting: 'that history is *not* a text, not a narrative, master or otherwise, but that, as an absent cause, it is inaccessible to us except in textual form, and that our approach to it and to the Real itself necessarily passes through its prior textualisation, its narrativisation in the political unconscious' (1984, p. 35). The structure of this argument is certainly borrowed from psychoanalysis and from Macherey's account of how, on the model of the way the unconscious is reproduced in the effects which deny it, history is present in the way the literary text represses it, an absent cause expressing itself only symptomatically. In invoking the Real as it does, Jameson's is also a psychoanalytic argument, for this is Lacan's real (as distinct from the imaginary and the symbolic): namely, that which exists outside signification.

Having bracketed history itself as real and knowable, and proffered instead only forms of narrative as knowable, Jameson now turns Marxism against post-structuralism and deconstruction, for historical materialism *is* the master narrative, the great narrative which 'subsumes other interpretive modes or systems' (p. 47). The epistemological problem thus apparently solved, history is able to return much as before, understood according to traditional Marxist categories as class conflict and the priority of collective, social being over individual consciousness. Such contradictions are unthinkable in the literary text and appear only as the political unconscious of the text, 'as what the text represses' (p. 48).

This line of argument is open to the same objections as when it was introduced by Macherey, namely, that the psychoanalytic conceptualisation is at best a model or paradigm and at worst no more than another metaphor. The concepts of the unconscious and of repression have a specific terminological force in psychoanalysis as they apply to operations of the mental apparatus. Thus the appearance in the subject of thoughts (especially thoughts of incest) is prohibited by the opening up of a split (*Spaltung*) between conscious and unconscious such that unconscious thought remains dynamically and actively repressed from entering conscious awareness. Now, it is certainly the case that for historical materialism class operates in a collective mode which exceeds or transcends the consciousness of individuals. Marx and Engels assert that class 'achieves an independent existence over against the individuals so that the latter find their conditions of existence predestined, and hence have their position in life and their personal development assigned to them by their class, become subsumed under it' (1970, p. 82). In this sense class is involuntary and acts against the individual's will but it is not *unconscious* or *repressed* in the psychoanalytic sense of these terms. Again, to take a second strand of the argument, if history is defined as

absent cause, as the Real, which persists necessarily outside signification and can only be encountered as narrative, this is an epistemological distinction between what can and can not be signified.
The real (like Kant's 'thing in itself') is indeed unthinkable but only
functionally so; it can only be referred to as repressed by a
considerable extension and attenuation of the term. In sum, the
objection to Jameson's notion of 'the political unconscious' is quite
simply that it is not unconscious.

A second relevant issue is raised by Jameson's whole attempt to
mobilise psychoanalysis towards an understanding of the social
formation and of literature. *The Political Unconscious* writes of
psychoanalysis as 'the only really new and original hermeneutic
developed since the great patristic and medieval system of the four
senses of scripture' (1981, p. 61). But the attempt to appropriate
psychoanalysis for – or rather incorporate it *into* – the great narrative
of historical materialism requires and corresponds to a sustained
critique of psychoanalysis in the name of history. This follows on
from Foucault's similar attack in *The History of Sexuality*. Noted
here, both will be kept aside for discussion in the concluding chapter
on the limitations of psychoanalysis.

Even if the engagement of *The Political Unconscious* with psychoanalysis is uneven and essentially imperialist, it nevertheless entails
a third topic in discussion of ideology that cannot be omitted.
Whereas traditional Marxism has envisaged ideology only as a mode
for the exercise of power, Jameson opens up the original proposal
that it must at the same time be necessarily utopian in so far as it takes
on the meaning of a universal value. Thus, if ideology has the effect of
rendering its subject passive, it must offer 'specific gratifications in
return for his or her consent to passivity' (p. 287). It does so, it is
argued, because '*all* class consciousness . . . is in its very nature
Utopian' (p. 289) in virtue of the fact that it expresses the unity of a
collectivity, even in the consciousness of the dominant class. This is
said of ideology as put to work in the products of popular culture but
there is no reason why it should not apply also to the high cultural
texts to be examined here and so it will be, though for reasons
additional to those Jameson gives in his account of ideology as
utopian.

This specifies only the concept of ideology but seems disingenuous
to present it only as it does, as a social effect. As a utopian hope for a
better world ideology actually functions as a vehicle for the

fulfilment of a wish and this is of course precisely the way psychoanalysis understands the nature and operation of phantasy. And so does *The Political Unconscious*, for, implicit in its own terminology, this is how the utopian side of ideology is described: the reader is offered 'gratifications', moved thus by 'impulses' and offered 'substantial incentives' for 'ideological adherence' (p. 287).

The nature of these impulses for gratification is not clarified in the discussion of ideology but elsewhere, in what may well be intended as a separate issue, a fourth point to remark here. Having shown psychoanalysis the front door or admitted it only in a revised form that can be incorporated into the great narrative of Marxism, *The Political Unconscious* lets it in at the back. A 'particular political fantasy' in a literary text may be structured as a 'libidinal apparatus' (p. 48). How far this is to be identified with the utopian wish of ideology is not made clear. But in Jameson's preceding work on Wyndham Lewis the concept of libidinal apparatus, derived also from Lyotard, was defined as a form or structural matrix 'in which a charge of free-floating and inchoate fantasy – both ideological and psychoanalytic – can suddenly crystallize' (1979, p. 95). Both ideological and psychoanalytic: though it does not adequately respect the difference between the two, this is the concept which most nearly coincides with the idea of social phantasy that will be advanced here.

Although this theoretical line from Macherey on constantly seeks a *rapprochement* between theories of ideology and the conceptual system of psychoanalysis, it has to be said that it comes no closer than other theoretical work to achieving a genuine synthesis of the two. Ensuing from this, the conclusion put forward here asserts, first, that we should not look for a synthesis, a unified theory comprehending ideology and the unconscious, and have no right to do so; second, that in a specific discursive form, such as poetry, both ideological significance and meanings analysable as phantasy are necessarily produced together and in relation.

A chapter of *Social Relations and Human Attributes* (1982) by Paul Q. Hirst and Penny Woolley contains one of the most serious and sustained attempts to assess together a sociological against a psychoanalytic account of what looks like the same area or object of inquiry. Its argument merits rehearsal in summary, its conclusion will be endorsed.

Hirst and Woolley set out to read against each other Freud's account of the incest taboo in *Totem and Taboo* (1913) and the classic anthropological study of Trobriand Island society in Bronislaw Malinowski's *Sex and Repression in Savage Society* (1937). Freud draws together three things: Darwin's thesis that in early societies a single male kept all the women for himself; W. Robertson Smith's view that the killing and ritual eating of a totemic animal is crucially important in the development of religion; Freud's own view that analysis of contemporary neurotics can illuminate the attitudes of primitive peoples (hence the subtitle to the work, 'Some Points of Agreement between the Mental Lives of Savages and Neurotics'). On this basis Freud constructs a hypothesis for the origin of human society out of a single event, a narrative he himself later referred to as a 'Just-So Story'. The hypothetical first father kept all the women to himself, expelling and destroying any sons who challenged him, so that they were driven to plot together to kill and eat him. Out of respect and guilt they symbolised the dead father in a totem animal and united to institute the law against incest.

Throughout, as Hirst and Woolley note, Freud assumes that the 'primary-process' of the unconscious is 'universal in its basic contents and mechanisms' (p. 150), that a Viennese member of the liberal professions and an Australian aboriginal are linked 'by similar mechanisms of unconscious thought' (p. 151). Freud is therefore not offering an explanation of the origin of human social life but rather of the incest taboo; and he is not concerned 'to explain institutions in the way a sociologist or anthropologist would' – rather 'he derives religion, law, and custom directly from the dynamic of the psyche' (p. 152) as though states of mind gave rise directly to institutions. This is fraught with problems, not least that Freud gives no explanation of how the process happens. Further, as they argue, in order to explain the formation of the Oedipal order Freud *presupposes* features instituted by this order (sexual identities, the place of the father), thus assuming patriarchy in order to say how it occurred.

In his account of a Polynesian culture Malinowski points out that the family structure is radically different from that supposed in Freud's account of the Oedipus complex. Descent is reckoned through the female line; the son inherits from his maternal uncle, and he, not the father, is an authority figure (the father is a nurse and playmate). Yet the child does not come into sexual conflict with his uncle or with his father as source of discipline. While paternity and sexuality are not strongly related in Trobriand Island society, a son is forbidden members of his uncle's clan and especially his sister so that sexual conflicts centre on the relation between brother and sister. Thus, against Freud, Malinowski can argue 'the building up of the sentiments, the conflicts which this implies, depend largely upon the sociological mechanism which works in a given society' (cited Hirst and Woolley, p. 155).

In his study Malinowski treats sexuality as inherently genital, deriving it effectively from the body; and he refuses Freud's concept of the unconscious, dismissing it as 'metaphysical' (cited Hirst and Woolley, p. 155). He thus can have no account of the libidinal attachments at work in families and social groupings, and, as Hirst and Woolley point out, while Freud's attempt in *Group Psychology and the Analysis of the Ego* to explain the organisation of institutions exclusively in terms of unconscious affections is inadequate, so is Malinowski's willingness to ignore them altogether. Freud relies on the concept of the unconscious, Malinowski on the body together with social relations, and so 'if Freud makes social relations the unmediated results of psychic states, Malinowski makes social relations, in the last instance, patterns of culture' (p. 156). It is not the case, then, that psychoanalysis and anthropology refute each other but rather that they are not in competition here, that 'we see two quite different forms of theory and investigative practice brought into confrontation' (p. 158). Hirst and Woolley conclude that what they term these two 'complementary human sciences' are in fact 'condemned for the foreseeable future to coexist in tension' (p. 160).

If this holds for the relation between psychoanalysis and anthropology it maintains for the same reasons for the relation with sociology and indeed historical materialism. But, crucially, though the objects of the unconscious and ideology, as theorised separately in the different scientific discourses of knowledge represented by psychoanalysis and historical materialism, are incommensurate this is not the last word. For as Hirst and Woolley point out, 'social relations, the customs and institutions of particular peoples, intersect with a general psychic domain' (p. 158), 'the psychic-symbolic domain interpenetrates with culture and social relations' (p. 159). Intersection, interpenetration: this is the crux of the problem of the relation between ideology and the unconscious.

Poetry as social phantasy

As theoretical forms of knowledge, psychoanalysis and historical materialism have different objects of study together with different methods and procedures for analysing those objects. They do so because their two objects – the unconscious and ideology within the social formation – are necessarily not identical and, as was proposed earlier, act according to their own specificities in different times. However, ideology and the unconscious, by nature incommensurable, are always brought together and produced together within history.

In this respect it becomes essential to envisage the relation between ideology and unconscious on the model of relative autonomy, in fact as the kind of interpenetration scrupulously summarised by Stephen Heath:

Psychoanalysis must be established within historical materialism. There is no subject outside of a social formation, outside of social processes which include and define positions of meaning, which specify ideological places. Yet this inclusion, definition and specification does not exhaust the subject: at once because it says nothing concerning practice and also because it says nothing about the material history of the construction of the individual for such inclusion, definition and specification. It is this latter area that psychoanalysis effectively identifies and opens up (the new 'continent'), that it takes as its province. Yet, to turn back round again, the real history with which psychoanalysis thus deals is still directly and immediately social, not 'before' or 'underneath' or 'elsewhere' to social processes, ideological places. There is a material history of the construction of the individual as subject and that history is also the social construction of the subject; it is not, in other words, that there is first of all the construction of a subject for social/ideological formations and then the placing of that constructed subject-support in those formations, it is that the two processes are one, in a kind of necessary simultaneity – like the recto and verso of a piece of paper. It is to the implications of such a simultaneity that psychoanalysis has often found it difficult to respond. (1976, pp. 61–2)

This account derives the articulation of ideology and subjectivity from three features. The autonomy of ideological formations is assumed; autonomy is attributed to the process of the unconscious since its inclusion and definition in the social process 'does not exhaust the subject'; yet a degree of unified relation between the two is affirmed since in history 'the two processes are one, in a kind of necessary simultaneity'.

The metaphor for this simultaneity is brilliantly adapted from the metaphor Saussure uses to describe the connection between signifier and signified in language:

Language can also be compared with a sheet of paper: thought is the front and sound the back; one cannot cut the front without cutting the back at the same time; likewise in language, one can neither divide sound from thought nor thought from sound . . . (1959, p. 113)

If we keep it sternly in mind that this is only a metaphor, having descriptive but not explanatory force, it is still an analogy of great accuracy. Thus, in language:

(a) signifier ('sound') and signified ('thought') are different orders, each proceeding separately according to its own logic and laws;
(b) their relation, therefore, is by nature only arbitrary;
(c) nevertheless, in practice, in the process of utterance, they are brought together in what Saussure calls the 'social fact' of discourse (p. 113);
(d) as such, a change in one plane brings about a change in the other.

In discourse:

(a) what is analysable as ideology and as phantasy follow their own autonomy;
(b) they are necessarily by nature distinct and incommensurate;
(c) but in history they are always produced together and in simultaneity;
(d) a change in one is simultaneous with and corresponds to a change in the other.

That simultaneity entails analysis of poetry as social phantasy.

Freud does not draw on a concept of ideology (consciousness socially determined in relations of power), the other side of the 'simultaneity' to which, as Heath remarks, psychoanalysis has found it 'difficult to respond'. Nor did he write a book on art. But he did write a sustained work on jokes.

The process of the joke has a very close affinity to that of art as phantasy, as was noted in chapter 1. Jokes in the form of the tendentious joke, the joke proper, have a social point and are effective in 'getting rid of inhibitions' (*SE* VIII, p. 134). Not a technical term (it does not appear in Laplanche and Pontalis 1980, though it is later given a different and specific definition in Freud's paper of that name of 1926) inhibition is used to mean the subjective internalisation of social values. Inhibition is an aspect of 'suppression', which at this stage in Freud's work is distinguished from repression because it is conscious and unconscious while repression is only unconscious. A joke relieves repression temporarily but only by also lifting an inhibition; the tendentious joke therefore works simultaneously with unconscious and conscious material, both psychically *and ideologically*. In acknowledgment of this latter factor Freud explains how 'every joke calls for a public of its own' (*SE* XIII, p. 151). In sum, then, the joke, like art, is an occasion for shared phantasy but only in conjunction with particular ideological meanings.

From here we may return to recapitulate the account of literature from the side of psychoanalysis set out in chapter 1. A dream as discourse of the unconscious expresses itself in thing-presentations; an aesthetic text as discourse of the conscious and pre-conscious is expressed in thing-presentations and word-presentations. A dream text is to be interpreted according to: (1) a shared intersubjective symbolism and (2) the context of the dreamer's life. Art has no dreamer but rather works publicly and intersubjectively as a shared symbolic expression which has a meaning for others; unlike the relatively (but not absolutely) asocial products of dreaming, art has a social function and social meaning, one that can be referred only to the concept of ideology and so to the concept proposed of literature as social phantasy.

The difference between dream and poem was clearly illustrated from the example in the previous chapter. Translated into textual discourse and read as poem rather than as dream, the same two-sentence narrative of 'A whole crowd of children' produced ideological meanings closely imbricated with phantasy meanings. Ideological significance accrued *inevitably* from the public production of a text as literature. This was the case with what started as a dream text but it happens to a much greater degree with the text which is already uttered, which starts as aesthetic text, designed through a special working of the signifier for public presentation as external discourse. Although the conceptual frameworks of historical materialism and psychoanalysis will remain distinct, resisting a synthesis we have no right to demand, *the literary text always produces ideological and phantasy meanings in a simultaneity* and both must be considered together as social phantasy: *nec tecum nec sine te* (neither with you nor without you). Any attempt to discuss a poetic text only with attention to one side is reductive and inadequate.

It will not be claimed that there is any generalisable form of this relation other than simultaneity. In every case except one, the relation appears to be one of close mutual support well short of active intervention by one plane in the other. One probable exception is *Paradise Lost*. In this, it will be argued, a phantasy effect is put to work in order to seek to make good contradictions and difficulties at the level of ideology, and this exceptional case of interaction may well follow from the fact that this is an epic poem with a sustained narrative. Most of the other texts conform to the lyric tradition and may be grouped together as instances of what will be termed 'confessional discourse', texts which aim to give the effect of an

individual voice speaking. They therefore dramatise a developing
state of mind rather than perform a narration. In these the relation
between phantasy and ideology is one of simultaneity and correspondence. And the least imprecise term to conceptualise this relation is
that of *imbrication*.

The Latin for a shower of rain is *imber* and the word refers also to a
pool in which a pattern is made up by the falling drops as they overlap
and intersect even while remaining distinct. A roof-tile which keeps
rain off by overlapping with others is *imbrex*. Thus any structure
made up by the close interleaving of separable items, as with scales on
a fish, is formed by imbrication. The term and the concept are
precisely what is needed here. For it will be argued that in the
outward, public mode of poetry the imbrication of ideology and
phantasy must be understood as a form of social phantasy.

Although no more precise or even form of organisation is argued
for, it should be stressed that the imbrications analysed are not
merely unitary but structural; that is, an ideological structure
produces meaning in correspondence with a structure of phantasy. It
is not simply the case that a signifier in a text opens on to two
meanings, as does for example 'wings' in the dream as poem [=(i)
angels and Christian ideology; =(ii) children wished as dead]:

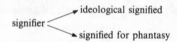

Rather the order of signifiers in a text produces at the same time an
ideological structure and a particular organisation at the level of
phantasy:

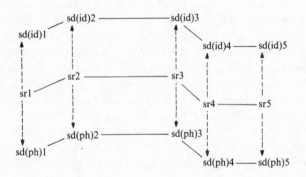

This diagram elaborates the previous one. In the middle are the signifiers of a particular text in a given order, sr1–sr5. But each of these opens onto an ideological signified and these together form a structure, an ideological structure represented above the signifiers of the text as sd(id)1–sd(id)5. Below the signifiers of the text are represented the signifieds for phantasy, also in a structure, sd(ph)1–sd(ph)5. No claim is being advanced that a given structure of ideology necessarily corresponds to a structure for phantasy in general and apart from a text or intertextual grouping; in fact evidence will be given the other way, that, for example, in the feudal period ideologies formed round courtly love are produced in relation to narcissistic phantasies but then again at the end of the eighteenth century so are very different ideologies associated with Romanticism. No general mode or form of correspondence between ideology and phantasy is being asserted here – only that specific correspondence ensured and in fact produced by the way a given order of signifiers in a text opens simultaneously onto ideological meanings on the one side and phantasy meanings on the other.

Although the ordering of signifiers in a given text can be read in terms of a local and particular set of meanings, a single poem cannot be considered apart from its intertextual relation to other texts in an ideological formation. Such intertextuality will be discussed as appropriate, though with a commitment to poetry as a relatively autonomous discourse. Within textual discourse itself, aesthetic discourse constitutes a specific mode; the requirements of poetic discourse exemplified in the material operation of the signifier in poetry through metre and verse form make for a further degree of particularity. Poetry as oral discourse – as the ballad, for example – has been excluded here since, with the exception of one Roman poem, all the texts examined are produced within one historical tradition, that originating with the courtly love poetry of the twelfth century. In this respect, as was argued in *Poetry as Discourse*, the 'canon' of poetry in the dominant tradition constitutes a single, epochal discourse and can reasonably be seen as an autonomous formation, having its *own time* as proposed by Althusser's account of history as discontinuous and differentiated.

The homogeneity of this continuous historical tradition is increased if, as happens here, attention is focused especially on lyric poetry (as noted, *Paradise Lost* is the main example of narrative poetry). It is this homogeneity which allows attention to concentrate on the poetic signified rather than on the level of the signifier and means of representation.

In order to defend the hypothesis that we need to understand poetry as a form of social phantasy it will be important to look at poems from across a number of different historical conjunctures. Each chapter will make some introductory reference to the ideological context for each example or set of examples. Rejecting the view that an articulation of ideology and the unconscious is to be sought in a single area or agency (such as that of the super-ego), the discussion will accept that in the social construction of the individual potentially every aspect of the construction of the subject in the split between conscious and unconscious can become activated. At the level of phantasy the study will inevitably concentrate on the two domains mainly theorised by psychoanalysis, narcissism and sexual desire, while looking for social phantasy across a range of unconscious operations: sublimation, idealisation, scopophilia, the Oepidus complex, neurotic obsession, paranoia and others. But in terms of the poems considered an argument will rapidly emerge that, far from there being some comprehensive range of phantasies enacted, there are in fact specific forms of phantasy local to this tradition of poetic discourse and that these correspond closely to certain ideological assumptions about individualism and about gender. That account can be left to explain itself as it arises with particular poems and will be saved for fuller exploration in a conclusion.

The next chapter will contrast two poems with three considerations in mind. One will be to acknowledge, albeit only in outline, a historical perspective stretching between ancient European culture and the Renaissance. A second is to establish the discursive form of the post-Renaissance tradition of lyric poetry by referring to the work of Foucault and his account of confessional discourse. But following on from this introductory reference to Foucault, a third consideration must be a preliminary critique of that work, indicating the limits of its applicability to the study of literature. As mentioned already, Foucault represents one of the most hostile opponents of psychoanalysis, and so discussion will open questions that will be more fully confronted in a final general chapter.

3

FOUCAULT, OVID, DONNE: VERSIONS OF SEXUALITY, ANCIENT AND MODERN

Our sex love differs materially from the simple sexual desire, the *eros* of the ancients.   Frederick Engels

The first two poems to be analysed as social phantasy are widely separated in time but seemingly very close in substance. Ovid's *Amores* were probably written down between 25 and 15 BC and Donne's 'Elegy 19' between 1593 and 1596. Usually known as 'To his Mistris Going to Bed', the elegy is an imitation of *Amores* I.5. Both texts conventionally fall into the category of forbidden poetry since they speak directly and explicitly about the sexual act, and on these grounds alone they are often treated as being much the same in effect and meaning. A psychoanalytic account will suggest that they offer somewhat different phantasies, differences that need to be understood historically. At the same time these two texts are particularly suitable to take up in the context of the first volume of Foucault's *The History of Sexuality*, *La Volonté de savoir* (1981), a text whose brave speculations contain numerous insights about the distinctions between sexuality ancient and modern. The other two relevant volumes, *L'Usage des plaisirs* and *Le Souci de soi* (1984), retreat disappointingly from the wider horizons of the first volume into a more detailed, more narrowly academic study of sexuality in the ancient world – Ovid, for example, finds no mention in *Le Souci de soi*.

Outside conventional literary criticism a Foucauldian reading now promises itself as a main alternative to forms of psychoanalytic interpretation, and so this chapter will in part sustain the theoretical concerns of chapters 1 and 2. While concurring with much of Foucault's analysis and indeed confirming it from the two examples, discussion here will aim to point out where that account needs to be qualified in its application to poetry and will argue that the notion of social phantasy is also needed to exhibit the particular content of literary texts.

The history of sexuality

According to Foucault, sexuality 'must not be thought of as a kind of natural given' but as the name 'given to a historical construct' (1981, p. 105). The history of sexuality in the West is generally viewed in terms of 'The Repression Hypothesis', that is, as Foucault summarises it, 'after hundreds of years of open spaces and free expression' (p. 5), the development of capitalism in the seventeenth century led to a repression of sex because of the imperatives of the work-discipline. His suggestion is that the opposite may be the case:

A first survey seems to indicate that since the end of the sixteenth century, the 'putting into discourse of sex', far from undergoing a process of restriction, on the contrary has been subjected to a mechanism of increasing incitement... [a] dissemination and implantation of polymorphous sexualities . . .

(p. 12)

This argument that instead of repression there has been for four hundred years 'a steady proliferation of discourse concerned with sex' (p. 18) is not meant to deny that there has been prohibition and censorship. Rather it is meant to dislodge the view (promoted by such writers as Reich and Marcuse, see Hussain 1981, p. 187) that sexuality should be thought of only in an opposition between expression and repression. Foucault's aim is to show: that sexuality cannot be defined like this along a single axis; that it must be conceived as a set of effects dispersed across many institutions and discourses; that power operates not only by forbidding but also in the ways it permits sexuality and permits it to be known. While previously sexuality had been constructed mainly in civil and canon law and in Christian pastoral teaching, increasingly from the end of the eighteenth century it was produced through such diverse centres as medical practice or the management and design of children's dormitories. To map a genealogy of these institutions and discourses will constitute a history of sexuality.

There have been, claims Foucault, 'two great procedures for producing the truth of sex', an *ars erotica* and a *scientia sexualis* (pp. 57–8). Since the middle ages the West has constructed sexuality as a science, as a knowledge of the truth, and has done so by means of various forms of confession, beginning from the Lateran Council in 1215, which imposed annual confession as a minimal obligation upon every member of the Church. The institution of individual confession instead of forms of group confession leads to a profound 'individualization by power' (p. 59). (There is plenty of support for Foucault's singling out of confession and the Lateran Council for emphasis here. For example, Colin Morris's book, *The Discovery of the Individual, 1050–1200*, gives evidence to support the view that it would be proper to speak of 'the Renaissance of the twelfth century' (1972, p. 7). Among the practices which encourage this early humanism Morris cites courtly love and the re-organisation of confession as instances of the contemporary movement 'away from regulations towards an insight into individual character', p. 75. See also Abercrombie *et al.*, 1980, pp. 80–1.)

Foucault's history asserts that the truth of sex was caught up in the discursive form of confession. At the Renaissance and especially after the Council of Trent (1545–63) confession and sexuality together come to express a further degree of inwardness. Previously the pastoral concern had been with the *act* of sexual intercourse – 'the postures assumed, gestures, places touched, caresses, the precise moment of pleasure'; now, that act itself becomes veiled as interest moves inward to 'thoughts, desires, voluptuous imaginings, delectations', so 'shifting the most important moment of transgression from the act itself to the stirrings – so difficult to perceive and formulate – of desire' (1981, pp. 19–20). From there confession spreads until by the twentieth century it plays a part 'in the most ordinary affairs of everyday life, and in the most solemn rites' (p. 59).

As vehicle and model for the discursive construction of sexuality, confession has a number of effective features. It is profoundly individual and individualising in that the subject or patient speaks about themselves; it presupposes that such speech is in address to an interlocutor in a position of authority; and it assumes that the outcome of confessing will be truth, a truth that at first is latent and tries to stay hidden but can by the very process of confession itself be extracted 'from the depths of oneself' and made to yield to 'the basic certainties of consciousness' (pp. 59–60). So the general adoption of confession as a form for the construction of sexuality has led Western man for three centuries 'to the task of telling everything concerning his sex' (p. 23).

The great watershed of the twelfth-century Renaissance leaves in question what form sexuality took before then. Foucault constantly refers to the inauguration of the modern tradition as a 'scheme for transforming sex into discourse' (p. 20, also 'transformation of sex into discourse' pp. 36, 61). But since sexuality is a historical construct, not a natural given, sex is *always already* transformed into discourse, as is made explicit when the book writes of the modern mirage of sex somehow given in and for itself as precisely a construction of sexuality and a deployment of power (p. 157, see also Heath 1982). The counterattack against this envisaged by Foucault is not yet another deployment of sexuality but 'bodies and pleasures' (Foucault 1981, p. 157). The before and after of the twelfth century should not be discriminated therefore as moving between sex and sexuality, between sex 'in itself' and as transformed into discourse but rather as an art of love giving way to a science of sexuality: 'We have had sexuality since the eighteenth century and sex since the nineteenth. What we had before that was no doubt the flesh' (Foucault 1980, p. 211). It is on the basis of this contrast between the discursive construction of the body, the flesh and pleasure as against its construction as the knowledge of inward truth that we may approach the poems by Ovid and Donne.

Ovid: *Amores* 1.5

The *Amores* tell the story of a love-affair with Corinna, a married woman. In Book 1.5 she is named for the first time and there is the first act of intercourse with her. The Latin text is given in 'A note on Marlowe's translation' (below, pp. 60–1); I have translated it fairly literally as follows. Semiramis is a famous Assyrian queen, Laïs an equally famous Corinthian courtesan:

> It was hot, and the time had passed midday;
>   I was lying on the bed for a rest.
> Part of the window was open, the other was closed,
>   almost the kind of light woods tend to have,
> 5   the kind of twilight that glimmers at sunset
>   or when night has gone but the day not yet come.
> That's the light that suits shy girls,
>   one their timid modesty hopes to hide in.
> Look, Corinna comes, with the belt of her tunic undone,
> 10   her hair loose over her white neck,
> like beautiful Semiramis was going to bed

(they say) or Laïs, who was loved by many men.
I tore off her tunic; being thin, it didn't do much,
   but still she struggled to cover herself with it;
15   Since she was struggling like someone who didn't want to win,
   she was won over easily and betrayed herself.
As she stood before my eyes with her clothes off,
   nowhere in her whole body was there a fault:
what shoulders, what arms I saw and touched!
20   the shape of her breasts how ready to be held!
What a flat stomach under her perfect bosom!
   What long, fine sides! What a young thigh!
Why list them one by one? I saw all was fine,
   and held her naked body close to mine.
25   Who doesn't know the rest? Tired, we both lay quiet.
   Let my middays often turn out like this.

Although the poem shows sexual intercourse mainly in terms of pleasure and the body, it does not deny a relationship between the speaker and Corinna, though, by staying close to concrete particularities, it leaves the nature of the relationship secondary and implicit. She wants to make love for she comes to him, in the dramatic phrase of the Latin, *ecce Corinna uenit*. She has untied the belt of her tunic and let her hair down (Roman women generally wore it up); her tunic itself is *rara*, loose in texture (l.13). Why then does he tear it off with violence? Lines 13–16 are offensive, an early illustration of the myth that male desire is best shown in physical violence and female desire when inner acquiescence overcomes overt reluctance. And why if this event did take place does he talk about it? There is an implicit address to a male audience, to a male friend ('Why list them one by one?' . . . 'Who doesn't know the rest?'), so that Corinna is treated as an object in knowing exchange between two men. But the poem is silent about what she thought and felt, not only because it reproduces a patriarchal assumption that she is to be an object for his pleasure, but also because its concern is with action and sexual pleasure rather than attitude and intention.

The distinction between an *ars erotica* and a *scientia sexualis*, says Foucault, consists in the fact that

In the erotic art, truth is drawn from pleasure itself, understood as a practice and accumulated as experience; pleasure is not considered in relation to an absolute law of the permitted and the forbidden, nor by reference to a criterion of utility, but first and foremost in relation to itself; it is experienced as pleasure . . .   (1981, p. 57)

In Ovid's poem sexual pleasure is treated 'first and foremost in relation to itself'. This can be seen negatively in the relative absence of guilt, social relationship or obvious fictionalisation surrounding the represented encounter; positively, in the degree to which the represented subject and object are imaged as relating almost without mediation, the man's desire excited and answered by the woman's body (and hers by his? but the poem excludes her point of view):

> what shoulders, what arms I saw and touched!
> the shape of her breasts how ready to be held!

The breasts, the feeling that seeing them provokes in him, his touching them, all are brought into a closely reciprocal relationship: *apta . . . premi*, 'ready to be held' (an epexegetic infinitive). Distance between sight and touching is minimal, as is well explained in John Barsby's commentary: 'the verb *uidi* is closely followed on its first appearance by *tetigi* (19) and on its second by *pressi* (24)' (1973, p. 69). 'I saw' (*uidi*) (ll. 19, 23) leads on directly to 'I touched' (*tetigi*) and 'I held' (*pressi*). In this text, vision itself offers little autonomous pleasure or mastery and functions as a simple intermediary to touching and holding. The poem is perhaps Utopian in that it imagines pleasure and satisfaction calling into play all the senses together.

Barsby says that the technique of the poem 'is exactly that of the film' (*ibid.*) yet that is precisely what the poem is not like. In Hollywood the dramatisation of sexual desire always approaches striptease – suspense in the narrative sequence, enumeration of details each hinting at the next. Ovid's syntactical juxtaposition of exclamations ('what arms . . .', 'how ready . . .') gives a direct and rapid account, a literal response that does not work through innuendo or circumlocution. It curtails a part by part description ('Why list them one by one?') in favour of the representation of bodily pleasure, *nudam . . . corpus ad usque meum* (l. 24), the inverted word order introducing *usque* ('through and through, at every point') between *corpus* and *meum*, between 'my' and 'body'. The climax is left unspoken, universalised, outside discourse – 'Who doesn't know the rest?'

Today it is likely readers will encounter a sense of absence in Ovid's text, a feeling that it is only of the surface, lacking depth and subtlety. It is so matter of fact and ends merely with the wish, 'Let my middays often turn out like this'. If this is the response it is caused by our expectation of an inwardness the text does not work with. Foucault's positive evaluation of 'bodies and pleasures' over against sexuality may help to reverse a little the habitual terms in which the text might be seen in comparison with Donne's imitation of it.

Donne: 'Elegy 19'

Donne's poem needs to be read in context with other English Renaissance poems that draw on the Ovid precedent: Nashe's 'The Choice of Valentines', Thomas Jordan's 'To Leda his coy Bride', Carew's 'A Rapture' and perhaps Herrick's 'The Description of a Woman'. It was refused license for publication in the 1633 edition of Donne's work and was not printed until 1669. It does not attempt an exact translation of Ovid but is rather an imitation, expanding Ovid's 26 lines to 48, drawing in ideas and material from its own time.

> Come, Madam, come, all rest my powers defie,
> Until I labour, I in labour lie.
> The foe oft-times having the foe in sight,
> Is tir'd with standing thou he never fight.
> 5 Off with the girdle, like heavens Zone glittering,
> But a far fairer world incompassing.
> Unpin that spangled breastplate which you wear,
> That th'eyes of busie fooles may be stopt there.
> Unlace your self, for that harmonious chyme,
> 10 Tells me from you, that now it is bed time.
> Off with that happy busk, which I envie,
> That still can be, and still can stand so nigh.
> Your gown going off, such beautious state reveals,
> As when from flowry meads th'hills shadow steales.
> 15 Off with that wyerie Coronet and shew
> The haiery Diademe which on you doth grow:
> Now off with those shooes, and then safely tread
> In this loves hallow'd temple, this soft bed.
> In such white robes, heaven's Angels us'd to be
> 20 Receavd by men; Thou Angel bringst with thee
> A heaven like Mahomets Paradise; and though
> Ill spirits walk in white, we easly know,
> By this these Angels from an evil sprite,
> Those set our hairs, but these our flesh upright.
> 25   Licence my roaving hands, and let them go,
> Before, behind, between, above, below.
> O my America! my new-found-land,
> My kingdome, safeliest when with one man man'd,
> My Myne of precious stones, My Emperie,

30   How blest am I in this discovering thee!
       To enter in these bonds, is to be free;
       Then where my hand is set, my seal shall be.
           Full nakedness! All joyes are due to thee,
       As souls unbodied, bodies uncloth'd must be,
35   To taste whole joyes. Gems which you women use
       Are like Atlanta's balls, cast in mens views,
       That when a fools eye lighteth on a Gem,
       His earthly soul may covet theirs, not them.
       Like pictures, or like books gay coverings made
40   For lay-men, are all women thus array'd;
       Themselves are mystick books, which only wee
       (Whom their imputed grace will dignifie)
       Must see reveal'd. Then since that I may know;
       As liberally, as to a Midwife, shew
45   Thy self: cast all, yea, this white lynnen hence,
       There is no pennance due to innocence.
           To teach thee, I am naked first; why than
       What needs though have more covering then a man.

Donne's poem begins as an imperative ('Come, Madam, come') telling the woman to undress, continues with the imperative to describe his touching her ('Licence my roaving hands'), and then shifts dramatically into the simple present with 'Full nakedness! All joyes are due to thee', though ends again with orders to her ('shew / Thy self'). Whereas Ovid's poem recalled the past in straight description, Donne's dramatises a present moment in which the woman is commanded to strip slowly while the man looks at her. In the first 24 lines the main pleasure comes from sight and vision. She is to take off her clothes item by item, girdle, breastplate, etc., and these objects are fetishised, the girdle 'glittering', the breastplate (or stomacher) 'spangled'. She is one army before a battle kept 'in sight' (l. 3) by another; her clothes stop 'th' eyes of busie fooles' but not his privileged gaze; the removal of her gown 'reveals' her beauty.

In the first paragraph the man's look is represented as always moving on from object to object. It is a movement of displacement or metonomy, whose effect is to suggest that once an object is mastered, seen directly, its interest is transferred to another object, one desired because it cannot be seen directly. Although it enumerates her clothes, the text does not list the parts of the woman's body. That is left over, an object of desire still not seen, ahead of the movement of the poem, which stops before it reaches there (she is called on to remove her linen shift four lines from the end). Similarly, and in firm contrast to Ovid's text, 'Elegy 19' is full of innuendo and irony, so much so that it needs no illustration here. This verbal effect is like the visual effect represented because it also works through displacement: meaning is kept hidden and suggested, caught in the implication sliding under the words rather than spelt out.

After the first paragraph there is an abrupt change from vision to touching with 'Licence my roaving hands'. But the metaphors in these lines (ll. 25–30) do not trade between two empirically perceivable objects (snow and skin for example) but exchange the body for something much more abstract, America, Newfoundland, Robinson Crusoe's island (or Prospero's), a diamond mine, an empire. In Ovid's text the body is referred only to itself ('what shoulders, what arms . . .') whereas the metaphors in Donne constantly relay the body and its pleasures to something that is neither, specifically to a spiritual dimension. Her girdle is seen as the Primum Mobile ('heavens Zone', l. 5), the bed as a 'hallow'd temple' (l. 18), he is 'blest' in discovering her (l. 30), women's naked bodies are like 'mystick books' (l. 41). Nakedness is compared to the resurrected body ('souls unbodied', l. 34), and with only her shift on, the woman is compared to an angel, though one not in the Christian garden but in 'A heaven like Mahomets Paradise' (l. 21). Such metaphorical substitutions of the body with something else add up to a single meaning: that the woman's body has spiritual value and that sexual intercourse has – will have – transcendent significance. The poem's metaphors imagine 'a far fairer world' (l. 6) than the real one, regions in which the experience of transcendence may take place: Eden before the fall, the utopia of the new world in America, heaven after the resurrection of the body.

From satisfaction to love

The differences between these two texts are made apparent because the same image of coitus figures in each in the place of an object of desire. In Ovid's text intercourse is desired very much in the form of a day-dream, the poem itself aiming to fulfil a wish, that Corinna should come to the speaker. In fact, it may well be read as the speaker 'indulging in erotic day-dreams while he takes his siesta' (Du Quesnay 1973, p. 11). Corinna arrives when he is already half-asleep and the poem ends with them both dozing. Maybe it is – was – all a day-dream. If so, the poem is alluding to its own status as a fictional text which makes possible this phantasy. And if that is the case the text undermines its own status as truth. In contrast, Donne's poem is profoundly committed to truth. It aims to exclude any fictionalising wish-fulfilment by dramatising its represented action as something really happening in the present ('Come, Madam, come'). And whereas the speaker of the Roman poem, if he is confessing, is also boasting and overtly fantasising for a male audience, the speaker of the 'Elegy' is *himself* advanced in the role of confessional interlocutor whose imperatives seek to elicit truth from the woman. As for his sex, that truth is there for all to see (e.g. ll. 4, 24, 47–8), but the truth about her body and her sex is hidden and must be revealed, something the power exercised in confessional discourse would compel into the open where it may be fully known:

> Then since that I may know;
> As liberally, as to a Midwife, shew
> Thy self . . .

This revelation is postponed continually during the poem and is still deferred when it ends.

This, I think, is as far as a Foucauldian analysis of the literary text will take us. It moves from the social formation and an account of social practice towards ideology, discursive practice and the positioning of the subject. In so doing it vividly draws attention to the discursive form of the 'Elegy' with its enactment of confessional discourse and its dramatisation of an individual voice 'really' speaking. And it marks well the contrast between Ovid's poem attending to the body and pleasure primarily in relation to themselves, and Donne's poem, which mobilises a proliferation and heterogeneous range of discourses for and around sexuality, dramatising a post-Tridentine inwardness of 'thoughts, desires, voluptuous imaginings, delectations' (1981, p. 19).

But Foucault's account, stopping with an external analysis of the social forms and functions through which subjectivity is exercised, does not pretend to analyse any further the *content* and dynamic of the operation of these inward thoughts and stirrings of desire, precisely the phantasy content which excites and gives them attraction by providing a scenario for fulfilment of a wish. His account quite deliberately halts at the frontier of the unconscious and aims to fold the space in which the unconscious becomes active back into the

social and ideological. In this respect, far from threatening psychoanalytic accounts with an alternative, Foucault's simply ignores
that possibility, and in application to literary effect is limited by its
reductiveness, as will be any analysis which faces the incommensur-
ability of ideology and the unconscious and then is prepared to settle
only for one. Inwardness is recognised, its boundaries marked out but
otherwise left substantially undefined. What needs to be explained in
Donne's text is the way it pursues its object of desire through a series
of substitutions for it, displacements of sexual drive into the pleasure
of looking, into verbal innuendo and witty circumlocutions, into
metaphors that persistently replace Ovid's concrete description of the
physical with some abstraction. The pleasures attaching to these
effects all start to become explicable in the psychoanalytic account of
narcissism and the ego.

Psychoanalysis distinguishes between ego libido and object libido.
The infant begins in a kind of unity, such that self-love and object-
love are not separated: the new-born subject loves its objects as itself.
He or she develops as a subject through the gradual separation and
redirection of drive onto either the subject's own self (narcissism) or
into an external object, especially when sexual drive is directed
towards another person. In explaining this separation, Freud puts
forward the view that a number of early causes in the development of
the psyche – the attempt to make up for objects that are lost as well as
the need to strengthen the infant ego and help it to control the id –
may lead the ego to force itself upon the id as a love-object, as though
saying, 'Look, you can love me too – I am so like the object' (*SE* xix,
p. 30). The result is a withdrawal of libido onto the ego which brings
about a 'transformation of object-libido into narcissistic libido', this
in turn implying 'an abandonment of sexual aims, a desexualisation –
a kind of sublimation, therefore' (*ibid.*). Sublimation remains a
permanent possibility for the subject and consists of the directing of
sexual drive 'towards an aim other than, and remote from, that of
sexual satisfaction' (*SE* xiv, p. 94).

That this account provides a valid context for understanding the
two poems can be appreciated immediately from the fact that Freud
first introduces the term 'sublimated' to explain how sexual drive can
be diverted into visual pleasure or *scopophilia* (*SE* vii, pp. 155–7).
Both texts represent the idea of sexual intercourse but Donne's differs
strongly from its precedent in the degree to which sexual drive has
been transformed or sublimated into narcissism. What appears to be

– is even notorious as – a poem with a sexual aim is in fact much more an expression of self-love, as Thomas Docherty notes in an excellent commentary when he remarks that what the speaker seeks is not at all the woman but rather 'recognition of his maleness' (1986, p. 82). The effect is produced when the poem's sexual object is desexualised by being constructed through a number of discourses which have an aim remote from the idea of sexual satisfaction, especially theology, political discourses concerning geographical exploration ('O my America') and imperialism ('My Emperie'), classical mythology ('Atlanta's balls'), even medical discourse (the reference to 'a Midwife'). The woman's body and making love to her are presented throughout as a metaphysical absolute, Eden, America, Paradise, heaven, altogether 'a far fairer' world. It is in such references that we may detect the poem's Renaissance Utopianism. Though rendered as attributes of the individual, the transcendence and mastery reveal their social derivation from the ideology of a class: freed from feudal hierarchy the bourgeoisie aims to master nature (as, implicitly, man does woman) and extend its imperialist domination across the world.

The pagan poem locates positive value on earth and in history; Corinna is compared to Semiramis and Laïs. In phantasy, Ovid's speaker wishes for sexual pleasure imagined as relative, transient, bodily, to be re-found and lost again on other afternoons. The speaker of the 'Elegy' wants above all to look at the object of his desire, to master it visually as a truth he must see 'reveal'd' so he may 'know' it completely. He desires neither the woman nor sexual satisfaction but rather a transcendent object, one whose perfect atemporal image may return to him an equally perfect reflection of himself.

Donne's text offers a sexual phantasy largely sublimated into narcissism, and this is why it is pre-occupied with the idea of looking at a naked woman while in Ovid sight at once mediates touch. Scopophilia has already been analysed brilliantly by Laura Mulvey as a form of social phantasy exemplified in Hollywood cinema (1975, pp. 6–18). The representation of and incitement towards visual pleasure becomes a constant feature in poetry from the Renaissance, for example in Petrarch (see chapter 4 below) and has recently had attention drawn to it in Shakespeare's sonnets of praise by Joel Fineman when he writes of 'the fundamentally *visual* modality of such idealising epideictic poetry' (1986, p. 68), so it may be set out here briefly.

Scopophilia begins auto-erotically as a pleasure in looking at one's own body, particularly one's own genitals: its 'preliminary stage . . . in which the subject's own body is the object of the scopophilia, must be classed under narcissism' (*SE* xiv, p. 1). It leaves narcissism behind in developing into voyeurism, the desire to look at others, but retains it fully in exhibitionism, the desire to be looked at. However, active scopophilia, looking at others, is narcissistic in so far as the subject *identifies* itself with and in the object of its own gaze, especially when this object is idealised and so able to give back to the subject a perfected image of itself (this identification of the subject with its objects forms the basis of Lacan's account in 'The Mirror Stage', 1977a, pp. 1–7, and is further discussed below, chapter 4). The scopophilia represented in the 'Elegy' is narcissistic in that the speaker uses the idea of the woman's body and intercourse with her as a vehicle for his own idealised image of himself, his Eden, his paradise. It is not the case that these elements are wholly absent from Ovid's poem – the speaker does seek a perfection for himself – but that there they are relatively unimportant.

A conventional reading of Donne states:

The Elegies are untouched by the idealization of women that distinguishes the courtly and Petrarchan traditions from the traditions of classical love-poetry . . . They show no trace of the conception of love . . . as a mystical union by which two souls become one. (Gardner 1965, p. xxiv)

Detailed examination of *Amores* I.5 and 'Elegy 19' has tried to show how far the object of desire in Donne is precisely mystified, sublimated and idealised in contrast with the classical love poem. While confirming Foucault's history of the way sexuality at the Renaissance is constructed with increasing inwardness, to reveal velleities beyond or beneath the act itself, the present argument has aimed to supplement this history with the concept of social phantasy. Although one text is based on the other, Donne's makes possible a narcissistic phantasy for which there is no precedent in Ovid but which conforms entirely to the ideological promotion of individual inwardness in the courtly love tradition. This will be explored further in the next chapter.

There may be one thing to add in connection with Foucault's history. In the second 'Contribution to the psychology of love' Freud writes:

In times in which there were no difficulties standing in the way of sexual satisfaction, such as perhaps during the decline of ancient civilizations, love became worthless and life empty, and strong reaction-formations were required to restore indispensable affective values. In this connection it may be claimed that the ascetic current in Christianity created psychical values for love which pagan antiquity was never able to confer on it. This current assumed greatest importance with the ascetic monks, whose lives were almost entirely occupied with the struggle against libidinal temptation.

(*SE* XI, p. 188)

Foucault's history, too, recounts how around 1215 the ancient possibility of 'satisfaction' gave way to the modern quest for 'psychical values'. It also holds the church responsible for the confessional discourse in which this shift of practices and meanings was effected. But Foucault reverses Freud's assessment. He advocates an art of love, celebrating 'bodies and pleasures', as a rallying point for a counter-attack against the regime of power deployed by a knowledge of sexuality (1981, p. 157). In the following pages the development of a poetic tradition promoting and enabling the social phantasy of what may be termed scopophilic male narcissism will be followed through and re-assessed, culminating in the argument that some versions of modernist poetry challenge the dominant lyric mode and seek to address phantasies around sexuality to a re-appropriation of the body and pleasure.

A note on Marlowe's translation of Ovid

The Latin text of Ovid's *Amores* I.5 is as follows:

> Aestus erat, mediamque dies exegerat horam;
>   adposui medio membra leuanda toro.
> pars adaperta fuit, pars altera clausa fenestrae,
>   quale fere siluae lumen habere solent,
> 5 qualia sublucent fugiente crepuscula Phoebo
>   aut ubi nox abiit nec tamen orta dies.
> illa uerecundis lux est praebenda puellis,
>   qua timidus latebras speret habere pudor.
> ecce, Corinna uenit tunica uelata recincta,
> 10   candida diuidua colla tegente coma,
> qualiter in thalamos formosa Sameramis isse
>   dicitur et multis Lais amata uiris.
> deripui tunicam; nec multum rara nocebat,
>   pugnabat tunica sed tamen illa tegi;
> 15 quae, cum ita pugnaret tamquam quae uincere nollet,

uicta est non aegre proditione sua.
ut stetit ante oculos posito uelamine nostros,
  in toto nusquam corpore menda fuit:
quos umeros, quales uidi tetigique lacertos!
20   forma papillarum quam fuit apta premi!
quam castigato planus sub pectore uenter!
  quantum et quale latus! quam iuuenale femur!
singula quid referam? nil non laudabile uidi,
  et nudam pressi corpus ad usque meum.
25   cetera quis nescit? lassi requieuimus ambo.
proueniant medii sic mihi saepe dies.

Donne's 'Elegy 19' is an *imitation* of Ovid's text, that is, a version
which makes little attempt to follow the original literally but will
remind the reader of it, and its effect is consistent with that mode. But
there is also a literal *translation* produced by Marlowe (almost
certainly while he was still at Cambridge). Ovid's poem is made over
suavely and accurately into heroic couplets:

In summers heate, and midtime of the day,
To rest my limbes, uppon a bedde I lay,
One window shut, the other open stood,
Which gave such light, as twincles in a wood,
5   Like twilight glimps at setting of the sunne,
Or night being past, and yet not day begunne.
Such light to shamefaste maidens must be showne,
Where they may sport, and seeme to be unknowne.
Then came *Corinna* in a long loose gowne,
10   Her white necke hid with tresses hanging downe,
Resembling faire *Semiramis* going to bed,
Or *Layis* of a thousand lovers sped.
I snatcht her gowne: being thin, the harme was small,
Yet strivde she to be covered therewithall,
15   And striving thus as one that would be cast,
Betrayde her selfe, and yeelded at the last.
Starke naked as she stood before mine eie,
Not one wen in her bodie could I spie,
What armes and shoulders did I touch and see,
20   How apt her breasts were to be prest by me,
How smoothe a bellie, under her waste sawe I,
How large a legge, and what a lustie thigh?
To leave the rest, all likt me passing well,
I clinged her naked bodie, downe she fell,
25   Judge you the rest, being tyrde she bad me kisse.
Jove send me more such afternoones as this.

Because the translation is generally so close, those points at which it
does diverge from the Latin become significant and tend to support

the earlier analysis of Donne. For example, Marlowe's translation of line 21 is not 'What a flat stomach under her perfect bosom!' but 'How smoothe a bellie, under her waste sawe I'; this interpolates a reference to sight not in the Latin and, corresponding to this scopophilia, moves the part of the body described down from between breast and hips to a more defined, fetishised object, the triangle of the lower abdomen. The tactile wholeness of the body in Ovid is replaced by a part, and a part to be seen. Each of Marlowe's last four lines brings a change in translation whose effect is to turn Ovid's simple rendering of the body into something more reflective. Ovid's *nil non laudabile uidi* (l. 23, 'I saw all was fine') becomes 'all likt me passing well' in a movement towards irony and male mastery; 'downe she fell' is added quite gratuitously and connotes both female resistance and original sin. The translation of *requieuimus ambo* ('we both lay quiet') as 'she bad me kisse' adds to the idea of her possible reluctance and wish for more in the way of relationship. And '*Jove* send me . . .' in the last line when the Latin has only 'Let my middays often turn out like this' calls on the approval of the symbolic father and reveals Marlowe's translation as caught in a Christian problematic it tries so hard to step outside: by invoking Jove when Ovid does not it introduces a *defiance* of the Christian God wholly foreign to the pagan text. As will be argued, at the nub of courtly love poetry is a struggle to negotiate between Christian ideology and sexual possibilities that are secular and humanist.

4

COURTLY LOVE AND
IDEALISATION

Women have served all these centuries as looking-glasses possessing the magic
and delicious power of reflecting the figure of man at twice its natural size.
                                                                Virginia Woolf

It is easy to state the intended argument of this chapter: to show that
social phantasy in the poetry of courtly love takes the form of self-
love rather than love for another. But the terms in which it is generally
construed mean that this discussion necessarily will have to follow a
complicated line. There are initial difficulties about the status of the
concept of courtly love and about courtly love as social practice as
against textual practice. Further problems concern the definition of
courtly love across historical periods and diverse places, controversy
(notably between C. S. Lewis and Peter Dronke) about whether
courtly love did appear 'quite suddenly at the end of the eleventh
century in Languedoc' (Lewis 1973, p. 2), the contradictory nature of
courtly love as at once feudal and bourgeois, and the differences
between courtly love and later Romantic love. In seeking to negotiate
these questions the chapter will begin by offering a definition of the
features of courtly love, follow a psychoanalytic account of it from
Freud and Lacan, turn via Lewis and Dronke to its ideological side,
and then, through the examination of three texts, move to a possible
distinction between courtly and Romantic love, concluding with
reference to Lacan's discussion of courtly love in the seminars of
1972–3. In the space of a chapter it is possible only to suggest a way of
reading courtly love poetry.

Courtly love defined

In an essay polemically entitled 'The concept of courtly love as an impediment to the understanding of medieval texts, D. W. Robertson denies that 'there was any such thing as what is usually called courtly love during the Middle Ages' (1968, p. 1). The phrase *cortez amors* is used once by one troubadour, Peire d'Auvergne. The term 'courtly love' was introduced by Gaston Paris in 1883, and there is no doubt its currency owes something to late nineteenth-century sentimentalising of medieval literature. However, under other names, as Roger Boase establishes (1977), the theme of love and its likely origin in the troubadour poets of Provence was widely written about in Europe from Dante onwards, for example in English by Thomas Warton in his dissertation 'On the origin of romantic poetry in Europe' prefixed to his *History of English Poetry* (1775–81). In 1884 Engels in *The Origin of the Family* refers confidently to 'the chivalrous love of the Middle ages' (Marx and Engels 1950, II, p. 208). That the concept of 'courtly love' is subject to construction in the present affects it no more and no less than any other concept used to describe a phenomenon which crosses between literary and extra-literary practices.

Courtly love poetry can be seen as an expression of courtly culture, which itself may be seen as determined by social and economic practices. Because of this, much writing feels unable to define courtly love poetry unless it can trace social and other origins for it with a degree of mechanical determinism that would make most Marxists wince (Boase 1977 summarises seven possible kinds of explanation by origin, from Hispano-Arabic influences to spring folk rituals). C. S. Lewis, having attempted a sociological explanation, urges that 'we abandon the attempt to explain the new feeling' (1973, p. 12). In one of the most authoritative accounts Moshé Lazar asserts that 'the origins of *courtliness, courtly love* (fin'amors) and Provençal poetry need to be examined separately' (1964, p. 13). Subscribing to this view, the present analysis will consider courtly love only as literary representation, both textual and inter-textual, and will bracket the social formation as an extra-textual cause for the reproduction of texts in a courtly culture.

Lewis writes:

Every one has heard of courtly love, and every one knows that it appears quite suddenly at the end of the eleventh century in Languedoc . . . an unmistakable continuity connects the Provençal love song with the love poetry of the later Middle ages, and thence, through Petrarch and many others, with that of the present day. (1973, pp. 2-3)

Courtly love poetry, courtly love in poetry, changes and develops as it moves north across France, south into Italy, and somewhat belatedly, arrives in Britain. For example, in northern France an important feature becomes altered, for there courtly love generally loses its exaltation of adultery, though the stories of Tristan and Lancelot form an exception to this. Nevertheless, a definition of courtly love can be put forward that will distinguish courtly love from the later development of Romantic love. It summarises a constellation of features marking a family resemblance and does not define an essence, and it does so by focusing in particular on the lyric tradition of courtly poetry and ignoring the treatment of love in medieval narrative verse.

Here are three definitions:

What is particular to [courtly love poetry] is to have conceived love as a cult directed at a supreme object and founded, like Christian love, on the infinite disproportion between merit and desire; as a necessary school of honour, which gives value to the lover and transforms a commoner into a knight; as a willing bondage which conceals an ennobling power, and makes suffering the essence of the dignity and beauty of passion.
(Bédier 1896, p. 172, cited in Dronke 1968, II, p. 4)

The sentiment, of course, is love, but love of a highly specialised sort, whose characteristics may be enumerated as Humility, Courtesy, Adultery and the Religion of Love. The lover is always abject. Obedience to his lady's lightest wish, however whimsical, and silent acquiescence in her rebukes, however unjust, are the only virtues he dares to claim. There is a service of love closely modelled on the service which a feudal vassal owes to his lord. The lover is the lady's 'man'. He addresses her as *midons*, which etymologically represents not 'my lady' but 'my lord'. (Lewis 1973, p. 2)

The novelty of Courtly Love lies in three basic elements: first, in the ennobling force of human love; second in the elevation of the beloved to a place of superiority above the lover; third, in the conception of love as ever unsatiated, ever increasing desire. (Denomy 1947, p. 20)

From these three accounts, seven defining features can be suggested. Courtly love is:

1 the love of a man for a woman
2 who is treated as a superior object,
3 producing in him unsatisfied desire
4 and secular virtue;

5   it is feudal,
6   adulterous,
7   and spiritual.

Each of these features is subject to some historical variation; each needs to be qualified in some way.

1   *Love of a man for a woman*   Courtly love is pre-eminently male and heterosexual. It is predicated on two sexes considered as essences, with man/male/masculine and woman/female/feminine lined up in confirmatory equivalences. The simple duality excludes and denies any possibility of manoeuvre or play within, across or outside these categories. Generally the only 'I' who speaks is a male voice, which, in a version of confessional discourse, seeks to tell the truth about his sexuality.

2   *Superior object*   In courtly love poetry the woman is imagined, as Bédier says, as a supreme object. Idealised, placed in a position of apparent superiority to the man's self-ascribed inferiority, she is fixed and immobilised as passive object of his active desire. The pedestal raises her so that she cannot move.

3   *Desire*   This is the most important feature, as the previous chapter suggested by contrasting versions of satisfaction and desire. Writing in 1912 in the same passage of the second 'Contribution to the Psychology of Love' as described how Christianity created 'psychical values for love which pagan antiquity was never able to confer on it' (see above, p. 60) Freud claims that 'the physical value of erotic needs is reduced as soon as their satisfaction becomes easy' and that 'an obstacle is required in order to heighten libido' (*SE* XI, p. 187), to turn satisfaction into love. From another quarter Johan Huizinga points to the same quality of non-fulfilment as defining courtly love:

When in the twelfth century unsatisfied desire was placed by the troubadours of Provence in the centre of the poetic conception of love, an important turn in the history of civilisation was effected. Antiquity, too, had sung the sufferings of love, but it had never conceived them save as the expectation of happiness or as its pitiful frustration . . . Courtly poetry, on the other hand, makes desire itself the essential motif . . .

(1955, p. 108; first published 1924)

Denis de Rougemont, in his eccentric but provocative work, *Passion and Society*, regards desire and the obstacle which produces it as central to courtly love. When King Mark finds the lovers asleep alone together in the forest, they have a sword lying between them. De

Rougemont takes this, the lovers' self-imposed refusal to consummate their passion, as epitomising the nature of courtly love:

Tristan and Iseult do not love one another. They say they don't, and everything goes to prove it. *What they love is love and being in love.* They behave as if aware that whatever obstructs love must ensure and consolidate it in the heart of each and intensify it infinitely in the moment they reach the absolute obstacle, which is death. (1956, p. 41)

Courtly love is desire, constituted by its own deferral. '*Fin'amors*', says Lazar, 'is always a lack, an absurd suffering without goal or end' (1964, p. 82).

4 *Secular virtue* It is love 'per cui a om pretz e valor' ('through which a man has price and value', Bernart de Ventadorn, cited Lazar 1964, p. 25):

Such love decides a man's destiny, it is what makes him act for good or for evil; *for good*, let us say at once, when it rewards the troubadour with what he desires; *for evil*, when it disappoints his hopes and patience.

(Lazar, *ibid.*)

In the Christian ethic the fate of the individual is determined by whether or not he or she loves God. Whatever the source and quality of its aim, the object of courtly love is not God but a woman. Such love is not Christian but secular and humanist, leading therefore to 'a secular state of grace' (Broadbent 1964, p. 31). It is thus able to operate as a criterion by which individuals can qualify for upward social mobility – its correct practice 'transforms a commoner into a knight' (Bédier 1896, p. 172).

5 *Feudal* Courtly love is

an amorous duty, modelled on feudal obligation. They called her *mi dons* (*mi dominus*), acknowledging in her the same authority which the vassal recognised in his lord. (Lazar 1964, p. 12)

In connection with the same feature, C. S. Lewis writes of 'a feudalisation of love' (1973, p. 2). But while courtly love is feudal – most obviously in its vocabulary – the fact that it is not simply or uncontradictorily feudal is implied both by its discursive effect of internalising individuality and its continuance in a modified form into the literature of the bourgeois epoch.

6 *Adulterous* Lewis makes this a definitive feature of courtly love and Lazar is similarly unequivocal when he says that in troubadour poetry 'the opposition between courtly and married love is absolute and irrefutable' (1964, p. 60). But this feature varies even as early as later medieval versions. In the structure of courtly love, adultery functions both to declare that such love is against the law, personal and individual not public and social, and also to introduce the redirection which constitutes the process as desire. What matters is not adultery so much as the obstacle.

7 *Spiritual* The spirituality of courtly love inheres in other features already mentioned: the distance the lady is set above the lover, the conception of love as desire that cannot be satisfied, the ethical price and value attaching to love. The issue is usually debated in literal terms as to whether or not sexual intercourse is supposed to take place. But as the previous chapter would show, the issue cannot be decided in a literal way. Lazar states that troubadour poetry always 'has as its object both the heart and body of a married woman' (1964, p. 61), and in general courtly love poetry reserves a genre, the alba, for the moment when the lovers wake together in bed at dawn. But the fact of physical consummation – as the previous analysis of Donne's 'Elegy 19' hoped to demonstrate – in no way prevents the spiritualisation of love. The idea of sexual intercourse and of the woman's naked body can be sublimated if other discourses are displaced onto it. In courtly love, sexuality is fixed and universalised as a spiritual essence.

Courtly love poetry, in which a speaker is represented as telling the truth about his love, puts to work the discursive form of confession, the mode noted by Foucault as that which renders sexuality as individual, inward, latent. And such poetry makes available what can be recognised as social phantasy from the ease with which it moves between the terms of desire and the vocabulary of feudal ideology. From the side of the unconscious the operation of this phantasy can be understood as idealisation (*Idealisierung*). Of necessity my summary will have to be sustained in some detail. Idealisation cannot be grasped adequately apart from an account of the structuring of the ego. Idealisation is crucial to Lacan's development of the Freudian analysis of the ego, and this too is directly relevant to the effect of what Freud refers to as 'being in love'. However, this technical rehearsal will be useful not only here but elsewhere, particularly in connection with the discussion of Romantic narcissism in chapter 6 below.

'Being in love' in Freud and Lacan

In the process of idealisation an object is valued as a form of perfection, as parents are by children or a hero or heroine by a group. If the tendency to idealisation is active towards a sexual object this is sexual overvaluation. As an example Freud mentions 'the troop of women and girls, all of them in love in an enthusiastically sentimental way, who crowd round a singer or pianist after his performance' (*SE* XVIII, p. 120). Idealisation is generally a feeling men direct towards women, and Freud observes that 'in typical cases women fail to exhibit any sexual overvaluation towards men' (*SE* VII, p. 151 fn.), though in 'A case of homosexuality in a woman' he notes that the patient displayed 'the humility and the sublime overvaluation of the sexual object so characteristic of the male lover' (*SE* XVIII, p. 154).

For psychoanalysis the 'I' is not a given but a construct and an effect: 'we are bound to suppose that a unity comparable to the ego cannot exist in the individual from the start; the ego has to be developed' (*SE* XIV, p. 76). The process is analysed in the papers 'On Narcissism: an introduction' (1914) and 'Mourning and melancholia' (1917). The account of being in love as an expression of narcissism is given in *Group Psychology and the Analysis of the Ego* (1921) and it may be summarised as follows:

1 As was noted in the paper on narcissism, the infant begins in a kind of unity, and accordingly, narcissism and the sexual drives, self-love and object-love are not separated – the new-born subject (to be) loves its objects as itself. It does so in a process of *identification* with its objects and this is 'the original form of emotional tie with an object' (*SE* XVIII, p. 107). But even when the ego becomes separated out, even in adult life, the subject can still regress to a version of this earliest narcissistic identification of itself with its objects.

2 The formation of the ego ideal (the voice of conscience and social obligation) is also narcissistic. As the ego develops and the child moves out of its first unity it seeks to recover the earlier identification of its objects with itself, 'the original narcissism in which the childish ego enjoyed self-sufficiency' (*ibid.*, p. 110). This retained sense of yourself as you were and you'd like to be is transformed into the ego ideal, 'a critical agency within the ego' (*ibid.*, p. 109).

3 The processes described in (1) and (2) can work together. Thus in adult life there can be regression to narcissistic identification of the

subject with its objects. And two different places or formations of the subject, both the ego and the ego ideal, can become the locus of this identification. Melancholia and being in love are two symmetrical but contrasted consequences of this identification. In each there is 'an impoverishment of the ego' (*SE* xiv, p. 246) when it submits to the idealised image of the beloved or, in the case of melancholy, to being 'judged by a special agency' (*ibid.*, p. 249). The states differ according to whether the object is identified with the ego or with the ego ideal.

Melancholia may result from the death of a loved one. The lost object may be kept alive for the subject if its place is taken by the ego – through 'an identification of the ego with the abandoned object' (*SE* xiv, p. 249). But this only happens on condition that the ego ideal becomes active in criticising and judging the ego (a similar process may explain the feeling of nostalgia, when an image of the subject's former self is mourned). By contrast, being in love may result if a loved one, rather than being lost, cannot be obtained and desire is not satisfied. The unattainable object can be possessed if, through identification, it is '*put in the place of the ego ideal*' (*SE* xvii, p. 113, italics original). Again, this can happen only on condition that the ego becomes impoverished:

The impulsions whose trend is towards directly sexual satisfaction may now be pushed into the background entirely, as regularly happens, for instance, with a young man's sentimental passion; the ego becomes more and more unassuming and modest, and the object more and more sublime and precious, until at last it gets possession of the entire self-love of the ego, whose self-sacrifice thus follows as a natural consequence. The object has, so to speak, consumed the ego . . . this 'devotion' of the ego to the object . . . is no longer to be distinguished from a sublimated devotion to an abstract idea . . .
(*ibid.*)

The lover subject to such sexual overvaluation shows 'traits of humility', even of 'self-injury'; because it has been established in the position of the ego ideal 'everything the object does and asks for is right and blameless' (*ibid.*). Like the sublimation noted in Donne's 'Elegy', the process concerns narcissism: through identification between object and ego ideal, the object comes to be 'treated in the same way as our own ego' (*ibid.*, p. 112). For Freud, the ego, ego ideal and object become discrete, though liable to regressive identification; for Lacan, the subject's identification in and with its objects is not contingent but constitutive: the subject's ego is 'that which is reflected of his [*sic*] form in his objects' (1977a, p. 194). The ego becomes fixed and identified in taking a likeness as itself: I come to see myself as single and unified – 'that's me' – by disavowing the universal process (the Other) through which my particular position is arrived at. Further, Lacan marks a distinction between the ideal ego and the ego ideal. The ideal ego is defined in the process by which the subject projects itself onto its objects, the ego ideal in that by which it introjects an external object (see Rose 1981, pp. 140–4). The subject's ideal ego appears at 'that point at which he [*sic*] desires to gratify himself in himself' (Lacan 1977b, p. 257), the ego ideal at 'the point . . . from which the subject will see himself [*sic*], as one says, *as others see him*' (*ibid.*, p. 268), a position achieved by internalising something from the field of the Other to support the first 'specular, immediate identification' (*ibid.*). In Ovid's story of Narcissus, an example which will prove immediately germane for the poetry of courtly love, the youth at first spontaneously loves his image in the water, then, acceding to language, says that image is himself.

Being in love effects an imaginary convergence between the ego and the Other, the terrain of intersubjectivity on which it is particularised; it appears to close the gap between the self and what is not the self, and to flatter the ego in doing so. 'Love is essentially deception', introducing 'a perspective centred on the Ideal point, capital I, placed somewhere in the Other, from which the Other sees me, in the form I like to be seen' (Lacan 1977b, p. 268). So, it is implied, in loving the perfect woman the man loves himself in his *ideal ego*; but in speaking about her view of him – how she loves or should love him – he installs her figure in the place of his *ego ideal*, using it to see himself at his best and as he hopes others see him, the perfect lover. Freud points to being in love as a male tendency towards idealisation; Lacan writes of it as a masculine prerogative and deception. Freud says that sexual overvaluation occurs when 'the sexual object attracts a portion of the ego's narcissism to itself' (*SE* xvi, p. 418); Lacan refers even more forcefully to 'its fundamentally narcissistic structure' (1977b, p. 186). In the masquerade of devotion to another, love is an expression of self-love.

This schematic and abstract outline is justified because of the purchase it gains immediately on the well-known ambivalance or paradox of the 'divided self' lying at the heart of the poetic tradition of courtly love and expressed in the famous oxymoronic oppositions (blindness/sight, fire/ice, prison/freedom, joy/tears, etc.): I love her and hate her, I love her but she doesn't love me, I love her and wish I didn't, I don't want to love her but I can't stop myself, I must love her but I get no return for it, I ought to love her spiritually but can't stop wanting her physically, and so on. Because of its fundamentally narcissistic structure, such love turns round easily into a complementary opposite. Masochism of the apparently submissive ego when the lady pleases reverses into sadistic aggression from the ego when she does not. (The effect is overdetermined; the shadow of incest always hovers over male heterosexual desire since any love for the figure of the bride threatens to recall the forbidden image of the mother, *SE* XI, pp. 177–90; idealisation of a good object produces as its antithesis a wish to annihilate its corresponding bad object, Klein 1973, pp. 198–236.) In courtly love poetry, idealisation of the lady masks an assertion of the ego. But since this duality is inseparable in such texts from an ideological contradiction they must be understood as operating with a form of social phantasy. Poetic expression of courtly love did not exist in the ancient world, and its inauguration with the troubadours of Provence is a historical innovation. This, however, is a matter of controversy.

Courtly love as social phantasy

C. S. Lewis argues forcibly, even polemically, that courtly love is a new historical departure. *The Allegory of Love* in 1936 claimed that the 'French poets, in the eleventh century, discovered or invented, or were the first to express, that romantic species of passion which English poets were still writing about in the nineteenth' (1973, p. 4), and that ' "Love", in our sense of the word, is as absent from the literature of the Dark Ages as from that of classical antiquity' (p. 9). This view that courtly love is a 'new feeling' (p. 12) has been specifically contradicted in Peter Dronke's book on *Medieval Latin and the Rise of the European Love-Lyric* (1968).

Dronke's critique says that courtly love 'is no "new feeling" ', while at the same time admitting that there are 'new elements in the medieval European lyrics of *amour courtois*' (I, p. 46); it does not clearly distinguish this 'feeling' from these 'elements'; it does not define courtly love in detail. However, it is clear in stating that

'the new feeling' of *amour courtois* is at least as old as Egypt of the second millennium BC, and might indeed occur at any time or place: that it is, as

Professor Marrou suspected, 'un secteur du coeur, un des aspects éternels de l'homme'. (p. xvii)

As evidence for this the book cites a comprehensive range of sources from pagan and Christian contexts, including Ancient Egypt, medieval Byzantium, twelfth-century Georgia, the seventh-century Islamic world, Mozarabic Spain, and tenth-century Iceland.

In so far as it takes as its object for study 'the human psyche', psychoanalysis and the previous account of love as idealisation might be thought to support Marrou's view as cited by Dronke that such love is 'one of the eternal aspects of human nature' ('un des aspects éternels de l'homme') (though more so in Freud than in Lacan). But in the case of the medieval literary *texts*, Dronke's argument can only sustain itself by denying that such poetry acquires meaning in a specifically Christian ideological matrix, one which is indelible in the features of courtly love poetry as summarised above, particularly in (2) the superior object, (3) desire, and (7) spirituality. In asserting that 'human and divine love are not in conflict with each other' (p. 5), Dronke's account simply sets aside the view put forward by Denomy in his aptly named *The Heresy of Courtly Love* and subsequently confirmed by Lazar, who says that courtly love 'is a conception completely opposed to Christian morality' (1964, p. 12). The reason why they are right was given conclusively by Etienne Gilson when he distinguished between courtly love and Christian love (or *caritas*):

. . . it is not enough to say that they do not have the same object, one must add that they cannot have the same nature precisely because they do not have the same object. (1934, p. 201, cited Lazar 1964, p. 82)

The object of Christian love is divine, that of courtly love is human. Dronke's case is that courtly love is not feudal but universal, though 'the universal range of metaphors of the lover "serving" his lady and becoming her "own man" may well in some circumstances have come to carry feudal connotations as well as erotic ones' (1968 1, p. 55). In the poetic expression of courtly love it is precisely these 'feudal connotations' that count, though, as will be argued, they are worked into a close relation with bourgeois connotations.

Desire, aspiration, transcendence: the poetry of courtly love releases a utopian impulse in the way Jameson's argument suggests. Individualist wishes to find in love a transcendent dimension outside society itself express in a displaced form a class aspiration, the shared, bourgeois hope of breaking with feudal order. Loving a woman as one should love the Lord anticipates the bourgeois conviction that a spiritual form may be given secular content. Man will master woman as culture overcomes nature: if the wish can be seen as collective and universal, it also reveals its origin in the exploitative content of the new class ideology, both in that 'mother' nature is regarded as merely passive material for use and in that one gender assumes the right to dominate another. However, the new culture matures in the womb of the old.

Considered from the side of ideology, the poetry of courtly love works with a contradictory formation, one in which feudal terms, concepts and obligations are articulated simultaneously with themes and attitudes that can be seen to anticipate bourgeois culture. Courtly love is most obviously feudal in two respects. The relation of superiority and inferiority between the lady and the man, the vocabulary for this (*mi dons* etc.) and the idea that the man's duty is to give a service she is obliged but not compelled to recompense, all matches exactly an ideological conception of the bond of feudal relation between lord and vassal. Secondly, the exaltation of this as a spiritual relationship of ultimate value reproduces the ideological forms of feudal Christianity and frequently speaks in its vocabulary. At the same time and in a contrary direction, courtly love poetry develops a tissue of ideas and elements tending to subvert feudal order. The object aimed at is not a heavenly or even an earthly lord but a woman; if the lover seeks an adulterous union he menaces the feudal idea of hierarchy since in loving her he must reckon to betray the lord she is married to (a main contention in the Tristan and Lancelot cycles). Such love contravenes the feudal code in defining virtue in service to the lady as an issue of personal merit rather than an attribute of birth. Throughout, courtly love treats the lover's feeling as a private motive, not a social and public one. His love for her is conceived as a truth lying in the depths of the self.

The poetry of courtly love must be considered as a social phantasy because this contradictory organisation of feudal and bourgeois (or proto-bourgeois) elements takes into itself the structure of idealisation analysed as 'being in love'. On the one hand, idealisation of the lady as a sublime and precious object and the apparent self-sacrifice of the self-love of the ego becomes inextricably imbricated with the terms of medieval Christianity and the idea of feudal hierarchy with its obligation to service. On the other, love as a form of narcissism, as an assertion of the ego, supports and is in turn confirmed by the bourgeois tendencies in courtly love ideology: a secular object rather than divine, threatened disobedience to the lord, personal merit rather than birth, pervasively the construction of sexuality as a mode of individuality and self. The possibilities of this proposed analysis of a social phantasy produced intertextually can be examined further in the poems of Bernart and Petrarch.

Bernart de Ventadorn: 'Can vei la lauzeta mover' (*c.* 1170)

One of the best known troubadour poems, this text retains its strangeness for us, even though it is less obscurely coded into the Provençal tradition than many others. It derives its force from the clarity, dignity and utter seriousness of direct, plain assertion, one that aims for a tight syntactical closure that selects and combines ideas loaded in the convention (*joi, doussor, lo cor, dezirer*) ('joy', 'sweetness', 'the heart', 'desire') rather than depending on metaphoric complexity and suggestion. The poem is thus one of the first in the tradition that attempts to dramatise the effect of someone actually speaking in the present. It does so by sustaining a coherent syntagmatic chain and using demonstratives to represent a consistent speaker across a string of first-person pronouns. He says 'I have lost myself' (l. 23) in full confidence that he can speak about and know the self he says he's lost, that he is as fully present in the enunciation as he is in the enounced. Thus represented, the speaker affirms the inner truth about his sexuality in an early form of confessional discourse. In line 57 *Tristans* is a *senhal* or cover name, either for a male friend or for the woman herself. In this way the poem explicitly provides a position for the interlocutor to whom his avowal is addressed.

The text here is considered apart from its music. The verse form is that of *coblas unissonans*, seven stanzas with eight lines each of eight syllables rhyming ABABCDCD on the same sounds in each stanza. Further, each stanza tends to be divided into two sets of two lines, the *pedes*, and four more lines as the *cauda*. The poem ends with a four-line *tornada*, this forming a *cauda* to the whole. Line 38 ('the fool on the bridge') is generally thought to refer to a proverb according to which a fool, unlike a wise man, does not get off his horse to cross a bridge and falls over; but T. D. Hill (1979, pp. 198–200) has found another parallel according to which a fool is said to stand forever on the bank waiting for the river to pass. Ezra Pound has translated the first two stanzas but regrettably only those (see 1963, p. 427). Mainly literal, my own translation tries to respect the terse dignity of the original:

Can vei la lauzeta mover	When I see the lark moving
de joi sas alas contra'l rai,	in joy its wings against the sunlight
que s'oblid'e·s laissa chazer	forget itself and let itself fall
per la doussor c'al cor li vai,	for the sweetness that comes to its heart,
5 ai! tan grans enveya m'en ve	oh! such great envy comes over me
de cui qu'eu veya jauzion,	for all I see rejoice,
meravilhas ai, car desse	I wonder my heart does not
lo cor de dezirer n·om fon.	just break with desire.
Ai, las! tan cuidava saber	Alas! I thought I knew so much
10 d'amor, e tan petit en sai,	about love but I know so little,
car eu d'amar no·m posc tener	for I can't stop myself loving
celeis don ja pro non aurai.	someone from whom I'll get nothing.
Tout m'a mo cor, e tout m'a me,	She has all my heart and all of me
e se mezeis et tot lo mon;	and herself and the whole world;
15 e can se·m tolc, no·m laisset re	and when she went she left me nothing
mas dezirer e cor volon.	but desire and a wanting heart.
Anc non agui de me poder	I have had no power over myself
ni no fui meus de l'or' en sai	nor am I my own since that time
que·m laisset en sos olhs vezer	when she let me look into her eyes,
20 en un miralh que mout me plai.	in a mirror which so delights me.
Miralhs, pus me mirei en te,	Oh mirror, since I saw myself in you,
m'an mort li sospir de preon,	the sighs from my depths have killed me,
c'aissi·m perdei com perdet se	and I have lost myself, as was lost
lo bels Narcisus en la fon.	fair Narcissus in the fountain.
25 De las domnas me dezesper;	I despair of the ladies;
ja mais en lor no·m fiarai;	I shall never trust them again;
c'aissi com las solh chaptener	as much as I used to proclaim them
enaissi las deschaptenrai.	so I shall now disclaim them.
Pois vei c'una pro no m'en te	For I see not one of help to me
30 vas leis que·m destrui e·m cofon;	with her who destroys and brings me down;
totas las dopt' e las mescre,	I doubt and distrust them all,
car be sai c'atretals se son.	for well I know they're all the same.

	D'aisso's fa be femna parer
	ma domna, per qu'e·lh o retrai,
35	car no vol so c'om deu voler,
	e so c'om li deveda, fai.
	Chazutz sui en mala merce,
	et ai be faih co·l fols en pon;
	e no sai per que m'esdeve,
40	mas car trop puyei contra mon.

This shows she is just a woman,
my lady, and I blame her for it,
for she does not want what one should,
and what one shouldn't do, she does.
I have fallen in bad favour
and I've done like the fool on the bridge,
and how this happened to me I don't know
except I went too high up the mountain.

Merces es perduda, per ver,
et eu non o saubi anc mai,
car cilh qui plus en degr'aver
no·n a ges, et on la querrai?
45 A! can mal sembla, qui la ve,
qued aquest chaitiu deziron
que ja ses leis non aura be,
laisse morrir, qu no l·aon.

All favour has gone, that's certain,
and I never knew it before,
for she who should have most of it
has none, so where shall I find it?
Ah, you'd never think when you see her
she'd let this poor man, sick with desire,
who'll never be well without her,
die, just die, and not help him.

Pus ab midons no·m pot valer
50 precs ni merces ni·l dreihz qu'eu ai,
ni a leis no ven a plazer
qu'eu l'am, ja mais no·lh o dirai.
Aissi·m part de leis e·m recre;
mort m'a, e per mort li respon,
55 e vau m'en, pus ilh no·m rete,
chaitius, en issilh, no sai on.

Since nothing can help with my lady,
prayers nor favours nor what rights I have
nor does it come as a pleasure to her
that I love her, I shall never speak again.
So I leave her and give it up;
she's my death and with death I answer her;
and I'm off, since she won't keep me,
poor man, in exile, I don't know where.

Tristans, ges no·m auretz de me,
qu'eu m'en vau, chaitius, no sai on.
De chantar me gic e·m recre
60 e de joi e d'amor m'escon.

Tristan, you'll have no more from me,
for I go, poor man, I don't know where.
I renounce and give up all singing,
and from joy and love I hide myself away.

Although for the definition of courtly love proposed earlier to make sense it is not necessary for any particular text to have all the seven features specified, this text does exhibit all of them. The love it discusses is male and heterosexual; it is for a woman conceived as a superior object; the man's desire ends only in death (*mort m'a*, l. 54); his loving is a secular virtue; she holds (though loses) her place as feudal superior (*ma domna*, l. 34); adultery is not explicit though the mention of the rejoicing of others (l. 6) hints strongly at the feelings of a husband; the love is spiritual without a hint of physical satisfaction, and indeed the woman's body is not described at all except for her eyes.

Several commentators have taken the image of the lark in the first stanza as determining the rest of the poem. Thus, the self-forgetfulness of the lark rising against the light figures a moment of transcendence the loss of which is thereafter lamented. Within the ideological formations of feudalism this transcendence would represent a fulfilled ideal in which the individual is completed by finding harmoniously their place within a social hierarchy. And the falling away then would suggest two things at once: either that the individual is aspiring beyond their station and so wrongfully placing excessive demands on the feudal order (a view that points back to feudal values); or that the aristocratic class is unjust because it doesn't reward individual merit as it should (a view that points forward to bourgeois values). Such a reading, concentrating on the social connotations of certain key words in the text, has been developed by Erich Koëhler's commentary on the text (1964, pp. 27–51).

The speaker in the first stanza, Koëhler argues, envies the lark's transcendence because in such a state it would be possible to forget the envy of others competing for the lady's favour. Without this transcendence the speaker feels himself to be weak in the face of a superior power (stanza three), a power which condemns him for pushing beyond his rank:

Through her scorn the lady punishes the arrogance of an ambition which has exceeded its limit . . . The poor knight . . . in return for his services hopes for a reward (*merce*) to which he could not lay claim. (1964, p. 49)

In line 41 'the text becomes very clear: *merce* means favour as well as pay (*salaire*)' (p. 50), and in line 46 *chaitiu* ('poor man') suggests loss of social position. The spiritual exile (*issilh*, l. 56) he suffers through not winning her love, the no-man's land he wanders in, connotes what Koëhler refers to as 'the space left empty in a society in which the ruling classes do not carry out their duty, which would be to reward fairly the contribution of the lesser nobility to the common good' (*ibid.*).

In support of this reading it might be added that at one point the text makes an overt and somewhat startling distinction between naming the lady as representative of her class (*ma domna* 'my lady') and as an individual member of her sex (*femna*, 'a woman' ll. 33–4).

Against it, one can argue that the tone and attitude of the poem are not so clearly and unambiguously weighted in the direction Koëhler supposes. Is the speaker's unhappiness due to wrongful exclusion – or is it due rather to excessive ambition? The question, and the ambivalence the poem dramatises, correspond to an ideological contradiction, and one which the poem does not resolve. If the aristocracy are at fault for not rewarding individual merit ('she left me nothing', l. 15), then the hierarchy is being criticised in a way that points beyond it to a bourgeois conception of individuality. If on the other hand his suffering is to be read as a personal fault due to pride ('I went too high up the mountain', l. 40) and he is *rightly* punished for it, then the justice of feudal order is reaffirmed. Yet against this in turn it can be argued that the poem itself expresses an individual voice and so begins to fill the void, to scoop out a space, outside the conception of feudal order altogether.

The contradiction – whether to blame himself or the aristocracy – intersects with what later become the conventionalised paradoxes of the Petrarchan tradition: I know and I do not know, to climb is to fall, reward is punishment, pleasure is pain, happiness is despair, home is exile, love is death. The poem represents a social phantasy in that its ideological contradictions are overlaid by – or superimposed on – versions of phantasy. In submitting to aristocratic order the speaker is also accepting the lady in the place of the ego ideal and so an impoverishment of the ego: 'I have had no power over myself (l. 17), 'I have lost myself' (l. 23), 'poor man' (l. 56, l. 58). But self-pity and self-disgust turn round into an aggressive self-assertion which rejects simultaneously the lady and the feudal hierarchy: 'I despair of the ladies' (l. 25), 'I know they're all the same' (l. 32), 'All favour has gone' (l. 41).

The whole text provides a narcissistic phantasy, and what was read ideologically must be re-read in these terms. At the start the speaker wishes to lose himself in the joy of the lark, which is itself lost in the sunlight. As a subject his desire is to love his objects as himself and return to identification with them. But that moment of primary narcissism is already irrevocably past as the poem begins. The lark's oblivious self-satisfaction is at once its fall (*s'oblid'e·s laissa chazer*), in the same act to 'forget itself and let itself fall'. Self-forgetting immediately lapses into a state of separated self-consciousness. In what follows, the poem aims to re-find this primary identification by other means, by installing her figure in the place of the ego ideal until it

'gets possession of the self-love of the ego'. She becomes his sole
moral authority, universalised into all women, all kindness. She will
be everything (*tot lo mon*, 'the whole world', l. 14) while he becomes
nothing. Or at least that is how he hopes to see her and himself in her.
All the paradoxes of the text reproduce the impossibility of this
project and resolve into: (a) he is her; (b) he is not her. For if he is her,
how can he see her (and himself in her)? And if he can see her, he is not
her. The movement of the poem struggles to anneal into a narcissistic
unity the two places between which the speaker's identity is
constructed. These two positions are articulated as: (a) where he sees
from; (b) where he desires to be seen from.

Scopophilia is thus constantly at work in the text in the form of a
phantasy of pleasurable mastery through looking. In the first line the
speaker sees the lark (*Can vei* . . .), he sees others rejoicing (l. 6), he
does not 'see [*vei*]' one who is of help to him (l. 29) (mastery in vision
coincides with mastery through the knowledge, ll. 9–10, 42, 58). His
desire is to see himself reflected in her eyes (l. 19) as he would like
others to see him:

> Oh mirror, since I saw myself in you,
> the sighs from my depths have killed me,
> and I have lost myself, as was lost
> fair Narcissus in the fountain.   (ll. 21–4)

Goldin's commentary explains very well what the speaker, casting
himself in the role of Narcissus, wishes to see in that mirror: 'It is his
own image perfected, his own form enhanced by every courtly grace
and virtue' (1967, pp. 97–8). As Koëhler notes, '*miralh* (mirror) is a
play on words with *mirar* (to reflect) and has subtle associations with
miralh (miracle)' (1964, p. 48). The woman is set up as both mirror
and miracle for the speaker; she is reduced to a point from which the
Other – all that is not the self – might see him in the form he likes to be
seen.

To read this text, and courtly love poetry in general, in terms of
narcissism, vision and the mirrorings of the ego lends an entirely new
interest to such already established work on the medieval period as
Frederick Goldin's *The Mirror of Narcissus in the Courtly Love Lyric*
(1967). The mirror as exemplum of the potentially idealising
properties of an image descends to the middle ages from Platonic and
Neo-Platonic sources. Ovid provides its most famous and influential
precedent, the story of Echo and Narcissus (*Metamorphoses* III,
318–510). Because he rejects her love and prefers himself, Narcissus is

cursed to fall in love with his own likeness in the water of a spring. At first he loves it believing it to be someone else but even after he recognises that it is an image of himself (*iste ego sum*, l. 463) he continues to be held by it until he dies. In Lacanian terms the progress would be from a primary identification of the ego in its likeness – *as* its likeness – when Narcissus desires 'to gratify himself in himself' (Lacan 1977b, p. 257) not knowing it is himself (the moment of the ideal ego) to a stage when the subject sees itself as others see it, when Narcissus recognises that he is looking at an image and says so (the moment of the ego ideal). It would therefore be true to note, as Geoffrey Hartman does, that with psychoanalysis 'The myth of Narcissius is given clinical verisimilitude' (1978, p. 92). (For a prose reading of Ovid's story alongside the Lacanian account of self-identification, see Brenkman 1976, and for a poetic reading of it, see John O. Thompson's poem 'Montana', 1980, pp. 75–8).

As Goldin argues, the mirror image also takes up a Christian meaning given to it by St. Paul: 'For now we see through a glass, darkly; but then face to face' (1 Corinthians 13: 12; ἐσόπτρου becomes *speculum* in the Vulgate). The figure is further developed by St. Augustine. As a consequence of this secular and religious tradition, Goldin concludes, the mirror 'appears in the writing of nearly every author of the Middle Ages' (1967, p. 3), not just in the poetry of courtly love. But it is in such poetry that the mirror continues to be a most powerful trope. And even when the mirror itself is not explicitly referred to, the lover still longs to win specular dominance over an idealised image retrieved from the Other. This kind of occasion for phantasy, instituted in the early poetry of courtly love, is developed and passed forward to the Renaissance in the work of Petrarch.

Petrarch: 'Rime 190' (*c.* 1374); Wyatt: 'Who so list to hounte' (*c.* 1535)

The *Rime Sparse* consists of 365 poems, mainly sonnets, together with one last one to the Virgin Mary. Of these, 263 are for Laura 'In Vita' and a further 102 to her 'In Morte'. In Latin on the fly-leaf of his copy of Virgil Petrarch gives this account of his love:

Laura, illustrious through her own virtues, and long famed through my verses, first appeared to my eyes in my youth, in the year of our Lord 1327, on the sixth day of April, in the church of St. Clare in Avignon, at matins; and in the same city, also on the sixth day of April, at the same first hour, but in the year 1348, the light of her life was withdrawn from the light of day, while I, as it chanced, was in Verona, unaware of my fate.   (Durling 1976, pp. 5–6)

So the everyday particularities of individual experience, located precisely at a point in space and time ('in the church of St. Clare in Avignon, at matins') – there, then, I, you – are subsumed into a kind of absolute category able to redeem the experience from all contingency ('I, as it chanced, was in Verona'). Truth lies in the depths of the self, in a desire which, even in the admitted absence of its object (Laura is dead) continues to move the lover. In the same record Petrarch writes of how the memory of Laura stirs him with *amara dulcedine*, 'bitter sweetness', a feeling which is articulated in the rhetoric of oxymoron particularly associated with his poetry.

'Rime 190' is a sonnet in the regular Petrarchan form, divided into four parts, two quatrains linked together by the repeated rhyme in the octave, and two sets of three lines in the sestet. English is hard put to convey a fair sense of the uplifted seriousness of the Italian, an effect brought about by the abstract precision of the vocabulary, the sustained inevitability of the syntax, the sonorous flow of the intonation running on across the hendecasyllabic line:

> Una candida cerva sopra l'erba
> verde m'apparve con duo corna d'oro,
> fra due riviere all'ombra d'un alloro,
> levando 'l sole, a la stagione acerba.
>
> 5   Era sua vista sì dolce superba
> ch'i'lasciai per seguirla ogni lavoro,
> come l'avaro, che'n cercar tesoro
> con diletto l'affanno disacerba,
>
> 'Nessun mi tocchi', al bel collo d'intorno
> 10   scritto avea di diamanti et di topazi.
> 'Libera farmi al mio Cesare parve'.
>
> Et era'l sol già vòlto al mezzo giorno,
> gli occhi miei stanchi di mirar non sazi,
> quand'io caddi ne l'acqua et ella sparve.

Translated literally, this becomes:

> A white hind on the green grass
> appeared to me with two horns of gold,
> between two rivers in the shadow of a laurel,
> the sun rising at the young season.
>
> 5   Her sight was so sweetly proud

that to follow her I left every task,
like the miser who in search for treasure,
with delight assuages his trouble.
'Let no one touch me', around her lovely neck
10   she had written with diamonds and topazes.
'It pleased my Caesar to make me free'.
And already the sun was turned at midday,
my eyes tired with looking were not sated,
when I fell into watery tears and she disappeared.

The poem is addressed from within a now thoroughly established
tradition and derives confidence from the intertextual range it can
rely on – the other poems in the sequence of the *Rime*, the poetic
tradition reaching from Italy back to the troubadours, the newly
revived classical precedents, especially Ovid. Whereas Ventadorn's
'Can vei la lauzeta' aimed to speak from an individual position
defined within a shared and publicly coded field of terms (*joi, doussor*,
etc.), Petrarch's love-lyrics seek in addition to evoke a realm of
unique and private feelings never made fully explicit. In part the
allusions and connotations are public and conventional, but they
slide away into uncertainty, as shown by the controversies between
different commentators. Through a metamorphosis Laura is turned
into a hind, like that which miraculously appeared to St Eustace in
the forest. A hind is a heraldic emblem, white because of her purity.
But the motif also reverses the classical story in which Actaeon was
changed into a stag and torn to pieces by his own hounds
(*Metamorphoses* III, 138–252, a story alluded to elsewhere in the
Rime, for example in 23, ll. 147–60 and 323, ll. 4–12). Although hinds
do not have horns, this one has two gold ones, like Laura's two
blonde tresses. The place between two rivers where all this happened
is usually explained as a reference to the Sorgue, near where Petrarch
met her, and the Durance, where he lived. That she is in the shadow of
a laurel tree contains the usual pun on Laura's name, as well as
connoting *l'auro*, gold (which the miser hunts, l. 7) and *l'aura*, the
breeze. Laura's transformation into a hind parallels Daphne's
change into a laurel tree (*Metamorphoses* I, 452–567, and also in the
Rime, for example in number 23, ll. 38–49 and number 29, ll. 40–2).

The story that hinds with collars saying they belonged to Caesar
were found three centuries after his death comes from Pliny
(Zingarelli 1964, p. 955, says it is also in Solinus though Minta 1980,
p. 69, says he cannot find it there). Writing on the collar repeats words
said by Christ to Mary Magdalene after the Resurrection (John 20:

17, *Noli me tangere* in the Vulgate) and the principle of rendering up to Caesar the money that is his and unto God the things that are God's is from Matthew 22: 21. According to Chiòrboli (1924, p. 453), the writing also alludes to something Beatrice says: when Virgil asks why she is immune to the flames of hell, she says she is made so by God, 'Io son fatta da Dio' (*Inferno* II, 91–3). Similarly here Laura has been made impervious to passion by her Caesar. A mundane point: the speaker is close enough to read the writing.

Sun reaching midday indicates the length of time passed since morning but also signifies that there are no shadows now (as there were in line 3, 'in the shadow of a laurel') and that allegorically the speaker's mind has cleared in the fullness of vision (Zingarelli 1964, p. 955). The expression *caddi ne l'acqua* is able to mean both fall into water – possibly that of one of the two rivers – and burst into tears. She disappears because his eyes are obscured with tears but *ella* refers both to the hind and to Laura (l. 14). The line suggests that the hind vanishes into the forest but may also foresee Laura's death (she was first seen with 'the sun rising', allegorically early in his life, and so midday means he is middle-aged when she departs).

The ideological significance of Petrarch's text can be measured against 'Can vei la lauzeta' in terms of the prominence or 'space' accorded to the individual in assumed opposition to the social order. In the troubadour poem the speaker's assertion of himself can find no adequate place in the existing order and is represented through metaphors as equivalent to exile; in 'Rime 190' the speaker's demands for himself are defined much more firmly, located (through the newly developed pastoral convention) somewhere outside the city, away from work (*lavoro*, l. 6), a place for utopian gratifications therefore, though one whose social derivation emerges clearly enough. For even here the speaker's demands cannot be met because the deer turns out to be private property belonging to someone else. 'Let no one touch me . . . / It pleased my Caesar to make me free': limits on the speaker's freedom are now set not so much by feudal hierarchy as law embodied in a sovereign individual. The decree takes on meaning within the ideological formations attached to absolutism, that is the transitional stage between feudalism and capitalism when the monarchy acquires some of the functions of the incipient bourgeois state. Although in the context 'Caesar' refers allegorically to God it still means Caesar, a wholly secular and indeed pagan representative of political power. And so inevitably in this Italian text Caesar will be felt as proleptic for the Prince and state power.

Just as monarch means father in terms of social phantasy, so the ideological assertion of individuality in this text is filled out by a more ample expression of narcissism than in Ventadorn's poem. Laura as the hind is set up in the place of the speaker's ego ideal and associated with a purity and spiritual transcendence guaranteed by God. Despite the speaker's apparent self-abasement, much more so than the troubadour poem this text renders the figure of the lady as the speaker's object, his ego ideal, his vision, the fixed point where he hopes to see himself perfectly imaged, immobilized in space and time (for a parallel account of the gaze in Italian painting, see Bryson 1983, pp. 87–131, 'The Gaze and the Glance').

Spatially the woman in this text is transformed into a fetish. John Freccero has summarised the treatment of Laura in the whole sequence:

Her virtues and her beauties are scattered like the objects of fetish worship: her eyes and hair are like gold and topaz on the snow, while the outline of her face is lost; her fingers are like ivory and roses or oriental pearls, her eyes are the pole stars, her arms are branches of diamond.   (1975, p. 39)

For psychoanalysis a fetish is an object established in place of the (missing) maternal phallus. Here that place is occupied by Laura herself turned into an animal and symbolically equated with her collar of diamonds and topazes. It is also taken by the details of her 'two horns of gold' (her hair) and perhaps more generally by the doubling of elements commentators have remarked on in the sonnet (two horns, two rivers, two kinds of precious stones). Phantasy fetishism can be linked with commodity fetishism (Heath 1974, pp. 106–8), implied here in the metaphor of the miser. The speaker tries to freeze Laura in his vision of her just as the miser seeks to reify the labour of production by changing it into gold (Laura = *l'auro*). Temporally the speaker aims to stop time through scopophilia, by mastering the woman with his look. What captivates him is sight of her, her figure seen (*vista* in l. 5 means both 'her appearance' and 'her being looked at'). His eyes are 'tired with looking' (*stanchi di mirar*) but not sated when they begin to fail (at the mention of Caesar?). Naturalistically, a hunter and a deer surprised in the forest would confront each other only for half a second before either he caught the deer or it ran off. Petrarch's sonnet provides the phantasy of the speaker's gaze holding the instant in suspension for nearly a whole day, perpetuating the desire to see. But this imaginary fulfilment is interrupted symbolically by the text on the deer's neck: vision is broken by writing and law imposed in the name of the father (here, Caesar). In its privileging of vision the poem recalls, along with its other allusions to Ovid, the story of Narcissus. Like Narcissus the speaker is captured by a beautiful image 'between two rivers', one which then 'disappeared' as the waters troubled his look (l. 14). Laura is presented as a perfect object in which the speaker as subject would see the form of his ego reflected. Ejected from culture into nature, changed into a hind, Laura can't look back, can't speak: 'the silent image of woman still tied to her place as bearer of meaning, not maker of meaning' (Mulvey 1975, p. 7).

Yet still the speaker can't see what he wants to see. Within or beneath the clear surface of the language in the poem a series of allusions and intertextual references open onto a more occluded version of the speaker's object of desire. The rhetorical strategy is to suggest this without explicitly naming it – in terms of vision to try to glimpse in the corner of the eye what could not be seen if looked at directly. Though not referring to 'Rime 190', Robert M. Durling has discussed this effect in the sequence as a whole, arguing that 'Ovid is omnipresent', that metamorphosis is not an incidental but a structural figure in that 'transformation . . . is a figure of sublimation' (1976, p. 27), contributing to 'a fundamental narcissism' (p. 31). In 'Rime 190' a subtext of implicit meaning is suggested through Ovidian metaphors (substitutions) and metonomies (juxtapositions). Thus in the sonnet the initial transformation is:

1　Woman (Laura) into hind (*candida cerva*).

This is assumed as the premise on which poem proceeds. It acts alongside and so intersects with the next.

2　Daphne into laurel.

Mentioned in l. 3 (*alloro*), Daphne's metamorphosis introduces but does not specify the idea of rape, since it was to elude Apollo that she was changed. The motif of sexual satisfaction is also contained in the next change.

3　Actaeon into stag.

Out hunting, Actaeon stumbles on Diana bathing naked; she splashes water into his face, he is turned into a deer and hunted to death by his own hounds. The converse of (1) and (2), this is picked up in the sonnet in that the speaker is a hunter who sees a female and whose eyes, in the last line, become wet with water.

Through these paradigmatic substitutions the text figures as an object of desire the sight of Laura naked and the possibility of sexual satisfaction (there may even be a distant allusion to Corinna in *Amores* 1.5, who like the hind here suddenly appears to the man, *apparve*, l. 2). But it is precisely the effect of Petrarch's text to displace this object by idealising it (exalting it into a sublime figure) and by sublimating it (linking it with aims remote from satisfaction). In terms of phantasy the effect is greatly to intensify the appeal of the text to narcissism. In terms of rhetoric, something else is brought about by the evocation of ideas not explicitly denoted on the surface of the language.

Ezra Pound writes derisively of how the poetic tradition deteriorates from the Italian followers of the troubadours, the poets of the 'new style' (epitomised by Guido Cavalcanti) down to Petrarch. In Cavalcanti Pound finds still a sensual and concrete rendering of 'realities perceptible to the sense' which is betrayed by Petrarch's surrender to 'ornament' (due to religious 'fanaticism' and 'asceticism') and leading to 'unbounded undistinguished abstraction' (1963b, p. 154). Metaphoric and metonymic displacements analysed in 'Rime 190' well fit this description, but they can also be read in context with the developments described by Foucault.

Confessional discourse at first, after 1215, concerns the act of sexual intercourse, 'the postures assumed, gestures, places touched, caresses, the precise moment of pleasure' (Foucault 1981, p. 19); but increasingly with the Renaissance such attention to perceptible realities gives way to an attempt to tell the hidden truth about 'thoughts, desires, voluptuous imaginings' (p. 19). It is a critical commonplace to say that courtly love poetry with the troubadours begins by trying to render a sense of the typicality of sexual experience but that by the Renaissance has become able to give a strong effect of its all but unique, personal implications. In contrast to the relatively literal statement of a generalised situation and a state of mind in 'Can vei la lauzeta', Petrarch's poem explores a specific event and its subjective correlatives. By creating a subtext of metaphoric transformations and equivalences – woman/hind, Daphne/laurel, Actaeon/stag – at some remove from the speaker's explicit surface, it thus deliberately aims to give an effect of private and unconscious motive. These latencies open a space for greater inwardness in the way Foucault suggests (though his account has nothing to say about the substantial content of this new inner space). Sublimation of sexual drive as it is displaced into spirituality, idealisation of the woman as a fixed object for vision: in both respects the Petrarchan text takes a more extreme form than the troubadour poem and so initiates poetic expression at the Renaissance of the masterfully self-sufficient individual, master both of what he surveys and, by implication, of the subjectivity he expresses.

Before moving on to Wyatt's imitation of 'Rime 190' discussion must touch on a complex issue. For in linking (1) scopophilia, (2) detailed visual description of a woman (as a deer), and (3) a body torn to pieces (Actaeon), Petrarch's text trenches upon a deeper level of phantasy. Active scopophilia is narcissistic and also, in seeking to dominate an object, is a form of the drive to mastery (*Bemächtigungstrieb*) which 'we call sadism when we find it in the service of the sexual function' (*SE* XII, p. 322). This sadistic drive to mastery through vision acts by dividing a woman's body into pieces: 'two horns of gold', 'her lovely neck' in 'Rime 190'; in a displaced way through the enumeration of items of the woman's clothing in Donne's 'Elegy 19'; explicitly through an inventory of parts of a woman's body in such poems as Carew's 'A Rapture' and Herrick's 'The Description of a Woman'. Dominating a woman's body by detailing it bit by bit is like 'dismembering a woman's body', as Francis Barker says with reference to the effect in Marvell's 'To his Coy Mistress' (1984, p. 86). And the allusion to Actaeon in 'Rime 190' is not unique for other poems in the series make mythological references – to Bacchus, to Orpheus – so that in all 'three men see women who are not to be seen, and are torn to bits' (Vickers, 1982, p. 99).

Lacan's paper on aggressivity and the ego outlines a way to associate these three aspects. In that the ego is constituted provisionally by an aggressive effort to bind and make cohere all that is not itself, it is constantly threatened with dissolution. The (masculine?) ego is like an image of the body as unity always defending itself against an image of the body in pieces (*le corps morcelé*) (see Lacan 1977a, p. 11). So the narcissistic drive to master a woman's body bit by bit emerges from a deep fear that the ego, like the body, may fall to pieces (like Actaeon's). And there may be a further complexity in this patriarchal scenario. The very idea of woman may pose a threat to the masculine ego if the feminine body is seen as the site of castration, in which case femininity is treated as the source of aggression (Actaeon is torn to pieces because of Diana) or aggression is projected onto it (pursued, Daphne is violently changed into a tree).

These topics, especially that of masculine projection, will be taken up again in the chapter on Victorian poetry.

Wyatt's sonnet 'Who so list to hounte' is not a literal translation of Petrarch's 'Una candida cerva' but an imitation of it, and one which may well owe something to Giovanni Romanello's own fifteenth-century imitation of 'Rime 190', 'Una cerva gentil'. Comparison of the two texts has been made before (Mason 1959, pp. 189–90, Lever 1978, pp. 26–7, Greenblatt 1980, pp. 145–53). It will be undertaken here to consider briefly how far Wyatt's text exemplifies the reconstruction of courtly love as Romantic love:

> Who so list to hounte, I know where is an hynde;
> But as for me, helas, I may no more:
> The vayne travaill hath weried me so sore,
> I ame of theim that farthest commeth behinde;
> 5   Yet may I by no meanes my weried mynde
> Drawe from the Diere: but as she fleeth afore
> Faynting I folowe; I leve of therefore,
> Sithins in a nett I seke to hold the wynde.
> Who list her hounte I put him owte of dowbte,
> 10   As well as I may spend his tyme in vain:
> And graven with Diamondes in letters plain
> There is written her faier neck rounde abowte:
> 'Noli me tangere for Cesars I ame,
> And wylde for to hold though I seme tame'.

Criticism has generally drawn attention to elements of parody and irony in Wyatt's poem, which convert Petrarch's transcendental idealism into a cynical, bourgeois realism. The lady is not so much a superior over the speaker as an equal, 'represented, not as a mystically untouchable paraclete, but as a wild and wilful beauty evading capture' (Lever 1978, pp. 26–7). Far from devoting himself to her he invites open competition for her from other men – addressing neither her nor an interlocutor but treating the woman as an object in exchange between men. He says he'll give her up, and although the speaker in Ventadorn's 'Can vei la lauzeta' also says that ('I leave her and give it up', l. 53), Patricia Thomson surely argues correctly that:

To describe the pursuit of an inaccessible lady as so much time spent 'in vain' is to aim a blow at the foundation of the sentiment of courtly love common to Petrarch and the Petrarchans.   (1964, p. 197)

As in Petrarch, the woman is to be pursued in the form of a deer, yet the tone of her words at the end is so provocative as to imply something predatory about her. If she is 'wylde for to hold' while seeming tame, then the mastery over her of Caesar, or of any man, cannot be strong. Religious connotations attached to Caesar in 'Rime 190' are missing from the equivalent reference in Wyatt's poem. Thus it takes its place in an ideological context in which political sovereignty is now almost wholly secular, an attitude confirmed if, as is thought, there is an allusion to Henry VIII as Caesar. Her 'Diamondes' are financial commodities and signposts of private ownership rather than spiritual emblems (Southall 1973, pp. 28–9). She and the speaker relate to each other in a world of competitive possessive individualism restrained by law rather than one bound by feudal loyalties or those of courtly absolutism.

Conventional accounts of the two texts frequently misconceive the contrast as between artificiality and realism, rhetoric and sincere speech. Certainly new strategies are introduced into English poetry in the sixteenth century to construct more persuasively the effect of confessional discourse, a voice really speaking from the heart. As in this example from Wyatt, these new elements include the innovatory use of iambic pentameter, of sustained syntax, demonstratives, personal pronouns and the present tense (an analysis of a Sidney sonnet is given in Easthope 1982, of a Shakespeare sonnet in Easthope 1983). A dimension of inwardness hidden from the speaker's fully conscious awareness is produced in the text by forms of irony and implication (see Greenblatt 1980, esp. pp. 115–56). Although the speaker says he has withdrawn from chasing the woman, a subtext like that governing the metaphors in Petrarch suggests the opposite, that she persists even so in the place of an object of desire for him. Far more vividly than 'Una candida cerva', Wyatt's poem dramatises a speaker in an imagined present.

Yet discontinuities between the contexts in which each poem produces meaning ('Petrarch's moral world is medieval while Wyatt's is Humanist and modern', Mason 1959, p. 190) have concealed the firm continuity linking the two texts. This can be appreciated if we review Wyatt's sonnet in relation to the seven features of courtly love poetry outlined above. Thus, in Wyatt the woman is no longer regarded as a superior object (2) but, rather, is placed in a supposedly mutual relation with the man, and the terms of feudal hierarchy (5) have made way for an apparently more bourgeois equality. The virtue inhering in service (4) has been fully replaced by a sense of individual merit. Adultery (6) is not explicit, though in Wyatt's poem there is still the obstacle represented by Caesar. But the feeling continues to be heterosexual love of a man for a woman (1), still an unfulfilled desire ('in a nett I seke to hold the wynde') (3), still a spiritual aspiration (7), within which the woman is idealised.

'Who so list to hounte' again presents the woman as a deer, a quarry to be hunted, subject to male desire. Whereas Petrarch's Laura is 'free', Wyatt's deer-woman is 'wylde', a term connoting 'not only elusiveness but the uncanny menace associated with the medieval tradition of the wild man or wild woman' (Greenblatt 1980, p. 147). Moving outside the conventions of masculine society – much more so than Laura – the woman here is exhibited as radically other. Her difference is not emphasised so that she can follow her own desire but rather so that she can be made to submit to his – provoking him to win her back, to hold her wildness like holding the wind (l. 8). For the speaker she makes possible a more dangerous yet desirable position of mastery if he can fix her essence as Caesar seems to have done. Then the words 'graven . . . her faier neck rounde abowte' (round her neck? *on* her neck?) would be a text summarising his identity, speaking *his* name not hers or Caesar's, and the diamonds would be like a mirror reflecting his image back to him in the form he desires to be seen. It is not the case that 'Who so list to hounte' is 'a radical criticism of Petrarch's whole attitude to women' (Mason 1959, p. 188), for this text supplies phantasy according to the same narcissistic structure as informed both 'Can vei la lauzeta' and 'Una candida cerva'. Once mastered by his look, the figure of the woman promises the speaker a point in which he may recognise himself with delight.

On the evidence of these three texts, scopophilic male narcissism presenting itself as love for another constitutes the main continuity between courtly and Romantic love. In Romantic love the woman is set up as mirror not for an elevated but a more level male gaze, a mechanism which further work could illustrate without difficulty from Sidney's 'Astrophel and Stella' and Shakespeare's sonnet sequence. Donne's *Songs and Sonets* constantly recur to the situation in which a lover is so close to the woman that his image appears reflected in the pupil of her eye, this becoming the metaphorical justification for a supposedly mutual recognition: 'My face in thine eye, thine in mine appeares . . .' ('The Good-Morrow'). As social phantasy, in its poetic articulation, love operates in a master/slave relation masquerading as its opposite. Displayed at first in feudal terms such that the adored lady and her loyal man coincide with the positions of ego ideal and ego, love secretes a narcissism able to launch it on a trajectory carrying far beyond the poetry of the middle ages. Just as the feudal elements mask the individualism within, so devotion to the lady masks self-love. Lacan's writing has foregrounded this continuity from courtly to Romantic love, and it is appropriate to end this chapter with some reference to his later work, which includes explicit discussion of courtly love.

Lacan and courtly love

There is, writes Lacan, 'no sexual relation' (1982, p. 143) because men and women desire different objects and desire them in different ways. To be what a man may want her to be 'a woman will reject an essential part of femininity' (1977, p. 290); the desire of a woman for a man is not the complement of his but rather represents 'the supplement of feminine over masculine' (1982, p. 93). Heterosexual feminine desire does have, he argues, a phallic function, but 'there is something more', he suggests, 'a *jouissance* beyond the phallus' (p. 145). In an attempt to deny this form of difference and reduce her supplementary desire into the complement of his own, man has tried to transform her into a spiritual essence, an absolute category, '*The* woman, where the definite article stands for the universal' (p. 144). This strategy is pursued in courtly love, which Lacan describes as follows:

It is an altogether refined way of making up for the absence of sexual relation by pretending that it is we who put an obstacle to it. It is truly the most staggering thing that has ever been tried. But how can we expose its fraud?

Instead of wavering over the paradox that courtly love appeared in the age of feudalism, the materialists should see this as a magnificent opportunity for showing how, on the contrary, it is rooted in the discourse of fealty, of fidelity to the person. In the last resort, the person is always the discourse of the master. For the man, whose lady was entirely, in the most servile sense of the term, his female subject, courtly love is the only way of coming off elegantly from the absence of sexual relation.   (p. 141)

The passage can be read as asserting a continuity between courtly and Romantic love. The avowed courtly relation of female mastery and male servility hides its reverse effect, that by which the man treats the lady as his female subject. That the lady does not return his love because she is superior provides an obstacle, like the sword found between Tristan and Iseult as discussed by de Rougemont (to whom

Lacan refers, p. 146), and so enables men to disavow the impossibility of the sexual relation. Love, whether courtly or Romantic, is phallocentric in that for men it promises a mastery of the intersubjective Other, appears to close up all difference in the figure of a complementary unity, The woman, with whom he may reassure himself by saying, 'You are everything and everything is you'. And so, in Lacan's conclusion: 'when one is a man, one sees in one's partner what can serve, narcissistically, to act as one's own support' (p. 157).

The patriarchal scenario of love is played out very much as a drama of vision. Here the Other is represented by the universal play of light, and the mastery apparent to the ego by a fixed position of sight particularised within that field. To see something presupposes someone could look back from there, that the object of my look could be a subject with me as object: 'I see only from one point, but in my existence I am looked at from all sides' (1977b, p. 72). Yet when in love I am tempted to believe I am seen as I wish to see myself and so that *'I see myself seeing myself'* (p. 80, italics original). Like the hoped for mutuality and complementarity of the sexual relation this aim is another impossibility, for

When, in love, I solicit a look, what is profoundly unsatisfying and always missing is that – *You never look at me from the place from which I see you.*
(p.103, italics original)

Absence of the self in the Other is particularly opened up when someone else looks at me, but a man may easily overlook this absence if he can believe his image is reflected back in admiration from a woman's eyes.

Formally, that is, at the level of the signifier, confessional discourse in the three poems examined here shows a chronological development towards ever more effective means to make the text appear as a voice, a person really speaking the truth about themselves in the present. But the same chronology also records increasing importance attached to the dramatisation of scopophilia – in the figure of Narcissus, the extended vision of a white hind, the clarity with which diamonds are seen on the lady's neck. The poems considered in the next chapter, English examples from the period after 1660, give evidence of a change in the forms of social phantasy.

No doubt with Descartes especially in mind, Lacan refers to 'the beginning of the seventeenth century' as 'that inaugural moment of the emergence of the subject, (1977b, p. 223); he also writes of 'the philosophical *cogito*' as 'the centre of the mirage that renders modern man so sure of being himself even in his uncertainties about himself, and even in the mistrust he has learned to practice against the traps of self-love' (1977a, p. 165), a description which would apply closely to Donne's 'Elegy 19' and to the developing structures of the tradition of poetry analysed here from Bernart de Ventadorn to Wyatt, a lyric tradition in which self-love masquerades as love for the figure of a woman.

But there is a historical distinction to be made. At first, in the social phantasy of courtly love poetry, there is a contradictory collocation between (at the level of ideology) feudal and bourgeois connotations in which, as was argued, the beloved figures respectively (at the level of phantasy) in the place of the ego ideal and the speaker that of the ego. The lady has a strong social meaning so that she is forbidden to the speaker by his feudal obligations at the same time as she is desired by his proto-bourgeois self. Nurtured inside this structure, narcissistic phantasy gradually breaks out to dominate the whole organisation, and the lady as prohibited social object gives way to presentation of the beautiful woman as impossible object of desire and reflective confirmation of the speaker's wish to see himself as he would wish to be. Accompanied as it is by formal changes dramatising ever more persuasively the effect of an individual voice really speaking, the tradition of love poetry retains the woman in the place of the ego ideal but only so as to recuperate the impossibility of the sexual relation – if she denies or proves unsatisfactory it is to efface the deeper impossibility the social phantasy seeks to conceal (and which Lacan so harshly unmasks). For even in its courtly origins – as with 'Can vei la lauzeta' – self-awareness and inwardness had always established itself implicitly on grounds of the Other by assuming an object of desire external to the self misrecognised as a point in which the (male) subject may image himself as he would like to be.

Now, in the seventeenth century the subject emerges in poetic modes which explicitly ignore inwardness by directing attention and mastery towards a rendering of the external world, though in doing so – there is always a subject of an object – they presuppose the conscious, rational subject as monarch of all he surveys. Confessional discourse seeking truth within the self is replaced by impersonal narrative modes which aim to represent truth in an objective reality.

The pleasure of looking becomes the pleasure derived from the seeming transparency of discourse; and, as will be argued, instead of the phantasy of male narcissism striving to guarantee itself by taking the figure of a woman as its object, the feminine is virtually displaced in favour of a privileged relation between father and son.

5

THE AUGUSTAN FATHER

Milton . . . the first of the masculinists.   Virginia Woolf

After 1660 a typical phantasy in poetry celebrates an equation
between the father and the state. So much at least is suggested by the
two poems to be considered in some detail here, *Paradise Lost* and
Absalom and Achitophel. It is also at work with significant historical
variations, in the three other poems that will be discussed briefly, *The
Rape of the Lock*, 'The Vanity of Human Wishes' and Gray's 'Elegy'.
Patriarchal and phallocentric values come to be asserted in poetry in
an exceptionally forceful and explicit version. This happens both at
the level of the signified and in the formal properties of Augustan
poetry. A would-be transparent style (and it will be claimed that
Milton's epic anticipates this) invites the reader to overlook the
operation of the signifier in favour of seemingly direct access to the
signified, to meaning (see Easthope 1983, pp. 110–21). Lacan's
assertion that 'the unconscious is structured like a language' (1977b,
p. 203) and Freud's account of the mechanism of fetishism make it
possible to argue that 'a plain and natural style' is itself phallocentric
or, in Woolf's term, 'masculinist'.

For Saussure, phonemes are characterised not by their positive
qualities but by the fact that they are 'opposing relative and negative
entities' (1959, p. 119), that is, by their mutual differentiation.
Phonemes, these elements which Lacan refers to as constituting 'the
synchronic system of differential couplings necessary for the discern-
ment of sounds in a given language' (1977a, p. 153), are always at
work in a text since there can be no signified without them. But in any
discursive form it is a matter of degree how far the phonetic elements
are acknowledged rather than denied. It can be argued that a

transparent style invites the reader to overlook the phonetic and the signifier in favour of the signified and that this effect constitutes a form of fetishistic disavowal.

For Freud fetishism is exemplified in the case of the young man whose fetish was a 'shine on the nose' or *Glanz auf der Nase* (*SE* XXI, pp. 147–57). Since the patient knew English as well as German, Freud understood that this shine on the nose was 'in reality a *glance* at the nose'. This represented a disavowal of the threat of castration arising from sexual difference: 'the fetish is a substitute for the woman's (the mother's) penis that the little boy once believed in and does not want to give up'. It is as though the little boy discovered his own loss in seeing that the mother did not have a penis but that his look, travelling on up her body, found the nose and set up looking at that as a substitute for what was imagined to be missing. Not just the nose becomes invested, but also vision and the play of language by which *glanz* comes to mean both 'shine' and 'glance'. This suggests that fetishism can reach into the domain of signification. Fetishism works through the process of disavowal (*Verleugnung*); the fetishist knows of the woman's lack but disavows the knowledge in the belief that 'the woman *has* got a penis, in spite of everything'.

The structure of fetishism is phallocentric in three respects. Since what the woman is presumed to lack is the phallus, fetishism privileges the phallus as signifier of sexual difference (as though male = +phi and female = −phi). Since the castration complex is brought about when a child learns the anatomical differences between the sexes (*SE* XIX, pp. 241–58), fetishism would deny woman's sexual identity to the extent that it disavows its participation in instituting castration. Thirdly, 'the patient . . . is almost always male' (*SE* XXIII, p. 202).

Structured like a language, the unconscious takes up sexual difference and linguistic difference together, so that the lack instituted by castration may be felt as the absence introduced by the mutual differentiation of the signifiers (phonemes are 'negative entities'). A transparent style aims to disavow the signifier and set up the signified in its own right as firm, self-consistent and solid – to treat meaning as a truth which is given rather than constructed, standing thus as a kind of fetish. Attempted transparency can be understood as a phallocentric style. Confirmation for this can thus be found in the phantasy that dominates both *Paradise Lost* and Dryden's *Absalom and Achitophel*, and which might be formulated as: the father produces sons with little mediation from the mother. It is as though this corresponds in the signified content to an effect brought about by the discursive form, an effect whose paradigm would be: a speaking subject produces signifieds without mediation from the signifiers.

Milton: *Paradise Lost* (1667)

It can be argued that language *is* foregrounded in *Paradise Lost* (in fact Leavis attacks the poem's style because it 'exhibits a feeling *for* words rather than a capacity for feeling *through* words', 1964, p. 48). However, the poem seeks to contain the work/play of the signifier in relation to the signified: sound is dictated by decorum, the requirements of theme and the epic genre, and it is also invariably iconic (that is, the reader is invited to perceive sound as imitating meaning) (these views have been rehearsed elsewhere with reference to a Milton sonnet, see Easthope 1987a). And though a reader must seek it out actively from within the word-order, a consistent meaning is sustained along the syntagmatic chain and across the line endings ('the sense variously drawn out from one verse into another', as Milton's note on 'The Verse' says), down the paragraph, on through the narrative ('It is the period, the sentence and still more the paragraph that is the unit of Milton's verse', Eliot 1957, p. 157). To be sure, the poem does not supinely offer to give the reader supposedly unmediated access to the meaning represented – rather, as Stanley Fish has convincingly demonstrated, the poem provides a test for the reader who must actively seek out its truth by discarding rhetoric for logic:

Rhetoric is the verbal equivalent of the fleshly lures that seek to enthral us and divert our thoughts from Heaven, the reflection of our own cupidinous desires, while logic comes from God and speaks to that part of us which retains his image. Through rhetoric man continues in the error of the Fall, through logic he can at least attempt to return to the clarity Adam lost.
(Fish 1967, p. 61)

The truth to be attained is not simply cognitive but also moral:

If the ways of God can be justified, it must be through a purification of the heart rather than by the reasonings of the intellect.
(Cormican 1960, p. 175, cited Fish 1967, p. 258)

Nevertheless, in a Ramist fashion rhetoric and logic are conceived antithetically in terms of falsity/truth, appearance/reality (carried through into the poem's meaning this opposition has the persistent effect of imposing the reality principle on the pleasure principle, in the best known example when Mulciber's balmy fall is countermanded by 'thus they relate, / Erring', I. 746–7). Split 'between commentary and analysis' the ambivalent procedure of the text is perfectly exemplified when the Deity speaks in person so that 'reason explains the stark givens of God's will' (Kendrick 1986, p. 136). Although *Paradise Lost* assuredly does not seek full transparency, the rigour of its 'rationalising mode of thought' (Milner 1981, p. 157) demands that the reader should learn to disregard rhetoric and the signifier except as a means to arrive at the logic of the signified, the final truth of God's ultimate mercy. Narrative, human history and the poem are meant to close once and for all in an understanding, simultaneously rational and moral, of the *felix culpa*, the fortunate fall.

Because it is a sustained narrative rather than a lyric, because it is an epic narrative and therefore necessarily committed to trying to speak for a whole society, because it is religious epic and an epic corresponding to the moment of the English Revolution of the seventeenth century – for all these reasons, *Paradise Lost* is a rich repository of utopian anticipations. In the first place it is the hope for Eden, Eden lost and refound as a 'farr happier place' (XI. 464). Nature and culture join in a reciprocal relation, time and place become perfected together as history achieves fulfilment in a spiritual and transcendental destiny. The religious expression gathers in collective hopes for a better world even though it arises from a sectarian rather than universal basis. As Marx argues, the speech and passions of the Old Testament were used by the English revolutionaries in the seventeenth century to pass off its class interests as a general good – once it had won power in 1660, as Marx comments sardonically, 'Locke supplanted Habakkuk' (1954, p. 11).

Although Adam seems to embody simple humanist and individualist ideals his very individualism reveals him as the representative of a class, for alongside the feudal world of God and his court, Satan and his host, Adam is clearly 'the first bourgeois', (Jameson 1986, p. 52). Adam's story of sin and repentance rewarded seems to unite the claims of social order and individual freedom, law and merit, authority and ability brought together in a just hierarchy where each finds his or her rightful place. In foreshadowing the possibility of Adam and Eve living together in a loving mutuality and equality between the sexes the poem tries to imagine 'a concrete vision of the community of free people' (p. 56). It is a utopian attempt to anneal the contradictions from which it is constructed.

'Milton's selection of the fall story both represses the revolution from the poem and reduces it to theological explanation' (Kendrick 1986, p. 92): at one level the ideological assertion of *Paradise Lost* is overt and conjunctural: having won the war but lost the peace, the paradisal Commonwealth has fallen to old corruption (Satan and Charles II), yet, as Michael predicts, God will win in the end. At a deeper level the poem works to justify this triumph by contrasting the sovereignty of God with that of Satan. While Satan's authority takes the form of personal power (he assumes 'Royalties' and is glad to 'Reign', II. 451), God's authority rests on individual merit and to some extent the rule of law (even Jesus gets to where he goes 'By Merit more then Birthright', III.309, and see Milner 1981, pp. 155–6). God's power is as hierarchic and authoritarian as Satan's in that neither is subject to democratic accountability but God's hierarchic order claims to be more fair since it derives from the apparently self-evident abilities of the individual. And far beyond any rational apology God's power is justified in the poem because he takes the place of the father in a narrative which performs in phantasy a version of the male Oedipal transition.

The little boy, in the face of the father's threat of castration, foregoes his incestuous wish for the mother and redirects his desire towards the bride. This process has to be negotiated between too much rebellion and too little: the task for the son 'consists . . . in reconciling himself with his father if he has remained in opposition to him, or in freeing himself from his pressure if . . . he has become subservient to him' (*SE* XVI, p. 337). Satan remains in opposition to God the Father and returns to where he came from; Adam frees himself from excessive subservience, loses Paradise but gains the promise of a 'farr happier place' (XI. 464).

Satan is at first like a newborn infant, expelled from heaven, enclosed in hell, then passing through the gates of hell. There he meets a female monster, Sin, who tells him how he fathered her, how they had intercourse whose product was a male monster, Death, who raped her, the outcome of that union being more monsters, who creep back into her womb when frightened (II.746–814). With some justice Sin is later referred to as 'the incestuous Mother' (X.602). Satan's 'envie against the Son of God' (V.662) may be a symptom of the same desire for the mother, a sibling rivalry which also leads him to attack the new favourites, Adam and Eve, whom he thinks of as God's 'darling Sons' (II.373). But in Eden Adam and Eve become like parents to Satan; with fierce jealousy for their mutual happiness he watches the primal scene of Eve 'Imparadis't' in Adam's arms (IV.506). Locked in his own narcissism, believing that his own thoughts make external reality ('The mind is its own place . . .', I.254), believing he made himself ('self-begot', V.860), Satan cannot grow up. He defies God the Father, seduces Mother Eve and sets free his incestuous desires (Sin, Death) against the world. Remaining infantile and polymorphous, Satan returns via incarnation as a 'Cherube' (III.636) to the gates of hell and ends up unable to talk, 'on his Belly prone' (X.514).

God's three sons – Satan, Jesus, Adam – form a combinatory: Satan errs because of excessive rebellion, Jesus errs because his 'Filial obedience' leads to excessive subservience (III.269), only Adam completes his choice of the bride. If Paradise represents the maternal body (IV.132–6), then Eve in Paradise is like a mother to Adam. Although formally there is sexual intercourse before the fall it is pretty childish. After the fall they experience desire with a difference when Adam tells Eve 'never did thy Beautie . . . so enflame my sense' (IX.1029–31). For Eve's sake Adam defies the father, loses Paradise and gains the bride. In the end, far from being a cause for mourning (as is suggested by Rapaport 1983), the fall is fortunate. On learning from Michael's prophecy that ultimately 'the Earth / Shall all be Paradise', that the lost object will be re-found, Adam cries out:

> O goodness infinite, goodness immense!
> That all this good of evil shall produce,
> And evil turn to good . . .   (XII.470–2)

An Oedipal phantasy and the fortunate fall are superimposed, the effect being to justify God's hierarchic supremacy. This hierarchy is thoroughly phallocentric.

The phantasy that women are failed men, a bad copy of them, is structured with extraordinary rigour down through the text of *Paradise Lost.* God the Father represents the principle of a supposedly unified *masculine* identity, and so Adam and Eve must necessarily relate differently to him: 'Hee for God onely, shee for God in him' (IV.299). God introduces Eve to Adam as 'hee / Whose image thou art' (IV.472); during her creation Eve is described as 'Manlike, but different sex' (VIII.471); one of the nicest things Adam can call Eve is 'Best Image of my self' (v.95), though later in private he confides to Raphael that she resembles 'less / His Image who made both' (VIII.543–4).

The poem struggles to contain recognition of feminine identity by reducing it into a kind of male attribute, particularly by treating Eve as Adam's *thing* (the word can mean phallus in Elizabethan English). Eve was produced out of Adam's side when God took a rib and left a wound. He touches the rib until 'Under his forming hands a Creature grew' (VIII.470) (what *is* God doing?) and the result is Eve. So created by a man from a man, Eve nevertheless first loves herself, or rather her image reflected in a pool (IV.440–91). God's voice breaks this visual plenitude with the reminder that it is only an image and that really she should address her affections to Adam, as though she were his 'mirror and shadow' (Froula 1983, p. 328). Presented with Adam, however, Eve continues to prefer her own image and turns away from him until he says she is part of him, 'His flesh, his bone', and she yields to him, conceding that 'manly grace' rather than 'beauty' is 'truly fair'. Eve's narcissism turns her off Adam yet it is just this narcissism that Adam loves in her – 'so absolute she seems / And in her self compleat' (VIII.547–8). His feeling for her is that of 'being in love': that is, she must be fixed as an object in the gap opened in him by the difference she represents. She is both wound and balm – for him. Like a test set for the lover by the courtly lady, Adam eats the apple as a 'trial of exceeding Love' (IX.961). She has come to figure in the place of his ego ideal and he is later reproached for treating her as his 'God' (X.145). It is because he must have her as his own thing that Adam falls: 'to loose thee were to loose my self' (IX.959).

The text's attempt to contain feminine identity becomes an expression of it as Eve exceeds the position assigned to her by the poem and the men in it. In her narcissism she worships her own image, a feminine image. What the poem regards as her difference, her otherness, is marked by Adam's feeling that she threatens his whole masculine self-possession. In sexual intercourse with her he fears that 'Nature faild in mee' (VIII.534), as of course it did in so far as Eve, being female, from her side opens up sexual difference and so fractures the supposed singularity of his male nature. Raphael tries to ward off Adam's fears by denying that Eve is properly human. Her femininity is only from the body ('An outside? fair no doubt') and sexual intercourse with her merely animal since 'the sense of touch whereby mankind / Is propagated' (as Raphael puts it) is shared biologically with 'Cattel and each Beast' (VIII.561ff.).

Only once is Eve tempted to be independently herself. After she has fallen she wonders whether she should tell Adam or rather

> keep the odds of Knowledge in my power
> Without Copartner? so to add what wants
> In femal Sex, the more to draw his Love,
> And render me more equal, and perhaps,
> A thing not undesireable, somtime
> Superior; for inferior who is free?   (IX.820–5)

The wording is troubled and exceptionally condensed. The words are meant to illustrate how a woman's sinful claim to equality subverts the given male hierarchy but through them Eve begins to ask, 'What does a woman want?' Must she and her desire be defined only by the thing she's got missing? Must she always be the complement to masculine desire? Or can she achieve a just relation in which her desire supplements his? The questions remain unanswered.

Phallocentrism is integral to *Paradise Lost* but especially in the way unity, difference and their origins are worked through in the text and dramatised in its narrative. In the poem's ontology the first unity is the self-identity of God with God, one that is affirmed for example when he refuses to change his mind about making Adam and Eve free on the grounds that to do that would be to 'revoke the high Decree / Unchangeable, Eternale' which he has ordained (III.126–7). There is no Mrs God, an absence the text draws attention to when Adam asks God for a wife and God facetiously pretends to take this as a rebuke to his own unmarried status:

> Seem I to thee sufficiently possest
> Of happiness, or not? who am alone
> From all Eternitie . . .   (VIII.404–6)

The angels exhibit a similar unity in their sexual intercourse for it consists of a 'Union of Pure with Pure' (VIII.627). When Raphael confesses this to Adam he blushes, either because he's shy, or, as has been suggested, because he's glowing with ardour, but it might relate to the embarrassing fact that there are no women angels (Catherine Belsey, however, gives a much more positive assessment of Raphael's heaven on the grounds that it envisages a world beyond traditional sexual difference, see 1988, pp. 66–7). The wish for masculinity to be universal is spoken in great bitterness by Adam after the fall: if God was able to people heaven with 'Spirits Masculine', why didn't he fill the world with men like angels 'without Feminine', or find (says Adam through clenched teeth) 'some other way to generate / Mankind' (x.888ff.).

Well, God might soon reply, I did my best. Imagined as the source
'from whom / All things proceed' (v.469–70), himself uncreated, God
tries hard to reproduce himself without the feminine and without
difference. He tries to get sons in the perfect image of their father,
beginning with the angels and Satan (all male). They are not enough
like him but encourage him to try again with Jesus: 'This day I have
begot . . . My onely Son' (v.603–4). One wonders how. Christ is the
good son, wholly submissive to his father, spoken of by the poem as a
perfect reproduction of his father, as though his father was trans-
parently visible through his skin or as a signifier perfectly com-
municating meaning:

> in him all his Father shon
> Substantially exprest . . .   (III.139–40)

Unfortunately for God's purposes, Satan envies his younger sibling
and so creates Sin out of his own head, just as Athene sprang armed
from the head of Zeus. Before then and after the fall of Satan there are
no females in Heaven. Sin is the only one there is and she doesn't last
long (she claims that 'All th'Host of Heaven' were amazed to see her,
II.759, but later, in his account of the same events Raphael makes no
mention of her). Satan's fall takes a bit of God's creation away from
him and so he makes another world, not from love but to 'repaire /
That detriment' lest Satan's 'heart exalt him in the harme' he has done
(VII.150–3). So God makes yet another son, Adam, 'in our image', by
speaking, with breath, without difference (VII.519ff.). It has been
claimed that 'God creates the son, the angels and mankind as
expansions from self to non-self, unity to otherness' (Hunter 1980, p.
190) but this is precisely what does not happen. God creates sons as
expansions of himself and his own unity. And, despite the troubling
intervention of Sin via Satan, there seems to be no reason why God's
masculine self-replication should not go on and on, producing 'men
innumerable' (VII.156), 'Happie men' and 'sons of men' all created 'in
his Image' (VII.625–7). But Adam wants Eve; she is feminine; and this
introduces difference into the unified system.

Because of the clarity the text aims to impose on itself it is easy to
see how the feminine enters the ontic and narrative world of the poem
at two points, both of them wholly problematic:

1   Satan imagines Sin, who is feminine. She tells him how 'Out of thy head I
    sprung' (II.758). But how? How could she come out as something
    different from him, not the same, as feminine, not masculine?

2   God creates Eve out of Adam's side. Male reproduces himself from male
    yet the result is feminine. How?

These questions are raised by the text's own logic, by the particular
economy it establishes for itself.

The project of *Paradise Lost* is to 'justifie the wayes of God' (I. 26).
Thematically the text labours to recuperate the contradiction between hierarchy and democracy, God's sovereignty and people's
freedom. It would justify its hierarchic conception of social order by
showing that it rests upon the merits of individuals. Adam's superior
status over Eve is to be justified because they are not equal in ability
('Not equal, as the sex not equal seemd', IV.296). The supremacy of
God is to be justified because he can see everything, knows everything
and is right, especially about the fall. It is the task of the narrative to
reveal how the appearance of a mistake gives way in the end to the
certainty that Adam and Eve are better having fallen. But the
narrative mobilises a phantasy version of the male Oedipal transition
to enforce recognition that the fall was fortunate. To make this work
Sin and Eve are needed, Sin so that she can enter Eve via Satan, Eve
so she can then lead Adam to want her and defy God. But the
feminine, once admitted as openly as it is by the poem, compromises
the very principle of hierarchy and God's supremacy it was supposed
to help to vindicate. Thus expressed, femininity exposes the phallocentric inequality of the hierarchic order, the structure reinforced
throughout the whole poem's genealogy and cosmology: female is an
adjunct or even product of the male. It might be summed up like this:
the text asserts the feminine so that Adam can be better for losing
Eden and gaining Eve; but it must deny the feminine by showing it
comes out of men so as to protect the hierarchy it was introduced to
support in the first place.

This reading of the poem has so far acquiesced to the view that the
fall is indeed fortunate. One should add: fortunate for some but not
for others. As Sandra Gilbert and Susan Gubar point out, there is an
imbalance even in the degree to which the fall itself weighs on the man
and the woman. Whereas Adam's fall is hardly a fall at all if it means
he will have to work ('with labour I must earne / My bread; what
harm? Idleness had bin worse', X.1054-5), Eve 'is humbled by
becoming a slave not only to Adam the individual but to Adam the
archetypal man' (Gilbert and Gubar 1979, p. 197).

Many of the patriarchal concepts in *Paradise Lost* do not originate with it but derive from a breadth of myth and ideology. For example, 'Hee for God onely, shee for God in him' reiterates the Pauline doctrine that 'the head of every man is Christ; and the head of the woman is the man' (I Corinthians II: 3). To present God as father of all but son of none, patriarchal mythology rehearses a traditional structure of ideas and tropes, as is put forward by Ernest Jones in a paper on 'The Madonna's conception through the ear' (1951, II, pp. 266–357). Instanced most famously in the Annunciation, there is a tradition, Jones notes, in which impregnation by the father god is imaged as an act of breathing or speech. It reappears in the everyday phrase in which a son is said to be 'the very spit of his father' (p. 273). But while any obstruction to breathing is unpleasurable, breathing itself is not positively pleasurable and there is no evidence of 'ideational interest' attaching to it because it does not call into play an erogenous area of the body. So, according to the logic of psychoanalysis, the investment attached to the idea of breath or wind cannot be explained in terms of breath – it must emerge from the representation of some association 'reaching back to childhood' (p. 276) in the oral, anal and genital stages, for these *are* pleasurably invested. Since anal pleasure is excited by the release of intestinal gas, the forceful, life-giving wind from male spirits and father gods looks as though it is a rationalised and sublimated version of what Jones refers to as *flatus*. Probably 'the sublimation of the original interest proceeded historically by a series of steps' (p. 320). Although noting that this view may seem at first sight 'repellent, highly improbable, and above all unnecessary' (p. 277), Jones adduces plenty of anthropological and mythical material from around the world to support it. Like fetishism, this phantasy structure is a masculine one in that it disavows the threat of castration – in fact the idea of insemination by paternal breath side-steps the genital and so sexual difference altogether. Hence Jones's conclusion that

the idea of gaseous fertilization constitutes a reaction to an unusually intense *castration-phantasy*. It is one of the most remarkable of the various modes of dealing with the primordial Oedipus situation.   (p. 351, italics original)

The total complex allows the male child to express an 'ambivalent attitude towards his father', both denying and affirming his supreme might (p. 353).

Another cliché which assumes the son to be made entirely of the same substance as the father is 'a chip off the old block' (a chip presumably cut with an axe). Jones's account helps to bring out the thoroughness with which the idea of paternal replication by breath is worked into the text of *Paradise Lost*. His explanation actually appears in the poem, disguised as a joke, when various monks are blown into limbo by a mighty wind from 'the backside of the World' (III.494). God's act of creating via breath – life is 'breath'd' into Adam's nostrils (VII.519) though Eve is made by hand (VIII.452ff.) – is linked to the idea that he creates by speech alone, 'by his word the mighty Father made / All things' (v.835–6). For God, his son Jesus is 'alone / My Word' (III.169–70), in him the father shone 'Substantially exprest' (III. 140). A single principle recurs in this cluster of ideas which see life as breath, the father's breath as able to inseminate by word alone, the son as perfect copy of the father, meaning as direct expression of intention. It is that the father can reproduce himself effectively without mediation, whether that mediation is thought of as the necessity for the mother in procreation (and so sexual difference) or the necessity for there to be signifiers in order to bring about signifieds (and so linguistic difference). The main phallocentric term in *Paradise Lost* can be understood as the presumption that 'Immediat are the Acts of God' (VII.176) a term that would comprehend both the capacity of the poem's form to effect truth in the reader and its presentation of God as father of all but son of none.

Dryden: *Absalom and Achitophel* (1681)

The argument that the plain style goes along with phallocentrism seems validated when we turn to the poetry of the Augustan period. Achievement of a would-be transparent poetic discourse issues at once, in the opening lines of Dryden's *Absalom and Achitophel*, into the exuberant celebration of a newly triumphant patriarchy:

> In pious times, e'r Priest-craft did begin,
> Before *Polygamy* was made a sin;
> When man, on many, multiply'd his kind,
> E'r one to one was, cursedly, confind:
> When Nature prompted, and no law deny'd
> Promiscuous use of Concubine and Bride;
> Then, *Israel's* Monarch, after Heaven's own heart,
> His vigorous warmth did, variously, impart
> To Wives and Slaves: And, wide as his Command,
> Scatter'd his Maker's Image through the Land.   (ll. 1–10)

Critics (male) generally succumb to this infantile phantasy of pleasure before and outside the law, referring only favourably for example to 'the openness and gusto of David's busy promiscuity' (Roper 1965, p. 185). Such a response is inadequate if it fails to recognise how the ancient myth of the sun as a male god (David's 'vigorous warmth') and of semen as seed actively sown in a passive mother earth is mobilised in this parade of phallicism. 'Concubine and Bride', 'Wives and Slaves' are put to 'promiscuous use', that is, 'without discrimination' (*OED*, cited in Thomas 1978, p. 19). Dryden's well-known exordium imagines a father perfectly producing children in his own image almost without intervention from a different sex.

This comically inflated phantasy at the beginning seems to go well beyond the poem's need to excuse Charles II's infidelities. But the text does require it, though not at the more superficial level of its ideological assertion in a conjuncture (hang Shaftesbury, support the king, stop the Exclusion Bill). In fact the text develops ideology at a deeper stratum. Speaking as a Whig, Achitophel pronounces that political sovereignty is conferred by the will of the people:

> . . . the People have a Right Supreme
> To make their Kings; for Kings are made for them.
> All Empire is no more than Pow'r in Trust . . .   (ll.409–11)

Against this conception of democratic answerability, with its dangerously radical implications (even today), the poem champions a notion of the sovereignty of law and the state as self-justifying, ultimately beyond election or dispute:

> If ancient Fabricks nod, and threat to fall,
> To Patch the Flaws, and Buttress up the Wall,
> Thus far 'tis Duty; but here fix the Mark:
> For all beyond it is to touch our Ark.
> To change Foundations, cast the Frame anew,
> Is work for Rebels who base Ends pursue . . .   (ll. 800–5)

Citing Dryden's work elsewhere to the effect that 'there must be in government an ultimate authority beyond which there can be no appeal', Brevold comments that this view has 'a thoroughly pragmatic justification', namely 'a vivid consciousness of the dangers of "innovation"' (1956, p. 147). In the poem the idea of political sovereignty is strengthened by being made inseparable from a phantasy of the father as fully masculine, fully self-present, engendering sons in his own image.

The text becomes entirely pre-occupied with the identification – and non-identification – of sons with fathers, the ability of sons to take their father's place and the father's capacity to provide that place. As this version of the male bond, the endless Oedipal negotiation of fathers and sons, becomes privileged over all other relations, women in *Absalom and Achitophel* are virtually effaced, reduced to tokens of exchange, as the opening passage predicts. The feminine is so marginalised that it appears only in the figures of Michal (David's wife), Bathsheba (David's mistress), Annabel (Absalom's wife), Absalom's 'mother' (unnamed, l. 368), the Muse (ll. 857–60) and in part-objects as Nature (l. 424), the moon (l. 217), fruit (ll. 258, 260), one of Zimri's leisure activities (l. 551), a viper's mother (l. 1013) and the buttocks of Grace ('Her hinder parts', l. 1008).

Suppression of the feminine and the smoothing over of difference may be a reason why *Absalom and Achitophel* is a less charged text than *Paradise Lost*. There is no Eve, and instead of Satan's seduction of her, Achitophel tempts Absalom. Narrative follows a simple course: at first there is no law, then there is. Initially the people, a 'Headstrong, Moody, Murmuring race' (l. 45), are led, like young children, by 'their wild desires' (l. 55), indulged by King David's 'mildness' (l. 77), which gives them 'all they crave' (l. 383). Their infantilism, unchecked, unformed, is figured in the narrative by Absalom, named as David's child, who similarly encounters no prohibitions from the father. Absalom says of David:

> His Favour leaves me nothing to require;
> Prevents my Wishes, and outruns Desire.   (ll. 343–44)

Like God for the unfallen Adam, David for Absalom 'made the Charming *Annabel* his Bride' (l. 34), in effect hardly a bride at all. In nurturing the childish narcissism of the people and Absalom, David's own narcissism is at work, for, instead of looking in his son for a copy of his own paternal authority, David secretly enjoys finding 'His Youthful Image in his Son renew'd' (l. 32). The King's 'Mildness' (ll. 327, 381), his lack of 'Manly Force' in the first half of the poem renders him as what might be called the feminine father. All that happens in the narrative is that David moves from 'effeminate passivity' until at the end he 'seems changed, a virile man again' (McFadden 1978, pp. 246, 249). Why?

In passing from the polymorphous perversity of the infant towards what may be a distinct heterosexual preference as an adult the human subject never abandons its 'constitutional bisexuality' (*SE* xix, p. 31). Accordingly, the Oedipus complex is both positive and negative: for males, positive in leading to competition with the father ambivalently resolved through identification with him, negative when for example the boy 'behaves like a girl and displays an affectionate feminine attitude to his father' (*ibid.*, p. 33). At the start Absalom feels only love towards David corresponding to David's own feminine mildness. Small and snake-like, a fiery soul that overflows the body (ll. 156–8), Achitophel as the phallus provides a motive for competition between father and son. In his first speech Achitophel fails to draw Absalom into opposition to his father though in his reply Absalom does discover some rivalry for his father's 'Lawfull Issue' (l. 351) and love for his mother (l. 368). Achitophel's second speech harps on the theme of rivalry, denies that Absalom is David's 'Darling Son' (l. 433), menaces him with 'the next Heir' (l. 441) and incites him to 'Self-defence' (l. 458). Absalom represents the son who, in order to submit to law, must first free himself from his father because 'he has become subservient to him'. But the form of his rebellion is complex and two-fold, bringing together both positive and negative elements in the relation of father and son, both masculine desire for the female and feminine desire for the male. It is 'by Force', says Achitophel, that David

> wishes to be gain'd,
> Like womens Leachery, to seem Constrain'd:
> Doubt not, but when he most affects the Frown,
> Commit a pleasing Rape upon the Crown.   (ll. 471–4)

By offering him rebellion as a means to 'possess the Prince' (l. 476) Achitophel tips Absalom into confrontation with his father. Possibly this stress on femininity in the male bond is needed to make good its suppression elsewhere in this poem of men without women.

Absalom's opposition to David is not sufficient to account for his change from negative to positive, from mildness to manly force. Rather, this is facilitated not by any dramatised change in David but by the repetition in the text of two contrasted patterns of relation between fathers and sons. Like Satan, Achitophel rebels excessively against King David and stays infantile, a fact expressed in his fathering of a son who remains embryonic, 'a shapeless Lump' (l. 173). Absalom's followers, the bad sons, who take up arms 'against their Fathers' (l. 720), are each in different ways childishly perverse:

Zimri is polymorphous, Shimei anally avaricious ('heaping Wealth',
l. 591), Corah a masturbator and possibly a sodomite (Thomas 1978,
pp. 112–13). In contrast, the text names the king's followers, the good
sons, who are independent yet obey paternal law: Barzillai, Zadock,
Sagan, Adriel, Jotham, Hushai, Amiel. This monotonous catalogue
even includes their sons, epitomised in Barzillai's.

Description of the ascent of Barzillai's son to heaven (ll. 831–53) is
the 'turning point of the poem' (Ramsey 1969, p. 101), marked in the
text by a shift from *histoire*, discourse of the third person, to
discours, discourse of the first and second person ('me', l. 816, l. 832;
'thy', l. 841). David's change of heart is hardly explained except in the
way the text recites the names of the good sons. As God's
representative on earth (according to the ideology of divine right)
King David is in a special sense the image of God the Father. His
mildness has turned him into a bad copy of his maker, weakened the
direct reproduction of Godhead in king, father in son. Its supposed
transparency is symbolically restored in Barzillai's son. Conceived
not in partnership with a woman but merely with a 'Bed', spoken of as
'perfect in thy Line', unnamed except as 'a Father's Name', faithful
unto death, Barzillai's son is said to have 'All parts fulfill'd of Subject
and of Son'. His ascent to heaven renews the direct line to God the
Father, David's manly force is confirmed. Henceforth David will be
masculine through and through, though the closing off of his
femininity leads to a touch of paranoia that comes out in the
condemnation at the end of all these enemies (ll. 937–1031).

'The God-like *David* spoke': like Milton's God, David's intentions
are imagined here to translate immediately into acts just as his
paternal will is imagined to reproduce itself completely and directly in
subjects and sons. The poem makes this phallic phantasy of the self-
constitution of paternal authority inextricable from the ideological
assertion that the legal sovereignty of the state is ultimately founded
on itself. What David says is that 'Votes shall no more Establish'd
Pow'r controul' (l. 993). So, in this social phantasy, state power and
the symbolic father coincide.

Pope: *The Rape of the Lock* (1714) and other poems

The ideological project of post-1660 bourgeois culture in England is
now well documented. Terry Eagleton, for example, in his account of
the novels of Samuel Richardson, argues that the new class set out to

exercise hegemony by carrying through its conquests not only into the visible areas of 'parliaments, law courts and industrial production' but into 'the more elusive textures of human subjectivity', including particularly that of gender (1982, p. 2) thus by means of a 'cultural revolution' establishing 'the bourgeois public sphere' (1984, p. 10, and see pp. 9–35). And Catherine Belsey shows how women in this period (as is anticipated in *Paradise Lost*) come to be offered contradictory subject positions both as free individuals and individuals subordinate to male hierarchy so that they display 'a discontinuity of being, an 'inconstancy' which is seen as characteristically feminine' (1985, p. 149, and see pp. 149–224).

Social phantasy, the structured imbrication together of the ideological and phantasy in public, and especially aesthetic texts, is a matter of the effect both of the single text and of that text in its intertextual relations. While recognition of the specific and differentiated effect of different kinds and genres of aesthetic production must be insisted on, it can still be proposed that poetry in the eighteenth century exhibits its dependence on these intertextual forms of social phantasy. For the ideological project already documented is accompanied by typical modes of phantasy as these concern: (1) attempted transparency; (2) sexual difference; (3) the imbrication of notions of state power with the image of the fully present father. In following through these related themes in an outline survey of some eighteenth-century poems it becomes possible – at the risk of a somewhat speculative tone – to suggest how Romantic narcissism is presaged and even rendered necessary in the forms of social phantasy poetically explored. Briefly: the father comes to be wished for as a dead father.

After the success of the bourgeois revolution in England, as Marx says, in ideology 'Locke supplanted Habbakuk' (1954, p. 11). Milton's rationalised supernaturalism gives way to the binary vision of *Absalom and Achitophel* in which the mythical legend of David and Absalom coincides with the contemporary history of the Exclusion crisis. Pope's *The Rape of the Lock* (1714) shows the everyday, contemporary world with supernatural machinery as its comic frontier to image the irrationality supposed to rule female sexuality 'to Fifty from Fifteen' (IV.58). The law of patriarchal authority is not represented within the narrative (hardly by the Baron) but rather in and by the minutely detailed transparency of the discursive form *itself*. The style of *The Rape of the Lock* invites the implicitly male reader to *see* perfectly, and so, in the structure analysed by Laura Mulvey, to take up position with 'woman as image, man as bearer of the look' (1975, p. 11). Styled accordingly, Belinda in particular is the object to be known by this determining male gaze: 'Look on her Face' (II.18).

But the troubling gap opened up by the difference between male and female is not so easily closed, either by the discursive form (despite its efforts, through innuendo and use of metaphor, to recuperate what remains unspoken outside what is said so distinctly) or by the way the figure of the woman is presented within the narrative. Like Clarissa in Eagleton's account of Richardson's novel (1982), Belinda resists, rests impervious to the penetrating male gaze. Like Richardson's Clarissa also, she is submitted to rape when the Baron cuts off a lock of her hair. Though domesticated to suit the decorum of the poem, the act may not appear so innocently sublimated if considered alongside Freud's assertion that *coupeurs de nattes*, men who cut off women's hair, 'play the part of people who carry out an act of castration on the female genital organ' (*SE* XI, p. 96). Belinda is also faced with the fact of castration under the guise of disease, ageing and death by the text's mother figure, its own Clarissa:

> But since, alas! frail Beauty must decay,
> Curl'd or uncurl'd, since Locks will turn to grey,
> Since painted, or not painted, all shall fade,
> And she who scorns a Man, must die a Maid . . .   (v.26–9)

It is appropriate that the threat of the law should come from this Clarissa since for women the castration complex is instituted via the image of the maternal body (*SE* XXI, pp. 223–43 and XXII, pp. 112–35).

Yet Belinda continues to resist. Housed inside her narcissism, her feminine identity returns to trouble and charge the text with an interest not available, for example, from *Absalom and Achitophel*. The stylistic effect of there always being something other beneath what is so clearly enunciated corresponds to contradictory positions offered to the reader in the narrative by the figure of Belinda, particularly in her long speech after the loss of the lock (III.147ff.):

> Yet am not I the first mistaken Maid,
> By Love of *Courts* to num'rous Ills betray'd.
> O had I rather un-admir'd remain'd
> In some lone Isle, or distant Northern Land;
> Where the gilt *Chariot* never marks the Way,

> Where none learn *Ombre*, none e'er taste *Bohea*!
> There kept my Charms conceal'd from mortal Eye,
> Like Roses that in Desarts bloom and die . . .   (III.151–8)

The text exposes this speech for condemnation within the pervasive lucidity of its moral over-view as self-dramatising, self-indulgent, self-deceived, yet at the same time, contradictorily, it thus contains a voice that exceeds the poem's masculine transparency. Belinda's speech is comparable to Eve's after she has eaten the apple.

If *The Rape of the Lock* can be read as an index of patriarchy triumphant over everything social and domestic except what is expressed in the figure of Belinda, then it is surprising how rapidly this confidence fades into melancholy, a melancholy which affects both the sad grandeur of the style and the represented content in Johnson's 'The Vanity of Human Wishes' (1749). In all but the last few lines this text consists of the naming over of a list of dead fathers, four in exemplary narratives (Democritus, Wolsey, Charles XII, Charles Albert of Bavaria) and many others mourned along the way (Villiers, Harley, Wentworth, Hyde, Lydiat, Galileo, Laud, Alexander, Xerxes, Marlborough, Swift). In the conclusion a somewhat feminised God the Father is promised in place of the lost object. However vain, the phantasy that the father is dead can never be wholly separated from the wish that he should be dead. It is this that we find, deeply inscribed, in Gray's 'Elegy Written in a Country Churchyard' (1751).

Again there is melancholy for the loss of the dead fathers (the churchyard holds no mothers, only 'The rude forefathers of the hamlet', l. 16). Again there is a desire for death, marked particularly in two features. First, in the famous crux of l. 93 in the text, the speaker, unequivocally 'me' at the end of the first verse, has slid away in the meantime to become 'thee' ('the speaker has lost his identity as an ego', Brooks 1968, p. 95). Second, in the speaker's absence two other voices – strictly a voice and a text – have to be interpolated in order to speak for him, the 'hoary headed swain' (ll. 98–116) and 'The Epitaph' at the end. Desire to return to the maternal *'lap of earth'* (l. 117) imports some guilt: the dead are better thus because it is assumed if they had lived, grown up and gone into the world, they would have become rebels and symbolic parricides like Hampden, Milton and Cromwell, guilty of cutting off the king's head (ll. 57–60). Being always already dead means that their lot 'Forbade to wade through slaughter to a throne' (l. 67), the text's one sweeping and rhythmically urgent line. This act, simultaneously prohibited and performed, neatly embodies a compromise formation between regression and aggression towards the father, and coincides with the poem's ideological project, a resigned endorsement of established power and wealth together with muted criticism of it from a position of individual alienation (the speaker has a place neither with the rich nor with the swains).

In *Paradise Lost* and in *Absalom and Achitophel* the over-rebellious son is condemned and paternal authority celebrated (in *The Rape of the Lock* it is the daughter); now Gray's 'Elegy' provides an attenuated and conditional assertion of opposition to the father. In Romantic poetry this becomes firmly joined with a form of narcissistic phantasy presaged in Gray's 'Ode on a Distant Prospect of Eton College:

> Ah happy hills, ah pleasing shade,
> Ah fields belov'd in vain,
> Where once my careless childhood stray'd,
> A stranger yet to pain!   (ll. 11–14)

Published in 1747, these lines come to mean much more when they are interpreted retrospectively from within the perspective of Romanticism (see below, p. 122).

6

ROMANTIC NARCISSISM

> O! the one Life within us and abroad . . .
> Coleridge, 'The Eolian Harp'

We may begin with three quotations:

Nothing was more difficult for me in childhood than to admit the notion of death as a state applicable to my own being . . . I was often unable to think of external things as having external existence, and I communed with all that I saw as something not apart from, but inherent in, my own immaterial nature. Many times while going to school have I grasped at a wall or a tree to recall myself from this abyss of idealism to the reality.
(Wordsworth to Mrs Fenwick, 1843: 1947, IV, p. 463)

I can at times feel strongly the beauties, you describe, in themselves & for themselves – but more frequently *all things* appear little – all the knowledge that can be acquired, child's play – the universe itself – what but an immense heap of *little things*? – I can contemplate nothing but parts, & parts are all *little* – ! – My mind feels as if it ached to behold & know something *great* – something *one & indivisible*.
(Coleridge, letter to Thelwall, 14 October 1797: 1956, I, p. 349, italics original)

Let us recollect our sensations as children. What a distinct and intense apprehension had we of the world and of ourselves . . . We less habitually distinguished all that we saw and felt, from ourselves! They seemed, as it were, to constitute one mass. There are some persons who in this respect are always children. Those who are subject to the state called reverie feel as if their nature were dissolved into the surrounding universe, or as if the surrounding universe were absorbed into their being. They are conscious of no distinction. And these are states which precede, or accompany, or follow an unusually intense and vivid apprehension of life. As men grow up this power commonly decays, and they become mechanical and habitual agents.
(Shelley, 'On Life', 1812–14: 1965, VI, pp. 195–6)

Each of these three prose passages writes of what in psychoanalytic terms would be understood as primary narcissism. This present chapter will discuss one short lyric, though one which is very well known and often regarded, in Judith Chernaik's words (1972, p. 125), as a 'classic statement of Romanticism': Shelley's 'To a Skylark'. Other Romantic poems will not be considered, but my hope is that the conclusions of a detailed discussion of one text can be generalised and applied to others from the period. As a means to outline a context for the social phantasy offered by Shelley's poem, two texts will be read together here, Lukács's analysis of the ideologies of Romanticism in *History and Class Consciousness* (especially as these are exemplified in a passage from Schiller) and Freud's exposition in *Civilisation and its Discontents* of primary narcissism as it gives rise to an 'oceanic' feeling recalled and re-experienced by the adult.

Romanticism in Lukács and Freud

The discussion of Romanticism by Lukács occurs in the section on 'Reification and the Consciousness of the Proletariat' in *History and Class Consciousness* (1971). For present purposes this has the distinct advantage of being written without reference to English literature or English poetry. Its starting point is the Marxist assumption that production 'not only creates an object for the subject, but also a subject for the object' (Marx 1973, p. 92), that the human species through labour creates itself in creating its world, and so, that the objective mode of production conditions subjective consciousness. This continues to be the relation even when subject and object become alienated from each other as they do within the capitalist mode of production in which people as active subjects become separated from the objective fruits of their labour because the means of production belong not to them but to private capital. Lukács describes how 'mechanisation and rationalisation are intensified' (1971, p. 88) during the development of the work-process from the Renaissance to modern mass-production through the introduction of machine industry, increasing division of labour, an ever more strict imposition of work discipline:

the process of labour is progressively broken down into abstract, rational, specialised operations so that the worker loses contact with the finished product and his [*sic*] work is reduced to the mechanical repetition of a specialised set of actions. (p. 88)

Since subject and object continue to come into existence simultaneously, this 'fragmentation of the object of production necessarily

entails the fragmentation of its subject' (p. 89). Consciousness tends
to become reified, appearing only in partial, specialised and rationalist forms. The sense of time, for example, sheds its variable and
flowing nature and 'freezes into an exactly delimited, quantifiable
continuum filled with quantifiable "things"' (p. 90). In sum,
standardisation, fragmentation and specialisation lead 'to the destruction of every image of the whole' (p. 103).

In a central section (3) the essay, after a critique of the philosophy
of the Enlightenment, considers forms of Romantic ideology as a
response to, and product of, the Industrial Revolution. Increased
reification of consciousness in the period means that 'even while
"acting" man [*sic*] remains in the nature of the case, the object and
not the subject of events' and consequently 'the field of his activity
thus becomes wholly internalised' (p. 135). A series of broad strokes
summarises the three areas by which Romantic ideology aims to
express this internalised activity – in Nature, Humanity, Art. Before
Romanticism the conception of nature had been 'the "ordered",
calculable, formal', while now, in contrast, as for example in
Rousseau, a reversal of meaning emerges and 'nature becomes the
repository of all these inner tendencies opposing the growth of
mechanisation, dehumanisation and reification' (p. 136). Further, by
extension, 'Nature' comes to refer to 'authentic humanity, the true
essence of man liberated from the false mechanising forms of society:
man as a perfected whole' (*ibid.*). And at the same time the accredited
status of art changes so as to confer 'upon aesthetics and upon
consciousness of art a philosophical importance that art was unable
to lay claim to in previous ages' (p. 137).

Lukács explains these ideological innovations with reference to
Schiller's work, *On the Aesthetic Education of Man* (1795). Schiller
defines 'the aesthetic principle as the play-instinct' and formulates it
as follows: 'For it must be said once and for all that man [*sic*] only
plays when he is a man in the full meaning of the word, and *he is fully
human only when he plays*' (1971, p. 139, italics original). This can be
understood better if more of the context is given from another
translation of 'Letter 15' from the *Aesthetic Education*:

But how can we speak of mere play, when we know that it is precisely play
and play alone, which of all man's [*sic*] states and conditions is the one which
makes him whole, and unfolds both sides of his nature at once . . . with the
ideal of Beauty that is set up by Reason, an ideal of the play-drive, too, is
enjoined upon man . . . Reason also makes the pronouncement: With beauty

man shall only play, and it is with beauty only that he shall play . . . For, to mince matters no longer, man only plays when he is in the fullest sense of the word a human being, and he is only fully a human being when he plays.

(Schiller 1967, pp. 105–7)

Schiller's assertion is expanded by Lukács when he says that on the one hand it 'recognises that social life has destroyed man as man' but on the other it

points to the principle whereby *man having been socially destroyed, fragmented and divided between different partial systems is to be made whole again in thought.* (p. 139, italics original)

To recapitulate: because of the alienation of object and subject, the subject expresses itself only via the fragmented forms of a reified consciousness; 'every image of the whole' is destroyed. However, in the structure of Romantic ideology, subject and object appear to be reunited and totality restored, though only on the side of the subject and 'in thought'. An abstracted conception of nature, humanity and art is mobilised to furnish images for this radically subjective project, to establish what Lukács refers to as 'yet another domain for the fragmented subject' (p. 140).

This account of the association between work discipline and the Enlightenment especially from 1750 overlaps considerably with Foucault's description of the formation during the same period of 'a disciplinary society' (1979, p. 193), and undoubtedly Lukács's text is an influence on *Discipline and Punish*. The analysis of Romantic ideology as both a reified reflection of the experience of the factory system and at the same time a compensatory reaction against that experience might lead us to recall the passage in Wordsworth's 'Preface to the Lyrical Ballads' (1800) which asserts that various causes 'unknown to former times', including urbanisation (the 'accumulation of men [*sic*] in cities') and the standardised division of labour ('the uniformity of their occupations'), in a reciprocal movement produce 'a craving for extraordinary incident' (1959, p. 376). Lukács's argument could be criticised for casting the net of definition too wide, for giving an account of Romantic ideology as broad as Althusser's subsequent identification of ideology with 'lived experience'. More seriously, it can be attacked for assuming that forms of economic relations (commodity production) have an immediate effect on forms of ideology, so denying that ideologies and discourses are produced in their own relative autonomy. Even if this criticism is accepted, it still would not discredit Lukács's analysis of Romantic ideology as a compensatory structure in which an awareness of fragmentation and partiality produces a need for a renewed sense of totality. This compensating structure, it is hardly necessary to add, has a Utopian character.

Another book would have to be written to show how far this analysis can be validly applied to Romantic ideologies in general. Here the proposal will be that this ideological formation is exemplified in Shelley's 'To a Skylark', but only operative there in the form of social phantasy, that is, in an indissoluble conjunction with meanings and effects ensuing from the process of the unconscious, specifically from primary narcissism as recollected by a subject who has already passed beyond it into a 'secondary' stage of separated self-consciousness. (Freud offers two somewhat different definitions of primary narcissism. Rather than be given a tendentious account of these here, the reader is directed to the account by Laplanche and Pontalis, 1980, pp. 337–8, and to the previous discussion of the development of the ego, pp. 57–8 and 69–71 above). Primary narcissism will be assumed with Laplanche and Pontalis to be an 'objectless' or 'undifferentiated' state, one 'implying no split between subject and external world' [1980, p. 338], and summarised here from one discussion that has a particularly cogent bearing on the kinds of social phantasy made possible in Romantic poetry).

At the beginning of *Civilisation and its Discontents* (*SE* XXII, pp. 65–8) Freud reports the response of his friend, Romain Rolland, to his book, *The Future of an Illusion* (1927). Rolland said the book had failed to understand the true source of religious sentiments. This consisted 'in a peculiar feeling', though one he supposed present 'in millions of people', a feeling he would like to call 'a sensation of "eternity", a feeling as of something limitless, unbounded – as it were, "oceanic"'. Freud understands this 'oceanic feeling' as being 'a feeling of an indissoluble bond, of being one with the external world as a whole'. And he offers to explain it as follows. Normally, there is nothing of which we are more certain than 'the feeling of our self, of our own ego . . . as something autonomous and unitary, marked off distinctly from everything else'. In certain pathological states and also 'at the height of being in love the boundary between ego and object threatens to melt away'. Of course a boundary cannot melt away until it has been established, and for the infant at the breast, for example, the distinction between subject and object does not yet apply since the infant does not 'as yet distinguish his [*sic*] ego from the external world'. This is one sense in which Lacan writes of the human infant as an 'hommelette', spreading like egg batter on a frying pan, as yet with no defined limit.

As the reality of the external world is learned (from loss, from unpleasure), so a separated ego develops and with it a desire to recapture what is now seen as a former state of unity (this sense of a better former self becomes the ego ideal). Freud's analysis is worth giving at some length, not least because its phrasing at one point comes significantly close to Shelley's ('there are some persons who in this respect are always children . . .'):

In this way, then, the ego detaches itself from the external world. Or, to put it more correctly, originally the ego includes everything, later it separates off an external world from itself. Our present ego-feeling is, therefore, only a shrunken residue of a much more inclusive – indeed, an all-embracing – feeling which corresponded to a more intimate bond between the ego and the world about it. If we may assume that there are many people in whose mental life this primary ego-feeling has persisted to a greater or less degree, it would exist in them side by side with the narrower and more sharply demarcated ego-feeling of maturity, like a kind of counterpart to it. In that case, the ideational contents appropriate to it would be precisely those of limitlessness and of a bond with the universe – the same ideas with which my friend elucidated the 'oceanic' feeling. (p.68)

For the infant in a state of primary narcissism no distinction between object and subject presents itself. It is only as this opposition itself develops and the ego becomes separated out that the subject becomes aware of a former oneness.

The process is reciprocal. Awareness of a former unity ('primary ego-feeling') is a 'counterpart' to awareness of increasing separation of the ego ('narrower and more sharply demarcated'). The 'oceanic feeling' tries to fill a gap that has now opened up, 'as though it were another way of disclaiming the danger which the ego recognises as threatening it from the external world' (p. 72). Exactly this compensatory movement is described when the paper 'On Narcissism' says that 'The development of the ego consists in a departure from primary narcissism and gives rise to a vigorous attempt to recover that state' (*SE* xiv, p. 100).

In 1941 in the course of an essay on Wordsworth's 'Immortality Ode' Lionel Trilling (1953, pp. 139–40) makes a cross-reference to the account of 'the oceanic feeling' in *Civilisation and its Discontents*.

Linking Romanticism with the phantasy wish to recover a state of primary narcissism is not unprecedented. However, reading together these two texts from Lukács and Freud suggests that Romanticism may best be thought of in terms of two reciprocal or dialectical structures – of ideology and of phantasy – which coalesce into a social phantasy. For Lukács, Romantic ideologies are organised into a reciprocal process by which a sense of humanity as socially divided between partial systems 'is to be made whole again in thought'; for Freud, the ego's increasing separation demands as its 'counterpart' a sense of 'oneness with the universe' (*SE* XIX, p. 72). One of the earliest examples of how these two structures are mapped onto each other is Gray's 'Ode on a Distant Prospect of Eton College'. When in the second verse the represented speaker says

> Ah happy hills, ah pleasing shade,
> Ah fields, belov'd in vain,
> Where once my careless childhood stray'd,
> A stranger yet to pain!

the idea of childhood has come to represent both primary narcissism and an ideological conception of totality, while the 'pain' of being an adult resonates both with a sense of the socially alienated individual and of the separated ego seeking to restore a previous psychic state.

Although analytically discriminated here, the two levels of structure are frequently run together in the social phantasy of Romanticism into a generalised sense of reciprocity between subject and object. This, with its ideological connotation of humanity restored to oneness, seems to be what is meant by the term 'imagination', for example when Wordsworth writes that in the *Lyrical Ballads* a 'certain colouring of imagination' has been thrown over 'ordinary things' (1959, p. 8) or in Coleridge's definition of poetic or 'secondary' imagination as active in the way it 'dissolves' the opposition between subject and 'fixed and dead' objects in a struggle 'to idealise and unify' (1949, I, p. 202). Modern literary criticism has responded to the same dialectical process even when it has not seen it as in part ideological, for example when Earl R. Wasserman claims that the four major Romantic poets all 'face the central need to find a significant relationship between the subjective and objective worlds' (1964, p. 33).

So far has this kind of account of Romanticism become a commonplace that René Wellek could look back over several generations of critical work attempting to define the Romantic project and confidently refer to the 'essence and nature' of European and English Romanticism as 'that attempt, apparently doomed to failure and abandoned by our time, to identify subject and object, to reconcile man and nature, consciousness and unconsciousness by poetry which is "the first and last of all knowledge" ' (1963, p. 133). It can be proposed then that Romanticism reworks intertextually a social phantasy in which (at the level of the ideological) an objective and social sense of totality has been destroyed but is to be restored subjectively, 'in thought'; in thought (at the level of phantasy) a state of primary narcissism is desired as a form of active recuperation (for the attempt is 'doomed to failure') by which awareness of the difference and separation between subject and object may be wished away.

Yet the whole of this account is subject to revision. A persistent failure, especially in British criticism, has been a refusal to admit to the real complexity of Romantic poetry. The situation will turn out to be not even so straightforward as in the provisional account proposed above, particularly when the two 'I's of the represented speaker are given adequate attention. Nevertheless, the analysis will stand as a preliminary and as a basis on which to look briefly at the language of Romantic poetry. For that arguably fits the account in that it itself seems to encourage forms of narcissistic phantasy.

Narcissism and language

With English Romantic poetry a syndrome of new poetic techniques is introduced in an attempt to deny any essential difference between poetic and non-poetic discourses, between fiction and non-fiction, between 'art' and 'life'. Lyric metres and blank verse replace the Augustan couplet, *discours* (I/you address) is preferred to *histoire* (he/she/it address), a sustained syntax imitates the rhythms and word order of speech, iconicity is extended into more aspects of the text than ever before as if to render it wholly expressive (Easthope 1983, pp. 122–33). The strategy is no longer to contain the signifier and the process of enunciation but rather to efface it altogether, to make language as though entirely transparent to the thoughts and feelings of a represented speaker. It was argued above that the attempted transparency of Augustan poetry could be understood as a phallocentric style in that it treats signified truth as a fetish. And one might add that the poetic forms of Augustan poetry also act out a fetishistic disavowal of the signifier in seeking to fix sound as an echo to sense and to contain the phonetic force of language in the couplet. While in Augustan poetry fetishistic containment of the signifier conforms to the demands of a paternal phantasy, the Romantic attempt to efface the signifier altogether corresponds to narcissism. Narcissus sees the image in the pool not as an optical effect but as himself (*iste ego sum*, p. 81 above). The represented image appears to be there for him without any means of representation acting to produce it. His state, therefore, is what Lacan defines as that of the imaginary insofar as the signified seems fully present for the subject independent of the signifier, *meaning* there without words. As origin for the castration complex, sexual difference and linguistic difference co-operate. Hence the vision of Narcissus is pre-Oedipal. And so the attempted effacement of the signifier in Romantic language must be understood as performing a regressive wish – to recover the imaginary and narcissistic plenitude that holds the subject before the institution of lack. An instance of this, one that proves very relevant to analysis of 'To a Skylark', is the dramatisation of a speaker in a state of excitement who apparently has access to a symbolic reality directly, immediately, without the intervention of the signifier.

A well-known passage in Coleridge's *The Statesman's Manual* distinguishes between allegory and symbol.

Now an allegory is but a translation of abstract notions into a picture-language, which is itself nothing but an abstraction from objects of the senses; the principal being more worthless even than its phantom proxy, both alike unsubstantial, and the former shapeless to boot. On the other hand a symbol (ὁ ἔστι ἀει ταυτηγόρικον) is characterized by a translucence of the special in the individual, or of the general in the special, or of the universal in the general; above all by the translucence of the eternal through and in the temporal. It always partakes of the reality which it renders intelligible; and while it enunciates the whole, abides itself as a living part in that unity of which it is the representative.   (1854, I, pp. 437–8)

The Greek phrase used means 'which is always tautegorical' and is explained when *Aids to Reflection* contrasts the allegorical , 'expressing a different subject with a resemblance', with the tautegorical, 'expressing the same subject but with a difference')1859, pp. 158–9). The distinction between allegory and symbol is open to several readings (see, for example, Schneider 1953, pp. 252–4, and Appleyard

1965, pp. 227–8). It – and this passage – have also been discussed in Paul de Man's essay, 'The Rhetoric of Temporality', though consideration of that will be left to the end of the chapter. Here I shall emphasise the claim that the symbol is transparent. Allegory, it is assumed, works through two orders of signification, 'abstract notions' and 'picture-language', each of which is autonomous, their relation being by nature arbitrary. Allegorical meaning is brought about when the two orders are lined up into correspondence. So, in *The Pilgrim's Progress*, the usual example, the characters and events of the journey are a concrete picture-language and ideas about spiritual development are the 'abstract notions'. Each detail of the first can be related to the second; meanings are produced from the pictures but these meanings could be put in another language – it's a question of 'translation'. The symbol is characterised not by its availability for translation but by its 'translucence'. While allegory brings one order into correspondence with another, the symbol 'always partakes of the reality which it renders intelligible', representing but at the same time being part of the represented. Rephrased in terms of signifier and signified the distinction would be between one discourse in which signifiers stood for signifieds and another in which signifiers were somehow the *same* as signifieds. This is impossible, though Coleridge elsewhere wishes for it: 'I would endeavour to destroy the old antithesis of *Words & Things*, elevating, as it were, words into Things & living Things too' (Coleridge, letter to Godwin, 22 September 1800, 1956, I, p. 626).

Shelley: 'To a Skylark' (1820)

Only through a wish ('as it were') can words become things, can signifiers partake of the signifieds they render intelligible, though this is precisely the rhetorical strategy of 'To a Skylark' (1820). It treats the world it represents as though it were symbol rather than allegory in Coleridge's distinction, seeking to present it as directly available outside any action of the signifier. In its poetic language the text would wish away the signifier, thus in this respect, as in others, providing a narcissistic phantasy for its reader:

> Hail to thee, blithe Spirit!
> Bird thou never wert,
> That from Heaven, or near it,
> Pourest thy full heart
> 5   In profuse strains of unpremeditated art.

Higher still and higher
 From the earth thou springest
Like a cloud of fire;
 The blue deep thou wingest,
10 And singing still dost soar, and soaring ever singest.

In the golden lightning
 Of the sunken sun,
O'er which clouds are bright'ning,
 Thou dost float and run;
15 Like an unbodied joy whose race is just begun.

The pale purple even
 Melts around thy flight;
Like a star of Heaven,
 In the broad daylight
20 Thou art unseen, but yet I hear thy shrill delight,

Keen as are the arrows
 Of that silver sphere,
Whose intense lamp narrows
 In the white dawn clear
25 Until we hardly see – we feel that it is there.

All the earth and air
 With thy voice is loud,
As, when night is bare,
 From one lonely cloud
30 The moon rains out her beams, and Heaven is overflowed.

What thou art we know not;
 What is most like thee?
From rainbow clouds there flow not
 Drops so bright to see
35 As from thy presence showers a rain of melody.

Like a Poet hidden
 In the light of thought,
Singing hymns unbidden,
 Till the world is wrought
40 To sympathy with hopes and fears it heeded not:

Like a high-born maiden
 In a palace-tower,
Soothing her love-laden
 Soul in secret hour
45 With music sweet as love, which overflows her bower:

Like a glow-worm golden
 In a dell of dew,
Scattering unbeholden
 Its aëreal hue

50   Among the flowers and grass, which screen it from the view!

Like a rose embowered
    In its own green leaves,
By warm winds deflowered,
    Till the scent it gives
55   Makes faint with too much sweet those heavy-wingèd thieves:

Sound of vernal showers
    On the twinkling grass,
Rain-awakened flowers,
    All that ever was
60   Joyous, and clear, and fresh, thy music doth surpass:

Teach us, Sprite or Bird,
    What sweet thoughts are thine:
I have never heard
    Praise of love or wine
65   That panted forth a flood of rapture so divine.

Chorus Hymeneal,
    Or triumphal chant,
Matched with thine would be all
    But an empty vaunt,
70   A thing wherein we feel there is some hidden want.

What objects are the fountains
    Of thy happy strain?
What fields, or waves, or mountains?
    What shapes of sky or plain?
75   What love of thine own kind? what ignorance of pain?

With thy clear keen joyance
    Languor cannot be:
Shadow of annoyance
    Never came near thee:
80   Thou lovest – but ne'er knew love's sad satiety.

Waking or asleep,
    Thou of death must deem
Things more true and deep
    Than we mortals dream,
85   Or how could thy notes flow in such a crystal stream?

We look before and after,
    And pine for what is not:
Our sincerest laughter
    With some pain is fraught;
90   Our sweetest songs are those that tell of saddest thought.

Yet if we could scorn
    Hate, and pride and fear;

      If we were things born
         Not to shed a tear,
95   I know not how thy joy we ever should come near.

      Better than all measures
         Of delightful sound,
      Better than all treasures
         That in books are found,
100   Thy skill to poet were, thou scorner of the ground!

      Teach me half the gladness
         That thy brain must know,
      Such harmonious madness
         From my lips would flow
105   The world should listen then – as I am listening now.

The ideological stance of the poem is well introduced by K. N.
Cameron's comment:

The message of *To a Skylark* is . . . that . . . in a 'despotic world' the song of
the soaring skylark becomes a symbol of liberty and happiness, a force from
nature that might, like the message of those 'unacknowledged legislators', the
poets, inspire others to produce a better world.   (1974, p. 295)

Lukács's analysis is substantiated. The liberty advocated by the poem
is personal rather than political – responsibility for producing a better
world is consigned subjectively to poetry and the poets because in the
objective domain the acknowledged legislators have turned despotic
(a not unduly pessimistic judgement of England in the year after
Peterloo). Whereas in the traditional, Christian scenario a supernatural force descends, like the Holy Ghost, from heaven to earth in
the form of a dove, here a 'blithe Spirit' embodied in a skylark
represents a pagan ascent from earth towards heaven. Because the
social dimension is felt as dehumanised, this natural image must
stand as repository for the true essence of perfected humanity, a
humanity that shares in both nature and art, since the bird sings both
like a skylark and 'Like a Poet' (l. 36).

    In poetry, 'in thought', as Lukács says, an image of the whole can
be restored – subject and object, represented speaker and symbolic
skylark, envisioned as caught up together and reconciled into a unity,
'I' and 'Thou' at one. This established, the poem hopes to move back
again towards the external world. 'Poetry administers to the effect by
acting upon the cause' (Shelley 1965, VII, p. 118), the objective effect
being social oppression, the subjective cause being reified consciousness which submits to oppression, and the necessary counter-action

being renewal of an image of the whole. Simultaneously political and poetic, utopianism here becomes a deliberate strategy. In an act of intervention the poem aims to win the world 'To sympathy with hopes and fears it heeded not' (l. 40) by itself re-producing for the reader just the sene of unity found by the speaker in the song of the skylark so that 'the world should listen then – as I am listening now' (l. 105).

In support of this ideological project the poem seeks to overload the reader with embedded representations of subject and object apparently reconciled or in active reciprocity. Analysis must try to disentangle some of these overlapping levels: that at which the symbol of the skylark combines internal and external; that at which the represented speaker as subject seeks a direct relation with the skylark as object; finally, that at which the reader supposedly moves directly through the transparent language of the text into the world of the poem. Narcissistic phantasy operates in each of these three 'registers' of the text.

The first aim of the poem is 'to embody the lark poetically, to fix its essence' (Chernaik 1972, p. 126), 'to capture the essence of the sky-lark's song' (Webb 1977, p. 212). The symbolic reality of the skylark is persuasive as reality partly because of its unconscious associations. If the skylark is phallic and its flying 'in defiance of the laws of gravity' (*SE* xv, p. 155) connotes male erection, then the melting landscape it flies through may evoke female genitals. Nathaniel Brown's *Sexuality and Feminism in Shelley* says that the sense of being 'dissolved into the surrounding universe' in a Shelleyan text implies orgasm (1979, pp. 130–1) and notes that the reference to 'love's sad satiety' (l. 80) is the only reference in his work to post-coital sadness (p. 73). Having argued for the many forms in which flatus is given sublimated expression, Ernest Jones (see above pp. 106–7) takes the skylark's flight as a multiply suggestive image for the breath-soul:

In Shelley's 'To a Skylark' most of the preceding associations are poetically illustrated. For example: soul (Hail to thee, blithe spirit – Bird thou never wert); fire (like a cloud of fire); invisibility (Thou art unseen, but yet I hear thy shrill delight); rising flight (thou scorner of the ground); voice (All the earth and air with thy voice is loud). (1951, II, p. 333)

Yet it would be doubtful to regard the skylark as symbolising specifically male phallicism rather than the pre-Oedipal phallic phase through which every human subject accedes to sexuality. For qualities of polymorphous perversity cluster around the skylark symbol. There is no gendered pronoun in the text, a decision side-stepped by the rhetoric of I/thou. The skylark is both 'arrow' (l. 21) and 'moon' (l. 30), masculine 'Poet' (l. 36) and 'high-born maiden' (l. 41), 'glow-worm' (l. 46) and 'rose' (l. 51) (for the femininity of the rose, see Janet Montefiore 1983).

As a symbolic reality the skylark is also given force by uniting aspects of object and subject, both the skylark as natural object from the external world and a significance deriving upon it from human subjectivity ('Bird thou never wert', l. 2). Features of the natural object are exploited throughout for their symbolic significance. When disturbed the tiny bird (*Alauda arvenis*) spirals upwards, singing to draw attention from its nest, and soon cannot be seen any more: this natural phenomenon in the external world is enlisted to yield subjectively the spiritual meaning of something beyond sense percep-tion, 'we hardly see – we feel that it is there' (l. 25). Similarly the idea of singing is used to comprehend simultaneously birdsong in external nature and the inward notion of the skylark's 'skill to poet' (l. 100).

Two other tropes help to establish the skylark as a symbolic unity between subject and object. One is the long sequence of metaphors, so important to the poem, which run together modes of perception normally separated in individual experience, as for example in the famous fifth stanza (attacked by Eliot but defended by Davie, 1967, p. 134, and King-Hele, 1960, p. 228):

> Keen as are the arrows
>   Of that silver sphere,
> Whose intense lamp narrows
>   In the white dawn clear
> Until we hardly see – we feel that it is there.

The piercing song of the bird is compared to the movement of an arrow which in turn becomes the light from the planet Venus as it appears brighter and smaller as the sky lightens at dawn. Such synaesthetic effects aim to make objective perceptions coalesce with subjective feelings, so that here, for example, sound has a tactile and visual equivalence.

The other persistent trope, explored most fully in *Shelley's Mythmaking* (Bloom 1969), is the poem's use of *discours*, of I/thou rhetoric. Shelley's 'A Defence of Poetry' distinguishes between 'a story and a poem' on the grounds that a story is 'a catalogue of detached facts' while a poem 'is the creation of actions, as existing . . . in the mind of the creator' (1965, VII, p. 115). We might now gloss the distinction as follows: whereas *histoire*, third-person discourse, tends to separate the matter narrated from its implied narrator, *discours*, first/second person discourse, would stage addresser and addressee in a direct relation. Subject and object constitute a close mutuality when the represented speaker as 'I' addresses the skylark as 'Thou', even towards the end of the poem invoking it through a form of prayer: 'Teach us, Sprite or Bird . . .' (l. 61).

Deliberately repeated and proliferating so as to saturate the reader's field of perception, this melding of subject and object, internal and external, serves to make available for the reader a phantasy of recovering the original, objectless state, primary narcissism, in which the bond between ego and surrounding world is so intimate as to appear non-existent. The represented speaker almost achieves identification with the skylark in the sense in which Freud defines identification as 'the original form of emotional tie with an object' (*SE* XVII, p. 107). In this respect the skylark as object for the speaker has at least four distinguishable meanings: (1) I am my objects; (2) I am my former self; (3) I am my best self; (4) I am my object of desire.

1   The skylark represents the very process of identification itself, for on its own terms it seeks to address and identify with its own objects, as when the speaker wonders,

> What objects are the fountains
>   Of thy happy strain?
> What fields, or waves, or mountains?
>   What shapes of sky or plain?   (ll. 71–4)

2   The skylark symbolises the perfection of the former self, that which is discriminated by Lacan as the ideal ego. The point hardly needs to be documented since the whole text works to do so but it is a meaning which emerges most clearly in the last nine stanzas when the 'I' contrasts the skylark with itself as transcending time and space, as eternally happy, without 'languor' (l. 77), not looking 'before and after' (l. 86).

3   In the development of the ego a sense of the former self is transformed into an idea of the better self: 'What man [*sic*] projects before him as his ideal is the substitute for the lost narcissism of his childhood in which he was his own ideal' (*SE* XIV, p. 94). Thus the

speaker represents the ego and the skylark his ego ideal. That the speaker is in fact implicitly masculine is evidenced not only by his quest for mastery but also from the fact that the skylark (itself, I believe, polymorphously perverse) is gradually brought under the aegis of that traditionally masculine symbol, the sun (linked with Hyperion, Helios and Apollo in Greek mythology, the sun is 'another sublimated symbol for the father', *SE* XII, p. 54). Just as the ego ideal becomes the internal, watchful agency for parents and other model figures from society, so in this text the skylark's flight takes it 'Higher still and higher' (l. 6) towards the sun. Jean Perrin has well brought out this feature of the poem when he argues that here, as elsewhere in Shelley's work, 'the *superego* is above all the eye of the Father' because 'the sun is the *universal eye*' (1973, p. 195, italics original).

4   As Harold Bloom says, the skylark moves 'in an upper paradise in which infinite desire is gratified' (1963, p. 318) and so it stands in the place of an object of desire for the speaker. What the speaker takes as object of desire is really himself as imaged in the versions just listed (1–3). It is as if he is in love with himself in the skylark, though to put it like that, intentionally recalling the discussion of being in love in chapter 3, indicates how much more enticingly narcissistic are the phantasies likely to be excited by this text. In wishing for a convergence between himself and the symbolic object figured in the skylark the speaker is looking for a mirror in which to identify himself in the form in which he likes to be seen. Insofar as the skylark is not even a whole person, a love-object like the lady in *Can vei la lauzeta*, but rather what psychoanalysis denotes as a part-object (here not so much the breast as faeces and phallus, see 'On Transformations of Instinct', *SE* XVII, pp. 125–33), the text discovers the speaker's narcissistic love for himself or rather a symbolic part of himself.

Again, around this point, analysis strikes one of the complexities of the poem (and Romanticism). On the one hand the subject/object relation dramatised is to be seen as actual, having a 'philosophic' definition, the perceiving subject over against an external object (skylark as skylark); on the other, the object is rendered as it is conceived by psychoanalysis, that is, as the object, whether real or phantasised, of a drive (the skylark as symbol). The aim is precisely to elide these two definitions of object: the skylark both as an object for a subject, the speaker, *and* a wished for reflection of the speaker himself, the subject-as-object we might say. Or to state it in other terms: the poem dramatises two points of identification for readers, that of speaker and that of skylark, and encourages us to respond to these as both subject/object and ego/ego ideal. How, one might ask, does it get away with it? How is the represented speaker contrived so that his presence is imposed on the Other which is not himself, specifically, on language and on us as readers? In answering this, the argument will be able to collect some topics previously left aside (symbol and allegory; the split subject; narcissism of language).

Recuperation

If the skylark is to incur the meaning of an achieved synthesis between subject and object, it can do so only at the risk of becoming, recursively, an object for a subject, namely, the represented speaker. For him 'the skylark is all but himself' (Wilson Knight 1943, p. 199). But that 'all but' makes all the difference. Except as the first, silent objectless or undifferentiated state of the infant, subject and object can never occupy the same space. So it is in 'To a Skylark' when the speaker thinks about the objects the skylark thinks about: in a process of infinite regress or rather *mise en abyme* those objects, if reached, would reveal themselves in turn as speaking subjects with their own objects (ll. 71–5). Moving in the opposite direction we have to recognise that the speaker's joy in the apparent synthesis of the skylark is only possible because he speaks from a position outside it, at a *distance* from it, 'near' but not there, as the poem stipulates:

> If we were things born
>   Not to shed a tear,
> I know not how thy joy we ever should come near.
>
> (ll. 93–5)

Therefore the poem works through allegory rather than symbol, as Paul de Man demonstrates in his essay, 'The Rhetoric of Temporality' (1983, pp. 187–228), a text no one could accuse of trying to simplify Romantic poetry (Frank Lentricchia, however, does accuse the essay of being 'peculiarly static and innocent of social and historical change', 1980, p. 298).

Against Gadamer's view in *Truth and Method* (1975) that Romanticism witnesses the growth of an aesthetics which values the symbol over allegory on the grounds that the symbol (in de Man's summary) 'refuses to distinguish between experience and the representation of this experience' (1983, p. 188), the essay, on the basis that you cannot have a signified without a signifier, argues that Romanticism depends upon allegory as it necessarily must but then strives to make up the difference:

Whereas the symbol postulates the possibility of an identity or identification, allegory designates primarily a distance in relation to its own origin, and, renouncing the nostalgia and the desire to coincide, it establishes its language in the voice of this temporal difference. In so doing, it prevents the self from an illusory identification with the non-self, which is now fully, though painfully, recognized as a non-self. (p. 207)

Reading this in terms of the previous discussion here and being less concerned with the intricate details of the essay than with what it may say about Shelley's poem, we may recall that the symbol supposes itself as a representation or signifier so wholly translucent to meaning that, in Coleridge's phrase, it 'partakes of the reality which it renders intelligible' and thus would coincide with it in a simultaneity. Allegory in contrast accepts 'temporal difference' in that it accepts the dependence of the signified on a temporary correspondence with the signifier, signifiers themselves being defined only in their mutual differentiation. From this opposition de Man's essay draws out a distinction that might best be grasped as one between two positions for the subject. Symbol would permit the subject to regard itself as substantial and self-present, coinciding with its own origin, since through the symbol the subject wins apparently direct access to meaning without recourse to the signifier (the non-self). In recognising the order of the signifier and acknowledging the dependence of signified on signifier, allegory precludes the subject 'from an illusory identification with the non-self'. The 'dialectical relationship between subject and object' itself is not in fact 'the central statement of Romantic thought' (p. 208). Rather allegory is, but in a special ironic form, as 'a defensive strategy' (*ibid.*) which tries to hide from the subject the painful fact that it cannot be fully present to itself, fully self-expressive in a symbolic reality.

For 'To a Skylark' the implications of this are two-fold, reflecting firstly on the relation between symbolic reality (the skylark) and the represented speaker and, secondly, on the position offered to the reader by the text (the first is considered by de Man, the second is not).

The speaker agonises to be present to himself in identification with the skylark, strives to render this object into a symbol for himself. Because he always stands at a distance from the skylark, he fails – but the poem seems to succeed in that this dramatised struggle constitutes the symbolic realm as a reality. Its paradigm might be: I cannot reach the symbolic reality of the skylark but *that* is the reality I cannot reach. In that all negation asserts (see Freud's paper, 'Negation', *SE* XIX, pp. 233–9), when the speaker says 'What thou art we know not' (l. 31) he denies only by presuming this other ('thou') as a knowable reality.

This effect in the dramatisation of the speaker explains the carefully organised rhetoric of the poem, though this is misrecognised by critics who read it as merely a spontaneous effusion (the poem 'goes tumbling on', Empson 1961, p. 157; 'the poem is a mere tumbled out spate', Leavis 1964, p. 179). Bloom's *Visionary Company* (1963) first showed how carefully structured the poem is, to be followed by Chernaik (1972, pp. 127–8) and Reiman (1976, pp. 115–16). Twenty-one stanzas are divided into three sections. In the first six (ll. 1–30) the speaker seeks to leap directly into identification with the skylark by describing it in metaphors. The strategy does not work, and a new one is announced when stanza seven asks, 'What is most like thee?' (l. 32). Six stanzas (ll. 31–60) approach the skylark through similes, each containing the idea of an excess or effluence as index of a covert source (the songs of a hidden poet, the music of a maiden in a tower, the light from a glow-worm, the scent of a rose on the wind). But the music of the skylark 'doth surpass' (l. 60) even these similes drawn from things which surpass, and the last eight stanzas change the mode of address altogether. Now the tactic is to speak directly in the form of prayer, 'Teach us', 'Teach me' (ll. 61, 101). He fails but the poem succeeds. Or does it? There is still the question of how the text presents itself to the reader.

The ideological project of the text is not just a statement but an anticipated form of practice – the poem is to act on its readers by itself being for them an embodiment of the lost totality, 'an image of the whole' inspiring them to find a better world. Just as the speaker seeks to identify with the skylark, so the reader is to identify with the speaker's struggle to identify with the skylark:

> Teach me half the gladness
> > That thy brain must know,
> Such harmonious madness
> > From my lips would flow
> The world should listen then – as I am listening now.

> (ll. 101–5)

It is the reader who is 'listening now' and has been throughout the poem and whose brain is expected to flow with 'harmonious madness' as a consequence of reading the poem. The strategy of this rhetorical politics assumes that the poem *as a whole* – speaker and skylark – can be a symbol, a reality to which the reader has unmediated access so that the 'real' of the poem can become at once the 'real' of the reader. This assumption cannot be sustained. What is at stake is an act of recuperation by which it can appear to be sustained.

The effect, I think, is brought about because the distance between speaker and skylark is admitted, in fact becomes the reason why he speaks. If he actually *was* the skylark, he wouldn't be able to try to identify with it, a contradiction the text seems to become aware of when it says that if 'we were things born / Not to shed a tear' we shouldn't be able to 'come near' the skylark's joy (ll. 93–5). The poem concedes the painful non-identity of speaker and skylark in order to conceal more effectively the process of signification which brings speaker and skylark into existence for a reader in the first place; a distance separating this subject and object is put in the foreground so as to recuperate the greater gap between reader and poem. In the following diagram the mediations constituting level 1 are admitted so as to efface those constituting level 2:

1	skylark/speaker object/subject	
2	object poem	subject reader

The reader is given apparently direct access to the represented reality of a subject in painful yet intense reciprocity with an object – intense because close to, painful because never close enough – so that the reality of the poem as a poem may be denied, so it may offer itself as represented without means of representation, signified without signifier. Allegory, one might say, is passed off as symbol, words elevated, as it were, into things in the performance of what earlier was identified as a narcissistic phantasy.

On the basis of this perspective the previous account of the social phantasy of Romanticism must be revised retrospectively. For it was proposed then that the two dialectical relations of subject and object – one ideological, one in phantasy – become imbricated together to make up the social phantasy. But if it is part of the working of Romanticism, as of Shelley's text, to present an external event in the social process of language (a poem) as though it were an internal reconciliation of subject and object (speaker and skylark), then it may be precisely an effect of Romantic ideology to *seek* to elide the two structures of the ideological and of phantasy, to make them appear to coincide. They do not, since one is in fact subordinate to the other, as a diagram may illustrate:

as phantasy	oneness/separation	
as ideology	'whole in thought'	'socially divided'

The whole manoeuvre to reclaim a state of primary narcissism takes place subjectively ('in thought') but is made more convincing because it seems to rework the larger structure on which it in fact depends. Once again this is an act of recuperation, in which oneness with the universe masquerades as the lost totality. Hence the self's painful isolation can be ascribed to loss of the bond with the universe rather than alienation from a social image of the whole.

To try to conclude more simply, more positively and with direct reference to the Shelley text: it was argued that a sense of unity between subject and object abounds in the poem, occurring in complex superimpositions at the level of meaning. But, crucially, the text offers positions for not one but two selves: a former unified self or ego ideal which is taken as an object and which another self as subject perceives from a distance and seeks to recover through identification. Identification fails. But the dramatisation of the two selves in the poem so vividly occupies the foreground that the reader is led to overlook the distance separating them from the text. If the reader treats the poem not as a poem but as a symbolic reality, this would deny the gap between reader as subject and text as object. Poetic language, therefore, would work to produce a narcissistic effect recalling once again the 'oceanic feeling'.

This analysis has rested on the assumption that Lukács's account of Romantic ideologies is valid, and of course it may not be. Claims have been put forward here about Romanticism on the evidence of a single, albeit central, text. But it might not be hard to justify those claims if other Romantic poems could be assigned to two categories:

those in which priority is given to a represented speaker, who then 'experiences' or recalls a state in which inner and outer worlds appear elided (as in Coleridge's 'Frost at Midnight' or Wordsworth's 'Tintern Abbey'); those in which priority is accorded to an intensely perceived object with which the speaker tries to find enraptured identification. Coleridge's 'Kubla Khan' stands at the front of this second category, as does Shelley's 'To a Skylark', 'Mont Blanc' and 'Ode to the West Wind', to name the more obvious examples, as well as Keats's 'Ode to a Nightingale', 'Ode on a Grecian Urn' and 'To Autumn'.

The degree to which the social phantasy presented in these texts is historical can be assessed if 'To a Skylark' is thought of in comparison with the troubadour poem discussed in chapter 4, for that opens with the image of a lark 'moving / its wings against the light' used to signify individual transcendence. To be sure, there is a continuity in that 'To a Skylark' reproduces the tradition of confessional discourse and also explores narcissism. But the contrast also is unmistakable. While the feudal poem begins with the lark and at once turns from it in an effort to scoop out a 'space' for the privatised individual through negotiation with the social, the Romantic text has always already surpassed the social in its assured journey into a realm conceived as uniquely personal (one therefore rendered especially in images – thing-presentations – whose relatively more unconscious privacy therefore always risks compromise if not complete betrayal when it is uttered as poetic discourse – word-presentations). And Shelley's text is far more pervasively committed to an idea of the recesses of subjectivity and the effect of narcissistic phantasy – through its language, as has been suggested, but also, for example, in that its speaker aims to recover an image of himself via a part-object (the symbolic animal) rather than a whole person (the lover's lady). If there is a hint here that Shelley's represented male speaker seeks a detour around sexuality, this may be a suitable thought to carry forward for the next chapter.

7

DARWINIAN CRISES

Do we move ourselves, or are moved . . . ?
Tennyson, *Maud*

'There is not a creed which is not shaken, not an accredited dogma
which is not shown to be questionable, not a received tradition which
does not threaten to dissolve': so Matthew Arnold cites his own work
in 1880 (1956, p. 1). There is in the nineteenth century a proliferation
in number and kind of discourses and ideologies, a growing dispersal
made less manageable (both for them and for any subsequent study)
because it took place in a centrifugal movement which called into
question the very possibility of a legitimating centre. It may also be
that during the period literature comes to manifest more and more
complex forms of phantasy. In response to such difficulties the
ambition of the present chapter is modest. It will discuss some
'Darwinian' passages in the poetry of Tennyson and Arnold, though
one must add immediately that they are in general Darwinian (the
shorthand adjective is useful) because they reflect anxieties about the
theory of evolution, what in the 1850s and 1860s was called 'the
Development Hypothesis', but cannot have anything directly to do
with the work of Darwin since *On the Origin of Species* was not
published until 1859. Granted the increasing plurality of Victorian
discourse, it may be appropriate to fix narrowly on one area of
poetry, especially since for nineteenth-century readers the issue of
evolution exemplified 'doubts that beset their whole culture' (Buckley
1960, p. 127). After posing the question of poetic language in the
period, the argument will be that Darwinism in poetry takes the form
of an ideology, one in fact brilliantly analysed by Freud, and comes to
constitute a social phantasy by trenching upon phantasy material at
some considerable distance from the explicit theme of evolution, the

nature of the universe and the development of the species *homo sapiens*.

Language in Victorian poetry

Alan Sinfield's close and incisive discussion of the language of Tennyson's *In Memoriam* ends with an inconclusive chapter comparing Victorian and modern poetry. While there is a continuity between them in 'Symbolist language' (the use of landscape to evoke mood, a preference for analogical syntax), the 'classical' poetry of the nineteenth century could 'claim to speak for the whole of mankind' whereas a twentieth-century poet 'is always conscious that any opinion may be their own' (1971, p. 197). More recently, Isobel Armstrong's *Language as Living Form in Nineteenth-Century Poetry* (1982) has tried to carry through a sustained account of poetic language in the period. Its thesis is that 'the language of nineteenth-century poetry can be shown to be idealist' (p. xi) in that in its 'concern with the relationship of subject and object' it assumes that 'the object is known as a category of mind' (p. xiii). Against what is taken to be the Hegelian view that the subject creates the object and 'dissolves as object the real sensuous world', the book advances what is taken to be a Marxist conception of the priority of 'vital, sensuous, concrete activity' (p. 43). Hence the argument made is that the idealism of poetic language in the nineteenth century gives way to what is implicitly a materialism in modernist poetry. A passage from Shelley's *Prometheus Unbound* and a lyric from Tennyson's *Maud* are assessed as follows:

If the poem appears to conjure objects merely as 'phantoms', if the language fails to construct the external world . . . the poet . . . is left with a poetry which is without a content, or which can only take mind as its content.

(p. 47)

In contrast, in modernism

the concentration on 'thingness' also enables the modernist poet to relieve himself [*sic*] of the notion of the subject and of subjectivity. It is almost as if things wrote poetry . . . (p. 208)

Although this analysis is persuasive in regarding the subject/object relation as crucial terms for approaching Romantic poetry and its inheritance, two major objections can be entered against its account of language as 'living form'.

A first difficulty is the assumption – precisely that which Althusser exposes in the early Marx – that the social formation is an 'expressive totality', a unity such that a *single* version of the subject/object relation expresses itself everywhere, in economic relations, in philosophic speculation, in poetic language. If there is no such mastering 'dialectic', then each level of the social formation will have its own specific effectivity (see Althusser 1977) and so as a specific discourse poetic language will act in its own separated, though relative, autonomy. Poetry works with its own complex enactment of the subject/object relation in its own way, as was suggested in the previous discussion of 'To a Skylark'. Second, the argument equates 'content', 'the external world' with 'object' (as 'thing' rather than as 'phantom'), and this cannot be supported. For it fails to mark the huge distinction between signified and referent, between the meaning of a word and a reality this meaning may or may not refer to. In itself as part of the internal system of a language, meaning *always* 'fails to construct the external world' in that reference to the external world is introduced through a local relation between meaning and reality. This condition prevails for all language, all forms of discourse, but it holds for poetic language with particular strictness. Insofar as it is literature and fictive, poetry never refers to the external world and its objects are always 'phantoms'. If the attempt to characterise nineteenth-century poetic language falls with these two objections, then the phantom/thing distinction resolves itself into the familiar opposition between 'abstract' and 'concrete' language, an opposition resting on an ideological commitment to a traditionally empiricist account of language (for a comparable instance, see the discussion of Hugh Kenner and Donald Davie on Pound's ideograms in Easthope 1983, pp. 140–1).

If Armstrong's analysis does not successfully elude these objections, then we are still left with the problem of Victorian poetic language. The proposals that follow here are hesitant and speculative, descriptive rather than analytic.

One might start with a text typical of the later Victorian period, the painting of 'The Knight-Errant' done by John Everett Millais in 1870 (see p. 142). On the one hand it portrays a heroic model of Victorian manhood, chivalric and gentlemanly, enclosed and uplifted in a sublime and historically remote setting, a knight rescuing a damsel in distress (she's tied to a tree). On the other, because of the detailed realism with which it is painted, the text becomes an occasion for

'The Knight Errant' by Millais, 1870 (reproduced by courtesy of the Tate Gallery, London)

erotic phantasy for it shows a fully clothed man (in armour in fact) about to release a naked woman from her bondage with his shining, phallic sword (the painting did trouble its audience at the time and could not be sold until the woman was re-painted in a less erotic posture). An example exactly similar to the painting would be the song 'Come into the garden, Maud', which concludes part I of the poem (xxII). This, with its flower imagery and ever more urgent and insistent rhythm leading up to the repetitions of 'She is coming' could well claim to be one of the most erotic lyrics in English poetry. Yet, set to music, it was sung at the time in drawing rooms throughout the country. (In 1896 Marie Lloyd was accused of singing suggestive songs and defended herself by saying anything could be performed in a suggestive manner, proving it by singing 'Come into the garden, Maud'. Her choice was shrewd.)

Psychoanalysis would understand the effect of the Millais painting and the song from *Maud* as an effect of rationalisation, a concept introduced by Ernest Jones and adopted by Freud to mean a procedure by which the subject gives a consistent and socially acceptable explanation for ideas and feelings whose motives are not perceived. If someone in a car is stuck behind a caravan in a narrow road and says that caravans ought to pay extra road tax, this would be a clear example of rationalisation (in this case for aggressive feelings towards the driver of the offending vehicle). Rationalisation has a function comparable to secondary revision, that which reduces dream images to a more consistent and plausible narrative. But the comparison immediately leads on to a second, associated psychic mechanism, for secondary revision is one of the functions of the dream work which disguises the latent content of a dream in its manifest content. And so it might be useful to think of Victorian poetic language as allowing the literary text to come closer to the operation of the unconscious, moving it along a continuum from one point, that of day-dream, towards (though never reaching) another, that of the night-dream. A third related mechanism may be at play. In a paper of 1940 Freud describes the way that the ego, in the cause of its own defence, may simultaneously recognise a reality and refuse it, 'two contrary reactions' which can 'persist as the centre-point of a splitting of the ego' (*SE* xxiii, pp. 271–8). The process tends to be pathological and is closely dependent on disavowal (*Verleugnung*) which itself is modelled on the disavowal of castration. A position taking account of reality and at the same time remaining detached from reality is most vividly illustrated by fetishism, for the fetishist knows it is not what it seems but thinks, 'All the same . . .' (see above, p. 97).

We do not find in the language of Victorian poetry the fetishistic disavowal of the signifier, characterising (so it was argued) Augustan poetry. What we do find, as Alan Sinfield shows in his revised account of Tennyson, is a defensive strategy aimed to fill the lack opened by the signifier:

The elaborate diction, the obtrusive syntax and the intense effects of sound and rhythm all act in the same direction. They offer not an enhanced transparency in the relationship between sign and referent, but an unattributed density *in the sign itself*. . . Tennyson creates, as it were, a plenitude of the sign. Language cannot be brought closer to the world, but it can be made more full and substantial *in itself*. In Tennyson's writing any particular word has, or appears to have, many reasons for being appropriate . . . Thus the arbitrariness of language seems to be controlled.

(1986, p. 86, italics original)

That arbitrariness is lack, disavowed via the seeming plenitude of the sign, and this effect at the level of the signifier promotes and facilitates a parallel rationalisation at the level of the signified: typically, *two levels* of meaning exist together but in unacknowledged disjunction.

Sketching in the related terms rationalisation, secondary revision and disavowal would enable analysis to avoid what happens in too many approaches to poetry of the later nineteenth century: it is read either innocently, as it seems to have been read then, or knowingly, giving vent to the tone of facetiousness which so easily attaches to accounts of Victorian art. Each of the three terms requires that both levels of meaning be brought together and understood together, even though they so obtrusively invite the reader to keep them apart, deciding between them. In addition the terms point towards defence of the ego as the strategy common to all three manifestations. And this brings the discussion directly home to the significance of the debate over evolution in England in the nineteenth century.

Susan Gliserman, whose work in the area is substantial and important, remarks how the contemporary claims of science subverted those of religion, and comments on the 'Darwinian' prose of the time: 'All the science writers Tennyson read were very much concerned to avoid precisely this implication of their own work' (1975, p. 453). If one were to ask what kind of textuality would best permit a reader to avoid the implications of what they were reading, the answer would be a mode consistent with the psychic effects of rationalisation and disavowal. It would be a textuality showing a marked disjunction between one level of meaning that was public, overt, rational, tending towards personification and abstraction, and another which was more personal and inexplicit, with meaning carried especially in allusion and metaphor. We may refer to these as 'manifest' and 'latent' levels, so long as it is kept in mind that their relation is like but not identical with the relation of manifest and latent in the dream-work. In Tennyson, the evolutionary hypothesis is canvassed in verse split between its explicit assertion and its subtextual implication. Such poetry exhibits a thematic link with the idea of the defence of the ego.

Evolutionary theory as ideology

Ann Wordsworth's finely suggestive essay on *In Memoriam* (1981) remarks with Yeats that a consequence of its evolutionary concerns is 'to lose the poem under summaries of nineteenth-century debates on science and religion' (p. 217). Another such summary is inescapable now, though it will be used mainly as a foundation on which to propose that as far as the poetry goes, the science is better understood as a version of ideology.

Growth in the sciences of botany, zoology, geology and cosmology contributed towards the Victorian crisis over the Development Hypothesis. The traditional Christian belief in divine creation was set out in Genesis; one calculation widely accepted in the nineteenth century was that God had made the universe in 4004 BC on 29 October at 9.00 a.m. GMT. Carl Linnaeus, the Swedish botanist (1707–78) established a binomial system for classifying plants and animals, and this, together with the work of various botanising clergymen, enabled William Paley, in *Natural Theology: or, Evidences of the Existence and Attributes of the Deity Collected from the Appearances of Nature* (1802), to demonstrate the benign providence of God the Father in designing every detail of the universe for human benefit. The eye, a favourite example, in its parts and the combination of its parts was perfectly shaped the way it is because people need to see with it. This kind of *post hoc ergo propter hoc* line of argument assumed that creation had been a single historical event and that the various species of animals, including the human species, were permanent. But this was, even in its own time, a matter of controversy, for example in the work of Erasmus Darwin (*Zoonomia*, 1794–96) and Jean Lamarck (1744–1829). Darwin believed in the mutability of species in response to changing circumstances; Lamarck's *Histoire naturelle des animaux sans vertèbres* (published from 1815), in struggling to explain why fossil species in one geological stratum were both like and unlike others in a separate stratum, formulated the first modern theory of evolution according to which the production of a new organ in an animal body resulted from a new need, these characteristics, acquired in a lifetime, being transmitted to the next generation.

None of these, as Susan Gliserman explains, was such an immediate influence on Tennyson as Roget, Whewell and Lyell. Peter Roget (author of the *Thesaurus*) in *Animal and Vegetable Physiology* (1834) seeks to extend Paley's argument from design with evidence collected from what would now be seen as biochemistry, and William Whewell, one of Tennyson's Cambridge tutors, does the same with evidence from the solar system and cosmic motions. All three – Paley, Roget, Whewell – are inevitably engaged in a process of disavowal, for, as Gliserman says, each is forced to recognise the material, self-acting autonomy of nature in order to deny it in the name of an originating deity. Texts by Lyell and Chambers made the recognition even harder to evade. Against the prevailing opinion that geological history was determined through successive universal 'catastrophes', Charles Lyell's *Principles of Geology* (1830–33) advances the 'uniformitarian' view that geological forces act in a uniform and regular manner through unlimited time. As part of this it admits the extinction of species only to reaffirm divine will in the form of successive creation of new ones. Published anonymously in 1844, *The Vestiges of the Natural History of Creation* by Robert Chambers relinquishes even this link with the argument from design. Bringing together material from astronomy, geology and zoology it claims that just as the inorganic world submits to the laws of gravity so the organic world follows a natural law of development which controls even the development of species. God is left to create, vestigially, through the exercise of such natural laws.

There is an opposition between science and ideology, the imaginary relation to the real, but it is not an absolute opposition. And it will in no way prejudice the scientificity of evolutionary theory to note its capacity, especially in the nineteenth century, to pick up a rich load of ideological meanings in a way which anticipates that particularly twentieth-century genre, science fiction. In judging this we may keep in mind the present situation. Hardly anyone in the 1980s is moved by Darwinism, one way or the other. But if evolutionary theory is almost a neutral topic, nature certainly is not. Exactly the same self-generating and self-balancing system of relations between plant and animal species that was felt by Victorian Britain to disclose a world which was 'other-centred, hostile and aggressive' (Gliserman 1975, p. 299) increasingly appears to the twentieth-century Western world as benign and harmonious, 'the food chain' or 'eco-system', object of 'green' politics. In an ideological transformation based on a contrast between nature and human culture, nature is now seen to stand in positive opposition to 'technological exploitation' (see, for example, Williams 1975 and Merchant 1982).

Writers agree about the main ideological significance of the debate over evolution. Its 'crux' is that it puts in question 'the position of man [*sic*]' and ultimately 'the reality of his soul and immortality' (Roppen 1956, p. 24). In Hillis Miller's account, the quest for personal certainty in the subjective dimension 'leads man [*sic*] back to an experience of the absence of God' (1975, p. 9) so that Victorian poets are 'stretched on the rack of a fading transcendentalism' (p. 359). This implication of evolutionary theory is summarised by Gillian Beer:

The all-inclusiveness of its explanation, stretching through the different orders of the natural world, seemed to offer a means of understanding without recourse to godhead. It created a system in which there was no need to invoke a source of authority outside the natural order: in which instead of foreknown design, there was inherent purposiveness.   (1983, p. 16)

Yet these explanations are too close to the very terms in which Darwinism was then discussed to be fully satisfactory. The idea that evolutionary theory meant that 'God is dead' in itself is too abstract and unreal to have much ideological weight – it must include a rationalisation for something else. Briefly, I shall name two other areas which magnify the impact of these scientific theories about nature by projecting them onto the screen of ideology.

1   Darwinism (to retain the shorthand) impinges deeply on the kind of ideological project analysed in the preceding chapter on Romanticism. For the aim of creating a 'living' dialectic between subject and

object (in whatever terms these are envisaged) will collapse at a stroke if it is confronted with nature as an object apparently entirely external, other-directed and impervious to human intention. *In Memoriam* attempts to answer the impersonality of nature as an object by asserting a personal faith, though this leads only to 'a thorough-going subjectivism which does not meet the difficulties raised by science, but simply bypasses them' (Hough 1947, p. 243). So the wish to anthropomorphise aims to recuperate the materiality of the extra-discursive – all that is the case – by projecting human meaning onto it and then presenting it negatively as a 'universe of death'.

2   In *Culture and Society* (1958) Raymond Williams gives only a page and a half to Darwinism. But the contemporary ideological connotations of evolutionary theory obviously intersect with the major ideological oppositions of the nineteenth century analysed there and in *The Country and the City* (1973): production/creation; public/private; material/ideal; mechanical/organic; rational/ emotional; use/beauty; science/poetry. When this ideological scenario is played out in the debate over Darwinism, the role of the first term is taken by a 'universe' which is at best coldly alien and at worst actively hostile, while that of the second is filled by a 'humanity' affirming simply 'I have felt' (*In Memoriam*, CXXIV). It is only via such feeble liberal humanism that a utopian assertion is made, one much more defensively one-sided than in Shelley's Romantic 'image of the whole'.

Though important, neither of these areas sufficiently explains the specificity and subversive vitality of poetic Darwinism. The work of Susan Gliserman, too soon curtailed, seeks to account for this affective power and justify the claim it makes that while previous 'critics and scholars see the scientific books Tennyson read as textbooks' it will treat them as 'mediating arguments between the data and the beliefs and feelings of a general audience' (1975, footnote p. 281). In harsh summary, her argument is that in the scientific writers who preceded Darwin (Paley, Roget, Whewell) the idea of willed design and a divine personality in the Creator implies the supremacy of a 'distinct, masculine person . . . a father-god, personal and caring' (p. 293) dominating a nature which is con- sistently rendered as feminine (Beer notes that 'personifying nature as female' is wholly traditional and has the effect in Darwin's work of distinguishing 'Nature from God' and making nature benign, 1983,

p. 70). The dethroning of this paternal deity by the account of evolutionary development as self-acting (for example in Lyell) and without design lends itself to the notion of (female) nature as 'animated, aggressive and erratically willful' (1975, p. 302). Gliserman can be read to suggest that Darwinian ideas gather force by being mapped onto ideologies concerning: (1) the sovereignty of the (paternal) ego; (2) the family and gender relations.

A progressive historical erosion of ideological notions of the transcendence of the human subject is Freud's theme when he talks about Darwin in 1917. 'A Difficulty in the Path of Psycho-Analysis' (*SE* XVII, pp. 136–44) describes how 'the universal narcissism of men, their self-love, has up to the present suffered three severe blows from the researches of science'. The first, a '*cosmological* one' was delivered when Copernicus showed that the earth was not stationary at the centre of the universe. The second came from Darwin. Previously man (and here it may well be appropriate to retain the masculine noun) had set a gulf between himself and animals on the grounds that he had an immortal soul and they didn't. However, as Freud recalls, 'A child can see no difference between his [*sic*] own nature and that of animals', and it was the task of 'Darwin and his collaborators and fore-runners' (these would include Lyell and Chambers) to demonstrate that:

Man [*sic*] is not a being different from animals or superior to them; he himself is of animal descent, being more closely related to some species and more distant to others.   (p. 141)

Very accurately phrased, this sums up 'the *biological* blow to human narcissism' and belief in the omnipotent ego. 'Man feels himself to be supreme within his own mind' but these 'discoveries amount to a statement that *the ego is not master in its own house*' (italics original). The third blow (Beer notices that Freud reserves the phallic third for himself) is 'the psychological one' revealing that the apparent self-presence of the ego depends upon an other, the process of the unconscious of which it is an effect. If Freud had been as familiar with the work of Marx in 1917 as he was by the time of the last of the *New Introductory Lectures* in 1932 he might have had to surrender his position as the third blow and accept that of fourth: for Marx also sets limits to human narcissism by showing how far individuals can be explained as 'the personifications of economic categories' (1974, I, p. 21).

'The ego is not master in its own house': metaphorically this refers to a paternal ego whose mastery is threatened by a wife and family who no longer stay in place. Chapter 5 above on 'The Augustan Father' sought to isolate in poetry the social phantasy of the full father, that is, the father conceived as transcendent. He appears so in a double respect: first in that as an 'I' he is fully present to himself in his intentions, uttering himself perfectly and completely and without mediation in his actions ('Immediate are the Acts of God', *Paradise Lost*, VII, l. 176), the source and origin of meaning; second in that he is able to reproduce himself perfectly in his sons as though without the mediation of the feminine, as though he were pure, unified masculinity all through, father of all but son of none. It is this inherited ideological notion of a designing and all-creating and fully self-conscious father which is shattered by the ideological implications of nineteenth-century Darwinism.

To argue that the poetic rendering of evolutionary theory sets in motion a social phantasy whose content is a threat simultaneously to the supposedly transcendent ego and to the full father accounts for two distinct features in the poetry. One is formal, the distance between the two levels of meaning. Earlier it was argued that a disjunction between 'manifest' and 'latent' levels of meaning was a rationalisation or disavowal, and these are mechanisms by which the ego seeks to defend itself. Another is the kind of phantasies promoted in poetry by the Darwinian material. Quite simply, these take the form of psychopathology, phantasies which are neurotic or psychotic. Both correspond to a disorder in which the ego is threatened and seeks to defend itself against that threat:

> . . . *neurosis is the result of a conflict between the ego and its id, whereas psychosis is the analogous outcome of a similar disturbance in the relations between the ego and the external world.*
> ('Neurosis and Psychosis', *SE* XIX, p. 149, italics original)

In the Darwinian poems the main pathological phantasies to be found are melancholia, paranoia and delusional jealousy. Details will be explored with reference to the particular texts.

Large scale deployment of pathological phantasy seems to be a historical novelty, at least in terms of the texts previously discussed in this present study. Ovid, Donne, poetry of courtly love, Milton and Augustan poetry (except for the melancholia in Johnson and Gray), Shelley – each of these has been understood mainly on the basis of the narcissistic and sexual drives (an exception is the phantasy of the body in pieces discovered in Petrarch). But since the very concept of phantasy rests on that of pleasure – in fact the present study aims in part to account for the pleasure of the poetic text – how could texts providing pathological phantasies ever give shared, public pleasure?

A brief answer is that phantasies, like dreams, fulfil wishes, and we do not always wish for what civilised life regards as acceptable. Hence, strictly, every dream is what Freud terms a compromise-formation, consequence of two forms of wish, one represented by the expression of unconscious thoughts, another by their repression, so that the dream always works by censoring and disguising its unconscious aim. This is the case for ordinary dreams – those for example expressing narcissistic and sexual drives in the ways noted in the poems so far discussed. With Victorian poetry a further two categories of wish-fulfilment became relevant, dreams of punishment fulfilling sadistic and masochistic wishes and anxiety dreams (see *SE* VI, p. 219). Phantasies with a strongly unpleasurable component may be like anxiety dreams, which Freud distinguishes from ordinary dreams by saying that while these are the *disguised* fulfilment of a repressed wish an anxiety dream 'is the open fulfilment of a repressed wish', one in which 'the repressed wish has shown itself stronger than the censorship' (*SE* XV, p. 217). The relevance of anxiety to Victorian poetry lies in Freud's argument that anxiety is a neurotic symptom and form of defence in which the ego makes an 'attempt at flight from the demand by its libido' (*SE* XVI, p. 405). What demands and what flight, analysis of the poems will investigate.

Developing at the end of the eighteenth century in the genre of the Gothic, the finding of pleasure in generally unpleasurable phantasies has become increasingly widespread and today attracts mass audiences to watch horror films in the cinema (the concept of anxiety has only been touched on in this present study though its relevance to literary analysis deserves much fuller exploration). Two points must be added on the question. One is that pathological forms of phantasy lie in the shadow of what Freud in *Beyond the Pleasure Principle* (1920) came to theorise as the death drive. The other is that a high degree of unpleasure can appear within a phantasy so long as the reader or viewer's sense of distance from the text is sufficiently secured, that he or she is enabled to live into its excitements without losing a position of mastery outside it.

Tennyson: *In Memoriam* (1850) and *Maud* (1855)

For *In Memoriam*, the death of Hallam is like the death of God: the poem 'associates with the figure of Hallam many of the ordering and nurturing energies which writers like Roget and Whewell attributed to God' (Gliserman 1975, p. 442). In a social phantasy this ideological conception is linked with the death of the father and loss of the phallus (in this respect comparable to *Hamlet* in Lacan's analysis, 1977c, pp. 11–52). The represented speaker of the poem feels himself to be unmanned by grief, and addresses himself from a feminine position when he says that the death of Hallam (or rather Arthur) has left him not so much a 'widower' (XIII.1) as 'widow'd' (XVII.20) (an aspect of the poem at last seriously discussed in Sinfield 1986). 'If the poem can give up wishing to marry Hallam . . . and establish him instead as the type of "masculine" authority, then it can establish its own sexual identity', as Eagleton writes in a Lacanian reading of the poem (1978, p. 105). And the course of the text does indeed work its despair through so that what comes about towards the end is an assertion of 'the transcendent importance of the individual soul' (Hough 1947, p. 248), a change of heart dramatised and expressed in the debate over whether the universe is self-purposing or designed by a Creator. It is the speaker's

subjective state of grief and shock at the beginning of the poem that causes him to see Nature as hostile and chaotic. As he comes to accept Hallam's death, and takes a larger perspective on human life, so he comes to perceive a larger order in Nature.   (Cosslett 1982, p. 48)

Movement at the level of ideology from doubt to faith corresponds at the level of phantasy (for they are relatively disjunctive here) to the working through of melancholia, as Ann Wordsworth has already argued most convincingly (1981).

The account of melancholia above (p. 70) did not stress that mourning, the normal working through of grief, is to be distinguished from the pathological tendencies of melancholia. Nor did it bring out what Freud mentions as 'the most remarkable characteristic of melancholia', its capacity 'to change round into mania' (*SE* XIV, p. 253). If the subject, through testing reality, does come to give up the lost object which has been kept 'alive' in the place of the ego, then a large expenditure of psychical energy, previously 'bound' by being withdrawn from the ego, now, suddenly, becomes available for discharge. A psychoanalytic account helps to draw attention to the way that in Tennyson's poem 'arguments about faith and doubt give way readily enough to an erotic and narcissistic triumph over death' (Wordsworth 1981, p. 217).

As Carolyn Merchant notes, traditionally Nature was thought of as feminine but with two aspects corresponding to the nurturing mother and the witch, one in which nature was identified 'as a kindly beneficent female who provided for the needs of mankind in an ordered, planned universe', and an opposing image of 'wild and uncontrollable nature that could render violence, storms, droughts, and general chaos' (1982, p. 2). It is in this second figuration that nature appears in the passages from *In Memoriam* concerned with the development of species. Through the voice of a personified female Sorrow, section III imagines the other-directed universe, one lacking God's design, to be waste and void. Nature, a female phantom, makes the stars 'blindly run' (l. 5) and is 'A hollow form' (l. 12), both metaphors (of blindness, emptiness) marking the feminine as a source and site of castration. And this becomes a crucial aspect to the phantasy structure as developed in LIV–LVI. In LV.4, love is what is 'likest God'; by 'type' is meant species; and the evidence of the fossils in cliffs and quarries (LVI.1–4) is that many species have become extinct:

LIV

Oh yet we trust that somehow good
    Will be the final goal of ill,
    To pangs of nature, sins of will,
Defects of doubt, and taints of blood;

5   That nothing walks with aimless feet;
    That not one life shall be destroyed,
    Or cast as rubbish to the void,
When God hath made the pile complete;

That not a worm is cloven in vain;
10   That not a moth with vain desire
    Is shrivelled in a fruitless fire,
Or but subserves another's gain.

Behold, we know not anything;
    I can but trust that good shall fall
15   At last – far off – at last, to all,
And every winter change to spring.

So runs my dream: but what am I?
    An infant crying in the night:

An infant crying for the light:
20   And with no language but a cry.

LV

The wish, that of the living whole
No life may fail beyond the grave,
Derives it not from what we have
The likest God within the soul?

5   Are God and Nature then at strife,
That Nature lends such evil dreams?
So careful of the type she seems,
So careless of the single life;

That I, considering everywhere
10   Her secret meaning in her deeds,
And finding that of fifty seeds
She often brings but one to bear,

I falter where I firmly trod,
And falling with my weight of cares
15   Upon the great world's altar-stairs
That slope through darkness up to God,

I stretch lame hands of faith, and grope,
And gather dust and chaff, and call
To what I feel is Lord of all,
20   And faintly trust the larger hope.

LVI

'So careful of the type?' but no.
From scarpèd cliff and quarried stone
She cries, 'A thousand types are gone;
I care for nothing, all shall go.

5   'Thou makest thine appeal to me:
I bring to life, I bring to death:
The spirit does but mean the breath:
I know no more.' And he, shall he,

Man, her last work, who seemed so fair,
10   Such splendid purpose in his eyes,
Who rolled the psalm to wintry skies,
Who built him fanes of fruitless prayer,

Who trusted God was love indeed
And love Creation's final law –
15   Though Nature, red in tooth and claw
With ravine, shrieked against his creed –

> Who loved, who suffered countless ills,
> > Who battled for the True, the Just,
> > Be blown about the desert dust,
> 20 Or sealed within the iron hills?
>
> No more? A monster then, a dream,
> > A discord. Dragons of the prime,
> > That tare each other in their slime,
> Were mellow music matched with him.
>
> 25 O life as futile, then, as frail!
> > O for thy voice to soothe and bless!
> > What hope of answer, or redress?
> Behind the veil, behind the veil.

At the 'manifest' level this is clearly enough a discussion of the universe without God and much less interesting than it becomes when considered at the 'latent' level it disavows, that at which it most insistently offers itself as phantasy. Granted the perspective already argued for, it may be sufficient to underline the main features thus brought out. In default of a full father with whom to identify, the male speaker feels himself regressively to be 'An infant crying in the night' (LIV, 18), an image sustained in the metaphors of walking (strictly, 'aimless feet', LIV.5, suggests a toddler), of falling ('I falter where I firmly trod', LV.13), and of crawling with 'lame hands' stretched for an absent father (LV.17–20).

It is a moment in the poem in which, as Eliot says, nature as a goddess becomes 'more real' than God (1961, p. 335). If the full father is missing, Nature as mother is 'careless' (LV.8), in fact actively aggressive towards her last male child, who should be her favourite ('her last work, who seemed so fair', LVI.9). Nature says, 'I care for nothing, all shall go' (LVI.4), disclosing unmistakably the figure of the castrating mother, bloodily biting and tearing like a shark, a tigress:

> . . . Nature, red in tooth and claw,
> With ravine, shrieked against his creed . . .   (LVI.15–16)

The figure is metaphorically enlarged, both by 'ravine', which must mean 'ravin', the 'act of seizing and devouring prey' (*OED*), but which spelt as it is connotes also 'a mountainous cleft' (*OED*); and by LVI.21–4 which read retrospectively mean 'fighting dinosaurs would be pleasant compared to the state of man without God' but which, while we read them, lead us to think of nature as 'A monster', 'A discord', a dragon (dragons *are* red in tooth and claw). Because

woman is seen as castrating, the sexes are in conflict: God the father
and mother Nature are 'at strife' (LV.5), she shrieks against the love
and law he stands for. While in a traditional patriarchal schema
'nature is God's handmaiden' (Tennyson, cited Shatto and Shaw
1982, p. 217), these sections portray the paternal ego as no longer
'master in its own house'.

They also form a turning point in the poem, one at which loss of the
object is worked through so that the speaker feels able to pass on – the
next section (LVII) begins, 'Peace; come away . . .'. But in another,
later passage drawing on evolutionary material, though this time
asserting faith against doubt, the same phantasy opposition between
castrating mother and full father reappears, though now the masculinity of the speaker is reaffirmed as he finds identification with the
father:

CXXIII

There rolls the deep where grew the tree.
　　　　O earth, what changes hast thou seen!
　　　　There where the long street roars, hath been
The stillness of the central sea.

5　　　The hills are shadows, and they flow
　　　　From form to form, and nothing stands;
　　　　They melt like mist, the solid lands,
Like clouds they shape themselves and go.

But in my spirit will I dwell,
10　　　And dream my dream, and hold it true;
　　　　For though my lips may breathe adieu,
I cannot think the thing farewell.

CXXIV

That which we dare invoke to bless;
　　　　Our dearest faith; our ghastliest doubt;
　　　　He, They, One, All; within, without;
The Power in darkness whom we guess;

5　　　I found Him not in world or sun,
　　　　Or eagle's wing, or insect's eye;
　　　　Nor through the questions men may try,
The petty cobwebs we have spun.

If e'er when faith had fallen asleep,
10　　　I heard a voice 'believe no more'
　　　　And heard an ever-breaking shore
That tumbled in the Godless deep;

> A warmth within the breast would melt
>   The freezing reason's colder part,
> 15   And like a man in wrath the heart
> Stood up and answered 'I have felt'.
>
> No, like a child in doubt and fear:
>   But that blind clamor made me wise;
>   Then was I as a child that cries,
> 20   But, crying, knows his father near;
>
> And what I am beheld again
>   What is, and no man understands;
>   And out of darkness came the hands
> That reach through nature, moulding men.

Mother nature continues to threaten castration, for in a world without God 'nothing stands' (CXXIII.6). In the void the speaker hears

> an ever-breaking shore
> That tumbled in the Godless deep;   (CXXIV.11–12)

Meaning is compressed and disturbed here. The shore doesn't break though waves do, and the surf surely tumbles at the *edge* of the sea, not in it. A consequence is that 'ever-breaking' comes to suggest that which makes something break, so that the whole is a metaphor for castration which combines the idea of the margin or littoral (to be recalled in 'Dover Beach'), of falling ('tumbled in'), of height like that in a ravine ('deep'). In the face of this danger, phallicism is reasserted, the speaker's heart 'Stood up' (CXXIV.16). There is no more falling, or falling over because he 'knows his father' (CXXXIV.20) and is able to achieve identification with him, 'what I am' becoming 'What is' (CXXIV.21–2). Restored once again, this is the symbolic figure of the full father, transcendent, masculine and only masculine all the way through:

> And out of darkness came the hands
> That reach through nature, moulding men.

When God makes Adam in *Paradise Lost*, the creature grows under his 'forming hands' (VIII.470). In this text God's phallic hands are able to pierce through nature, through the feminine, because he has recovered the capacity of God the Father in *Paradise Lost* to produce sons perfectly moulded in his own masculine image.

The possibility that masculine phantasy has recourse to a fear of woman, *horror feminae*, (see *SE* XVIII, pp. 231–2) has already been mooted in discussing the body in pieces in Petrarch and fetishism in

Augustan poetry. Psychoanalysis in offering not 'a recommendation *for* a patriarchal society, but an analysis *of* one', as Juliet Mitchell says (1975, p. xv), does have an account of why in such a society 'the victimization of women is the inevitable consequence of their double role as objects and analogues of desire' (Barsani 1978, p. 13). The argument opens onto some difficult ideas and so, at the risk of labouring it, I shall set it out in four steps:

1 The castration complex is brought about for both sexes through sexual difference, a symbolic structure in which the sign for each sex acquires meaning by not being the sign for the other sex, the difference between the two terms instituting a lack in the subject (see *SE* xiv, pp. 241–58 and Lacan 1977a, pp. 262–3).

2 But such a structure is also always culturally determined. Patriarchy recasts sexual difference on the basis of a masculine symbol, seeking to define castration in terms of having or not having the phallus. Thus she becomes different from him.

3 In trying to say why such societies, primitive and civilised, regard women not just from their particular actions but as 'altogether taboo' (*SE* xi, p. 198), Freud's paper on 'The Taboo of Virginity' concludes that masculine dread of women is 'based on the fact that woman is different from man' (*SE* xiv, pp. 241–8). Only the effort to co-opt the feminine to a male norm will explain how masculine phantasy attributes a phallus to the mother and to women, and feels threatened when it is subsequently discovered to be missing: 'the phantasy of the maternal phallus represents difference as absence, the Other as a variant of the Same' (Weber 1982, p. 124) (elsewhere I have followed what this account entails for the way masculinity in the dominant definition strives to maintain itself as masculine and only masculine, and have included a critique of Freud in 'The Taboo of Virginity', see Easthope 1986, pp. 161–73).

4 The same strategy for domination by universalising suggests why the feminine is held responsible for not having what it never could have. One of the psychoanalytic concepts which has been most successful in gaining currency is that of projection. A wish or feeling the subject rejects inside is expelled by being located outside: I condemn in another what I dislike in myself. So masculine dread of the feminine because it seems to threaten castration can become projected *back* onto the feminine as the phantasy of the castrating mother, the castrating woman ('red in tooth and claw').

It should not be too surprising that this argument discloses an approach to Tennyson's *Maud* (and, later, Eliot's *The Waste Land*).

Since for psychoanalysis the subject is constitutionally bisexual, there is always both a positive and negative response in the Oedipus complex (see above pp. 109–10). Faced with castration the little boy can challenge the father and win the bride (a 'positive' trajectory); or, in a complex organisation of drives, fear of castration may persuade him to take up a feminine position towards the father (a 'negative' trajectory) and, in addition, to set such a high value on the phallus that he can't 'tolerate its absence in a love-object' (*SE* XVIII, p. 231). For Freud this is the psychical aetiology of male homosexuality. And, further, the subject's attempt to defend itself against its own homosexual desire is a causal factor in paranoia and delusional jealousy. In paranoia a male subject would believe the man he loves to be a main instigator of general attack, its defensive paradigm being: 'I do not *love* him – I *hate* him, because HE PERSECUTES ME' (*SE* XII, p. 63); in delusional jealousy, in which (say) a man constantly imagines the infidelity of the woman he loves, the paradigm becomes: '"*I* do not love him, *she* loves him"' (*SE* XVIII, p. 225).

   Maud can readily be understood as a paranoiac phantasy. The poem's ideological project, in narrow terms, is to denounce the culture and society of Victorian laissez-faire as 'a world of the dead' (II.v.3). Sections at the beginning particularly focus on the idea of an economic war of each against each, in which 'the poor are hovell'd . . . like swine' (I.i.9), chalk is sold for bread, the mother 'kills her babe for a burial fee' (I.i.7). In a way consistent with this, the natural order is envisaged as Godless and therefore as a Darwinian struggle for survival:

> For nature is one with rapine, a harm no preacher can heal;
> The Mayfly is torn by the swallow, the sparrow speared by the shrike,
> And the whole little wood where I sit is a world of plunder and prey.
>
> (I.iv.4)

This, in the main passage alluding to evolutionary theory, reworks in little the kind of phantasy structure already described. The death of the father is symbolised in the extinction of the dinosaurs, of one that 'was of old the Lord and Master of Earth' (I.iv.6) and who felt himself 'to be Nature's crowning race', his sovereignty being supported then by mother Nature. But he is gone, man will go, 'the drift of the Maker is dark, an Isis hid by the veil' (I.iv.8): the power of God the Father is uncertain, as is his masculinity, for he is seen as equivalent to Isis, the great nature goddess of the Egyptians. 'Seen as' is critical here. In ascribing to the evolutionary conception of the self-purposing development and extinction of species, including the human species ('is he the last?' I.iv.6), the speaker projects his 'internal catastrophe' into a vision of 'the end of the world', as does Freud's classic case of paranoia (*SE* XII, p. 70). The melodramatic narrative of *Maud* anchors the Darwinian perspective in a radically subjective point of view, makes it in fact an expression of madness.

Ruined by a speculative venture, the unnamed hero's father has committed suicide (or has he?) by throwing himself into a 'dreadful hollow'; the hero is engaged to Maud even though her father and brother may have had a hand in his father's death; they prefer a rich and aristocratic suitor for her. The hero woos Maud while her brother is in town; on his return, the brother finds Maud and the hero in the garden together and they have a fight in which the brother is (perhaps) killed; the hero flees to France, passes time in a madhouse, Maud (perhaps) dies; the hero returns to fight for Britain in the Crimean War.

This narrative – and my recounting of it – cannot be trusted because as readers we have access only to the speaker's monologue, and this fluctuates uncertainly between external discourse (writing imitating the oral) and inner speech, between neurosis and psychosis, between fact and fantasy so that 'everything becomes a symbol' (Priestley, 1973, p. 110). One consequence of this mode is that a firm demand is imposed on readers to follow through the speaker's phantasies. Another is that the text is able to speak social criticism that otherwise would not be spoken. But a third, one in line with the proposals about poetic language made earlier, is that both the discomforting ideological assertion and the pathological phantasies can be disavowed; the reader can live through the text and at the same time dismiss it (as the speaker himself does) as a 'hysterical mock-disease' (III.vi.3).

The phantasies we live into via the speaker's stream of consciousness are more than hysterical. The text dramatises the ego's loss of transcendence, first of all in the form of neurosis, in the way wishes and obsessions press in from the unconscious upon the hero's self-consciousness. As with *In Memoriam*, a main theme is the dead father. The hero is fixated on his father's death in 'the dreadful hollow' from the first line of the poem, a void we might associate with the 'hollow' of *In Memoriam* (III.11–12). He hates Maud's father, is unable to identify himself with adult male sexuality, cannot achieve a satisfactory relationship with Maud, seeks masochistic punishment, is overwhelmed with feelings of guilt and wishes for death, 'the doom assigned' in the last line of the poem.

Secondly, his disorder takes the form of psychosis, a disturbance in the relations between the ego and the external world. Throughout, obsession and phantasy take the place of external reality for him but there is a definite break-down into psychosis in the section spoken in an asylum (II.v.1–11), 'Dead, long dead . . . And my heart is a handful of dust'. Paranoia is present throughout. The hero hears his 'own sad name in corners cried' (I.vi.8), believes Maud's brother 'plots against me still' (I.xix.8), that the brother 'shouted at once from the top of the house' a 'private affair' he had whispered to him (II.v.4). It is even present in classic form in that the man the speaker feels most persecuted by is the one he desires:

> His face, as I grant, in spite of spite,
> Has a broad-blown comeliness, red and white,
> And six feet two, as I think, he stands;   (I.xiii.1)

Paranoia as an attempted defence against homosexuality in a male is a denial of femininity. The hero of *Maud* imagines that before he was born people wondered 'if it prove a girl' (I.vii.2). And in some extraordinarily compressed lines at what Christopher Ricks acknowledges is 'a nub' in the text (1972, p. 254) all the speaker's wishes come to be expressed together:

> And ah for a man to arise in me,
> That the man I am may cease to be!   (I.x.6)

At what may be the deepest level of the text, one presented in its images and metaphors, the origin of male homosexuality in the dread of castration, a fear projected onto the idea of woman, may even have some indirect expression. There is a fear that the garden of love, Maud's garden, is really the same as 'the dreadful hollow' which killed the father, that the roses that so often image Maud's sexuality 'are not roses, but blood' (II.v.8).

Only the hero speaks in *Maud*, its mode designed to ensure her point of view appears in his terms. Nevertheless, three things might be said about her position. The hero demands that she conform to an extreme version of traditional femininity: fragile, passive, aesthetically perfect. She is imaged for him as flowers, as animals, as feminine

and only feminine (she is 'only the child of her mother', I.xiii.3, not
her father). Yet the hero fears that she is somehow active, masculine,
not traditionally feminine. And it may be that she is not, though
ambiguously so. After the fight between the hero and her brother
she gives 'A cry for a brother's blood' (II.i.1). This must mean that she
complains against the hero for shedding her brother's blood. But it
might also mean that she wants the blood of her brother, her father's
surrogate, who arranges a marriage for her.

Arnold: 'Dover Beach' (1867)

Written the year after the publication of *In Memoriam* in 1850,
Arnold's poem writes discursively and sententiously about the
decline of 'The Sea of Faith'. The landscape/seascape it presents is
implicitly Darwinian, as Ruth Pitman has shown (1973, pp. 109–36).
Lyell's *Principles* in 1830 'had explained in detail the threatening
relationship between sea and land' (p. 111) and had specifically
discussed the 'sea's encroachment on Dover cliff' (p. 112) to illustrate
the changes wrought by geological transformation. Clearly the text
treats this as an instance for the erosion of religious faith by
materialist doubts. The complex image in lines 21–3 is glossed by the
Allotts, who cite G. H. Ford to the effect that the forces of the sea are
gathered up round the land

like the 'folds' of bright clothing ('girdle') which have been compressed
('furled'). At ebb tide, as the sea retreats, it is unfurled and spread out.
                                                        (Allott 1979, p. 256)

If the date of composition is kept in mind, the last lines can be taken
to allude to the various European revolutions of 1848.

       The sea is calm to-night.
       The tide is full, the moon lies fair
       Upon the straits; on the French coast the light
       Gleams and is gone; the cliffs of England stand,
5   Glimmering and vast, out in the tranquil bay.
       Come to the window, sweet is the night-air!
       Only, from the long line of spray
       Where the sea meets the moon-blanched land,
       Listen! you hear the grating roar
10   Of pebbles which the waves draw back, and fling,
       At their return, up the high strand,

Begin, and cease, and then again begin,
With tremulous cadence slow, and bring
The eternal note of sadness in.

15 Sophocles long ago
Heard it on the Ægæan, and it brought
Into his mind the turbid ebb and flow
Of human misery; we
Find also in the sound a thought,
20 Hearing it by this distant northern sea.

The Sea of Faith
Was once, too, at the full, and round earth's shore
Lay like the folds of a bright girdle furled.
But now I only hear
25 Its melancholy, long, withdrawing roar,
Retreating, to the breath
Of the night-wind, down the vast edges drear
And naked shingles of the world.

Ah, love, let us be true
30 To one another! for the world, which seems
To lie before us like a land of dreams,
So various, so beautiful, so new,
Hath really neither joy, nor love, nor light,
Nor certitude, nor peace, nor help for pain;
35 And we are here as on a darkling plain
Swept with confused alarms of struggle and flight,
Where ignorant armies clash by night.

In this text ideological meanings seem to arrive in three waves. In the first an attempt to ground experience in the permanencies of eternal human nature, albeit tragic, albeit only Eurocentric ('Sophocles', l. 15) stalls in the face of historical development. Something has happened in the nineteenth century to change human nature once and for all ('once'/'now', ll. 22, 24). To counter this, a second ideological assertion aims to relegate and exclude such public despair by setting it against the certitudes of private happiness ('Ah, love . . .', l. 29). Although the social world is equated with meaningless conflict, 'Where ignorant armies clash by night' (l. 37), in a subtle manoeuvre implicit throughout in the geographical setting the poem is able to draw on nationalist ideology to insinuate that even if confusion reigns on 'the Continent', north of the white cliffs of Dover in some degree England retains its insular quietude.

Any further analysis shows how disunified the text is, particularly how it is fissured by three uncertainties or anomalies. How is the landscape/seascape to be read? The text itself imposes an allegorical reading on it (surf = despair, sea = faith) but it suggestively exceeds its own account of itself in that reading, for example in the troubled lines about the girdle (ll. 21–3). Why does the sea, which ebbs and flows in the second section (ll. 15–20), in the third section (ll. 21–8) ebb but not flow back, something seas do not do? And why does the speaker (presumably male) suddenly address a plea for fidelity to his (presumably female) lover (ll. 29–30)? The text's explicit level of 'manifest' discursive statement ('the Sea of Faith' and so on) dissociates itself entirely from the 'latent' level at which these incoherencies arise, a level which makes more sense if it is approached as phantasy.

Norman Holland's psychoanalytic account of 'Dover Beach' (1968, pp. 114–30) reads it in terms of infantile sexuality and the figures of the mother and the father. Without necessarily rejecting this, my reading here will stress those features highlighted in the text by the context of what might be called the Darwinian phantasy, that is the imbrication of ideological reference to the universe, faith and doubt with pathological forms of phantasy.

As Holland and others have remarked, the poem rests upon a series of dualities: England/France; land/sea; light/dark; sight/sound. There are reasons for supposing these oppositions are symbolically assigned to masculine/feminine. Thus, 'the cliffs of England stand' phallically in line 4 as land, as England, and as what is clearly visible in the light ('moon-blanched land', l. 8). In fact these are grounds for presuming the speaker is male since in a traditional scenario he stands at the window seeking to exercise mastery over his field of vision. If France is feminine, she is dark ('on the French coast the light / Gleams and is gone', ll. 3–4), she is across the sea, and in the implied allusion of the last two lines she is a place where you hear war but cannot see it properly. The meeting ground or overlap or area contested by these dualities is represented by the tide and the foreshore, the part of the beach between high and low water marks. While each domain is autonomous and secure in itself, this littoral or margin marks the difference between the two. It is this that compels him to turn to her as sight is forced to give way to sound ('Listen! you hear the grating roar . . .', l. 9) and it is here he hears an 'eternal note of sadness'. His masculine transcendence, like that of paternal Sophocles, seems threatened by this place of 'turbid ebb and flow' (l. 17). The difference at the margin can only be sexual difference.

But that was alright. Although not enjoying it very much, via identification with a classic father, he could live with the endless ebb and flow, in and out, either/or. But now the sea goes out and, against all laws of physics, stays out (ll. 21–8). It removes its protective clothing, its girdle, from the (male) loins of the land, it withdraws, it retreats, giving itself (herself) up

> to the breath
> Of the night-wind, down the vast edges drear
> And naked shingles of the world.   (ll. 26–8)

It would surely not be fanciful to gloss this by noting a series of consequences. Since the feminine is no longer securely in place, sexual difference is brought forward so re-instituting castration, which, in a version of masculine phantasy, is then projected onto the feminine, transforming it into the figure of the castrating woman (perhaps it is in response to this that Anthony Hecht, in rewriting the poem, renames it 'Dover Bitch'). The 'vast edges drear' of 'Dover Beach' expose the same threat as the 'ever-breaking shore' in *In Memoriam* (CXXIV).

The space between section three and section four, between the 'naked shingles' and the plea for fidelity, might contain the kind of sequence outlined in the main part of this chapter: for the supposedly transcendentally masculine ego the threat of castration may lead to a preference for the negative Oedipal pathway which leads to homo-sexuality which in turn becomes foreclosed as delusional jealousy: '*I* do not love him, *she* loves him'. How otherwise, in a reading of the text as phantasy, can one explain the speaker's sudden, urgent cry,

> Ah, love, let us be true
> To one another!   (ll. 29–30)

and why should he demand fidelity unless he feared her unfaithful-ness? Before this pathological mechanism was set in train, sexuality and sexual relations were bad enough for him, a 'turbid ebb and flow'; now, following some novel affirmation of the feminine, they have become a nightmare to and fro, an aggressive struggle in which 'ignorant armies clash by night'.

One of the most difficult issues in psychoanalysis is the way narcissistic and sexual drives, though distinct in their operation, constantly interact with each other in their effects, as they do in these nineteenth-century poems. So there is a danger of simplification even

in a clarifying summary. However, it has been suggested that
Victorian poetry in the first place is characterised by a poetic form
seeking to disavow lack in an impossible plenitude of the sign, seeking
therefore to defend the ego through rationalisation and a split
between 'manifest' and 'latent' levels of discourse. Developing on this
basis, the Darwinian passages in Victorian poetry evidence a social
phantasy in which the paternal or masculine ego reveals itself to be in
crisis. The would-be transcendental ego feels itself threatened when
the subject, faced particularly with the other-directed materiality of
nature, can no longer find support for itself in a reflecting object. As
the full father comes into question, so the son's identification with
him weakens and becomes more troubled. From this undermining of
the father ensue forms of phantasy that are pathological: melancholy,
paranoia, delusional jealousy.

When the aetiology of these is traced, a further step in analysis
becomes possible, if it is the case that, in contrast to the situation in
Augustan poetry, in Victorian poetry the feminine can no longer be
subordinated to the masculine. The would-be self-sufficient 'I' falls
typically into a state of anxiety in fleeing from a libidinal demand, 'the
open fulfilment of a repressed wish'. That wish at its deepest level
seems to be a form of male homosexual desire, activated in a complex
causality. A greater assertion of the feminine and of the idea of
woman (as perhaps when Maud cries 'for a brother's blood'), affirms
sexual difference and reintroduces in another way a challenge to the
masculine phantasy of a supposedly fully present and fully masculine
father. Male fear of castration is increased, leading in some extreme
expressions to *horror feminae* (when the threat is projected back onto
the idea of woman), to the son taking up a feminine position towards
the father, and to that in turn being expressed and defended against in
paranoia and delusional jealousy. An ideology denying that the
world is designed by God the Father becomes imbricated in a social
phantasy with wishes and fears well summed up in the idea that – in
every sense – the paternal ego is 'no longer master in its own house'.
We are at some distance now from Lyell, Chambers, geology and *The
Vestiges of Creation*. But it is a distance that brings the argument
right up against the topic of modernism in poetry.

8

MODERNISM/POSTMODERNISM: ELIOT/POUND

Most people have lost the nostalgia for the lost narrative.
                                                    Jean-François Lyotard

Thinking the present is the hardest yet most necessary task. Even Eliot's poetic modernism of the 1920s surrounds any attempt to analyse it, as water does a fish. In the first place it is difficult to give a plausible, general account of modernist ideologies. Then there is the dilemma, one signalled by the opposition between Lukács and Brecht (Brecht's side of the case is put in his polemic 'Against Georg Lukács', 1977, pp. 68–85) about whether modernism is to be preferred to realism: should we denigrate modernism because it sacrifices social awareness to an abstracted and universalised sense of the individual or welcome it because its formal techniques subvert the position of the supposedly transcendental subject? In touching on Lukács's powerful critique of modernism the present chapter will seek to argue that the critique is inadequate in its account of the signifier but valid for the level of the signified; nineteenth-century versions of ideology and phantasy in poetry are continued into some versions of modernism, and *Maud* does anticipate *The Waste Land*. This point reached, then the argument will try to go a step beyond it. If modernism, exemplified by *The Waste Land*, remains committed to the transcendental subject, albeit, as it were, in negation, then postmodernism, at least such postmodernism as is provisionally and partially instanced by Pound's 'Pisan Cantos', has forgotten there ever was such a possibility. And accordingly the kinds of phantasy structures offered by postmodernism may have moved beyond those enacted by the modernist text.

Georg Lukács's *The Meaning of Contemporary Realism* is a blow by blow attack on modernism. It begins by contrasting the novels of

Joyce and Thomas Mann in terms of the 'stream of consciousness' technique, which in Mann is mobilised for certain specific effects. But

with Joyce the stream of consciousness technique is no mere stylistic device; it is itself the formative principle governing the narrative pattern and the presentation of character. Technique here is something absolute . . . the perpetually oscillating patterns of sense- and memory-data, their powerfully charged – but aimless and directionless – fields of force, give rise to an epic structure which is *static*, reflecting a belief in the basically static character of events.   (1963, p. 18)

In a chapter entitled 'The Ideology of Modernism' these views are developed. Modernism reflects a static, universalised and unhistorical sense of human life in society and, on this basis, treats solitariness as a universal human condition: in modernism 'the hero himself is without personal history . . . he does not develop through contact with the world' (p. 21). Drawing the distinction from Hegel (see 1969, pp. 541–53), Lukács contrasts 'abstract' and 'concrete' potentiality:

Abstract potentiality belongs wholly to the realm of subjectivity; whereas concrete potentiality is concerned with the dialectic between the individual's subjectivity and objective reality.   (p. 22)

With modernism, via such techniques as the stream of consciousness, 'abstract potentiality achieves pseudo-realisation' (p. 24). Nevertheless, even in this abstracted and alienated form subject and object continue to come into existence together, and so, in such literature a sense of 'the disintegration of personality is matched by a disintegration of the outer world' for this becomes 'inherently inexplicable'. But 'attenuation of reality and dissolution are thus interdependent' (p. 26) – this dissolution of personality in modernist literature is dramatised through versions of abnormal psychology, psychopathology, neurosis (Lukács gives examples from Robert Musil's novels).

Lukács's critique must itself be criticised. It rests on a mimetic or reflexive conception of art and so is fully prepared to judge modernism as a true or false reflection of reality (it's false). It assumes the social formation to be a totality expressing a universal dialectic uniformly active in every practice and discourse, including the specific fictional discourse of literature. And it derives its account of the formal modes of modernism from the preceding view that art reflects reality and so form should be more or less transparent to meaning. These might be good reasons to reject Lukács altogether if it were not for the fact that his work does offer some outline of an ideology of modernist literature. Abercrombie, Hill and Turner assert that in the twentieth century, under 'Late Capitalism', the 'dominant ideology is much less well defined, is made up of a number of disparate elements and contains several internal inconsistencies' (1980, p. 128); and it would be consistent with Lyotard's position in *The Postmodern Condition* (1984) to accept that in the modern period ideologies were flattened out, as it were, so that none was dominant. In default of a clearly better alternative Lukács is useful in claiming that modernism goes along with a definable ideological assertion: that the 'human condition' is timelessly unchanging, that the individual is isolated in that condition, that the social world is inexplicable, and that the dissolution of the self is manifested in various forms of psychopathology. Modernism is represented for Lukács mainly by Joyce, Kafka and Musil, not Eliot, and his analysis of its ideology is thus all the more interesting when tested, as it will be, with reference to *The Waste Land*.

Modernist language and subject position

Against Lukács's reaction to modernist literary language as formalist and static ('perpetually oscillating patterns of sense- and memory-data') it can be urged that, on the contrary, such discursive modes are progressive and dynamic because they foreground the signifier and put into question the position of the reader along with that of the text providing that position. Already with *Maud*, for example, an unprecedented attention to the signifier leads to consciously artificial variety in the metrical forms, so denying the reader a position of simple and coherent identification with the represented speaker – and that speaker is in any case incipiently dispersed and disunified ('different phrases of passion in one person take the place of different characters', Tennyson 1897, I, p. 396). With poetic modernism – constituting its main definition – such effects are radically extended. Argued in *Poetry as Discourse* (1983, pp. 134–59), this view may be recapitulated briefly here.

The traditional poetry of the canon relies on sustained coherence in the syntagmatic chain and the attempted effacement of the process of the signifier to give the reader seemingly unmediated access to the represented, especially access through identification with the 'presence' of a consistently represented speaker. In this, such poetry offers the reader a position as transcendental ego, a position produced by denying that production. In contrast, modernist poetry reminds the reader of its own textuality as writing; breaks the coherence of the syntagmatic chain with indentations, fissures, *lacunae*; slides unevenly between *histoire* and *discours*; brings the phonetic force of words to attention through the use of free verse or 'intonational metre'; opens the text to a polysemic interplay of meanings in which no syntagmatic chain achieves automatic privilege. In sum, through these means, modernist poetry refuses to provide a speaker represented as 'really' present; it denies a position to the reader in apparent identification with the position of a transcendental ego and compels the reader to encounter the text and its representations from and in a place that is relative rather than absolute, to acknowledge that position as effect rather than origin of discourse. To reaffirm this argument against Lukács does not preclude the later possibility of discussing the limitations of modernist poetry as they develop in the signified, rather than the signifier.

Eliot: *The Waste Land* (1922)

The textuality of Eliot's poem perfectly exemplifies the modernist text. Fissured with isolated quotations, half-lines, broken phrases, snatches of song, citations from foreign languages, interjections, truncated dialogue, onomatopoeic bird-song, unexplained juxtapositions, uncompleted scenes, with disruptions and *lacunae* of all kinds, the text releases words, writing, from its prison in any determinate context, surrounds it with space on the page and leaves it to attract a swarm of suggestions, overtones, connotations, resonances. Like the pauses in Beckett's *Endgame* or a play by Pinter, the gaps in the text become silences which amplify the meanings, the possible contexts, for the words on either side. Almost every line and image thus becomes free to associate with almost any other in the poem through a network of floating fragments and synaptic connections. There is some warrant for this effect in Eliot's critical writing, when it distinguishes between 'emotions' and 'feelings'. While emotions are 'actual' and pertain to 'the person who suffers', feelings inhere 'in particular words or phrases', so becoming available to produce meaning for the reader in excess of personal intention (1961, p. 18).

An essay by Barbara Everett ('Eliot in and out of *The Waste Land*') denies the poem any organising principle whatever and stakes out what may be a limit position in this way of approaching the text as almost completely open:

> The only rhetorical rule is the extreme discreteness of its mixed and broken formalism: hardly a word in the whole that does not rest within a local convention, but hardly a convention that is not violated and confused. All the attempts to rectify the poem by imposing upon it unifying categories that improve this situation merely distort its essential medium. *The Waste Land* has neither 'story' nor 'narrator' nor 'protagonist' nor 'myth' nor 'themes' nor 'music' nor 'locale': these are exact and technical terms which the poem includes only to fragment and deny.   (1975, p. 14)

Most criticism attests to the openness of *The Waste Land* since little of it seems able to advance a clear line of argument about the text and relapses into elucidating allusions (*Women in the Poetry of T. S. Eliot* by Tony Pinkney, a reading in terms of Kleinian psychoanalysis, is an important exception, 1984).

Everett's position is similar to that of Shoshana Felman discussed in the first chapter and is liable to the same objections. All readings impose categories on texts; outside readings texts remain silent; as essence (or 'essential medium') the text only exists as it is distorted in the process of reading. What follows, then, is a reading of *The Waste Land*, though one which tries to acknowledge the polysemy of the text even as it argues for a more limited and partial interpretation of it. It will claim that the poem is not simply to be read as an endlessly open play of textuality but that it is also, at the same time, mimetic, having a provisional and qualified centre in the 'emotions' of a protagonist, a represented speaker. A conclusion will relate this feature back to the transitional status of *The Waste Land* as a modernist rather than postmodernist text.

Two independent essays, both published in 1960, contradict each other about the poem. One, treating it as a reflection of reality, says it is not true but is merely the expression of an individual viewpoint:

> T. S. Eliot's *The Waste Land* is one of the outstanding cases in modern times of a work which projects an almost defeatist personal depression in the guise of a full, impersonal picture of society.   (Craig 1960, p. 241)

(Terry Eagleton attacks the poem on similar grounds because it 'smuggles private attitudes into what postures as impartial wisdom',

1970, p. 159.) At the same time as the poem was criticised for being only a personal statement, Graham Hough argued that the poem had no 'unifying principle' and no represented speaker at all (Tiresias being the only, unsuccessful, candidate):

Who was Tiresias? A man who had also been a woman, who lived for ever and could foretell the future. That is to say, not a single consciousness, but a mythological catch-all, and as a unifying factor of no effect whatever.

(1960, p. 25)

The appearance of the manuscript in 1971 tended to support the former reading, for while in a note it denied that the poem was 'an important bit of social criticism' it did affirm that it was 'a personal . . . grouse against life' (Eliot 1971, no page number given). And this is consistent with the note to the poem which attributes a speaker to it and names that speaker as Tiresias: 'What Tiresias *sees*, in fact, is the substance of the poem' (note to line 218).

The poem obviously contains distinct voices, usually set off as such by quotation marks (Marie, the 'hyacinth' girl, Madame Sosostris, the cockneys in the pub, the three Thames-daughters). But this is not incompatible with there being a single, consistent speaker; Browning's Andrea del Sarto, for example, hears or imagines the voices of several other people, as does Prufrock for that matter. Difficulties really arise from the note naming *Tiresias* as the speaker throughout (and the willingness of critics to treat this note as a final authority). It is arguable that there is a represented speaker in *The Waste Land*, that like the hero of *Maud* or Beckett's *The Unnameable*, he (it is a he) has no name, that like Prufrock who assumes the roles of John the Baptist, Lazarus and Polonius, he speaks at different points in the poem in the voices of others: Ezekiel ('Son of man') and Iachimo in Imogen's bedroom, Phlebas the Phoenician and a Vedic seer. Each is adopted for temporary, local reasons, including the mask of Tiresias, put on while the speaker is a voyeuristic witness to the sexual encounter between a typist and a young man (ll. 214–56).

The first person singular ('I' twenty-nine times, 'me' twice) is used throughout *The Waste Land* to identify a single voice and a single subject. This might have been clearer if – as Eliot proposed – the text had been prefaced by 'Gerontion' or given the epigraph from Conrad's *Heart of Darkness*, 'The horror! The horror!' directing the reader to its context in that novel:

Did he live his life again in every detail of desire, temptation and surrender during that supreme moment of complete knowledge? He cried in a whisper at some image, at some vision – he cried out twice, a cry that was no more than a breath – 'The horror! The horror!'

Just as a drowning person is supposed to re-live their whole life (as in Golding's *Pincher Martin*), Kurtz re-experiences his life in the moment of death. The speaker of *The Waste Land* mingles 'Memory and desire' (l. 3), recalled perception and fantasy, and if we needed to fill out this state of mind with literal and naturalistic explanation, it would be with that kind of situation, or like that in *Maud* when the speaker, confined to an asylum, imagines himself to be dead and buried alive but still thinking as 'the wheels go over my head' (2.v.1). Or like that of the Ancient Mariner in Coleridge's poem who experiences death-in-life until he is won by 'The Night-Mare LIFE-IN-DEATH'. Though hardly linear in the strict sense, there is a narrative development in *The Waste Land* from the speaker's crucial moment of vision on the way back from the hyacinth garden to the image of the typist and young man and on to the end. The first three sections correspond to Death-in-Life, the fourth is a death, 'Death by Water', and the fifth crosses into another territory, a kind of Life-in-Death (it will be suggested below that this can be seen in psychoanalytic terms as a transition from neurosis to psychosis).

The Waste Land offers itself as one man's consciousness: 'I will show you fear', 'I had not thought . . .', 'I saw one I knew . . .', 'I remember . . .', 'I Tiresias . . .', 'I sat upon the shore . . .' But it represents a speaker whose consciousness is constantly under pathological invasion from his unconscious. As C. K. Stead well demonstrates, in the famous essays published just before completion of *The Waste Land* Eliot was wrestling with 'the problem of conscious direction and unconscious process in the writing of poetry' (1964, p. 127), and it is not inappropriate to consider these critical texts in relation to the poem. The aim of poetry 'is not to find new emotions, but to use the ordinary ones' so that poetry may 'express feelings which are not in actual emotions at all' (1961, p. 21). If we may take 'emotions' to refer to a subject's conscious and pre-conscious, then 'feelings' seems to specify the unconscious. The rhetorical strategy of *The Waste Land* is to dramatise a speaker whose emotions are constantly disrupted by feelings in the sense just described, so that beneath the speaker's self-awareness – to repeat a series of well-known formulations from the criticism – the poem will do its work on the reader, unconscious may 'respond to unconscious', 'swarms of inarticulate feelings are aroused', all in a dimension beneath self-consciousness in which the words have 'a network of tentacular roots reaching down to the deepest terrors and desires' (1961, p. 155). At this depth the reader cannot ascertain whether the words are to be followed mimetically or textually, as an expression of the speaker's unconscious or as writing.

At the level of ideology the significance of the poem is very much what literary criticism has seen it as from the start, even if much of that criticism believed its own account was true rather than ideological. Symbols of drought and rain, sterility and rebirth, suggest that under the accidents of civilisation mankind lives essentially, as F. R. Leavis said in 1932, in 'a harmony of human culture with the natural environment' (1972, p. 72); but the development of modern life, urbanisation and industrialism, has cut people off from their roots and brought them to a state of self-consciousness, boredom, automatism, anomie, spiritual death. So *The Waste Land* 'gives evidence of social disintegration' (Matthiessen 1968, p. 116). The dehistoricising of human history into some mythical contrast between the soil and civilisation, between the country and the city, the notion that older 'organic' ways of life, typified by the eighteenth-century village, were natural compared to the development of urban, class-society – all of this is, as David Craig shows (1960), a form of ideology rather than truth. It is also very much what Lukács's analysis locates as the ideology of modernism though that account disregards a Utopian side of the poem, which imagines transcendence in sexuality (romantic love), in social relations (the ritual) and in a harmony with the natural world (fertility) as possibilities, though possibilities always already lost.

In *The Waste Land* rapid juxtapositions between the contemporary and the ancient, between modern London and Elizabeth and Essex on the Thames, contrive to suggest some unchanging condition of human nature. Within this condition the hero or represented speaker is wholly solitary. In 'A Game of Chess' his inner speech continues but he thinks only silently to himself ('we are in rats' alley') in reply to '"Speak to me . . . Speak"' (l. 112). In an image which recurs throughout modernist literature, the speaker later describes everyone as being locked inside their own selves, 'each in his prison' (l. 411), where 'the whole world for each is peculiar and private to that soul' (note to line 411). The social world is meaningless, inexplicable. The city is 'Unreal' (ll. 60, 207), the office-workers crossing London Bridge to the City from London Bridge Station on the south bank are like zombies, the walking dead: 'I had not thought death had undone so many' (l. 63). Loss of meaning in the social routines of modern life is matched by a sense that romantic love, that central innovation of bourgeois ideology as chapter 4 suggested, has lost all value. Coming back from the hyacinth garden the speaker found that in the place of love and its transcendence he 'knew nothing' (l. 40). The sexual relation between the typist and the young man is automatic rather than lived, mechanical rather than organic, material not ideal, sex not love. Adding this feature from ideologies of gender to Lukács's summary brings out well how far the ideology of modernism is predicated on a sense of loss: the loss of a human essence, of a significant historical narrative, of communal relation, of social purpose, of private fulfilment through 'being in love'. As discussion turns towards the phantasy structures put to work in the poem it will become clear that these, like the poem's ideological structure, rest on a foundation, take their shape from a point of supposedly absolute origin. The loss is a loss of transcendence such that its absence can be treated as a transcendent absence in a kind of *negative theology*.

Cataphatic ('speaking about') or positive theology is distinguished from apophatic ('denying') or negative theology. Thus while positive theology draws on terms from human experience – God is good, God is love – to describe God, negative theology says what God is not. From the perspective of negative theology and the *via negativa*, any such affirmation is not false but inadequate, since God transcends all qualities applied by the created to the Creator. It therefore 'tells us that God excels in everything' so that 'the absolute terms that are common to the mystical tradition (*emptiness, void, darkness, nothing-ness*) are paradoxically positive in content' (see entry under *Via Negativa* in Eliade 1987, xv, pp. 252–9, italics original). Prevalent rather in the Orthodox than the Catholic tradition, negative theology is distrusted in the West: because it is not particular to Christianity but shared by the Hindu and Tao religions, among others; because it introduces into faith a dangerous element of paradox and play; and because finding support for the presence and existence of God in absence and non-existence can almost as easily show God's non-existence *tout court*. Eliot's poem exemplifies a negative theology in suggesting that God is dead and his death has left a god-shaped hole.

Insofar as *The Waste Land*, like Tennyson's *Maud*, is a monologue, we are led to follow the speaker's thoughts and feelings from within. After the introductory paragraph the speaker dons the mantle of

Ezekiel ('Son of man') to pronounce a final truth, a scene in which he will show us 'fear in a handful of dust' (l. 30). Framed by quotations from Wagner, the passage begins with 'the hyacinth girl' recalling a moment of love in the hyacinth garden. But what matters to him is what he saw afterwards in the act of love, on the way back:

> . . . I could not
> Speak, and my eyes failed, I was neither
> Living nor dead, and I knew nothing,
> Looking into the heart of light, the silence.   (ll. 38–41)

He has encountered something ultimate and transcendent. In the act of sexual intercourse he *knew* nothingness itself and felt what Dante felt when he saw the Devil:

> . . . I write it not
> Because all speech would fail to tell,
> I did not die, and did not remain alive . . .
> (*Inferno*, XXXIV.23–5)

Looking into what should have been 'the heart of light', a paradise, he found a brilliant and silent void, *'Oed' und leer'* (l. 42), waste and empty, more like a heart of darkness. The scene and his response to it appear in some respects to be 'the romantic absolute, love' (Leavis 1972, p. 84) especially in the phrase 'heart of light'. But all the other terms connote an experience of transcendent *horror*, and this is confirmed by the rest of the poem. It was the retrospective vision of what had happened in the hyacinth garden that has brought the speaker to his present state of living death; the scene recurs in different images throughout the poem; and it remains responsible for his state at the end of the poem since he cannot progress from this vision in which his eyes failed by being turned to pearl and he came to see the organic as mineral, the world as a desert.

The social phantasy at work is well indicated by a passage in an essay on Baudelaire in which Eliot distinguishes the spiritual from the animal:

Baudelaire has perceived that what distinguishes the relations of man and woman from the copulation of beasts is the knowledge of Good and Evil . . . Having an imperfect, vague romantic conception of Good, he was at least able to understand that the sexual act as evil is more dignified, less boring, than as the natural, 'life-giving', cheery automatism of the modern world.
(1961, pp. 428–9)

In the absence of a spiritual dimension the world is seen ideologically as mechanical and meaningless. But this transcendent absence is discovered in the same remembered or imagined experience as originates the speaker's pathological phantasies.

To name this state as obsessional neurosis would simplify the congeries of ideas and feelings that track across and beside each other through the text. It is not enough to refer as Pinkney does, within a Kleinian problematic, to 'regression – with a vengeance – to the paranoid-schizoid' (1984, p. 95). Nor is it adequate to stipulate, as does Hugh Kenner, that 'the guilt of the protagonist seems coupled with his perhaps imagined responsibility for the fate of a perhaps ideally drowned woman' (1959, p. 162). If all the women in the poem 'are one woman' (note to line 218), the speaker does wish the woman dead but equally thinks of her as already dead and himself as dead. His experiences make up an over-determined structure: obsession, compulsive repetition, doubt, guilt, anxiety, fear of castration, regression (especially from the genital to the anal), the wish for death. Like the patient in Freud's 'Notes upon a Case of Obsessional Neurosis' for whom the image of the rat condensed several phantasies, so in *The Waste Land* the same image provides a range of phantasy possibilities (see 'rats' alley', ll. 115; 'A rat crept', l. 188; 'the rat's foot', l. 195; Stallybrass and White are very good on the rat phantasy, though don't refer to Eliot, see 1986, pp. 143–8). The rat represents: dirt and the anal; the wish to be dead (and eaten); if phallic, with 'the rat as a male organ of sex' (*SE* x, p. 214), then the wish to be penetrated – or to penetrate by entering a (dead) woman's body sexually; if phallic, also the equation of genital and anal; the threat of castration, for if 'rats' alley' symbolises the vagina, that's where the 'dead men lost their bones' (l. 116). And so on.

Yet to the extent that the text privileges a strand of meaning that originates in the idea of the woman and the hyacinth garden, then one interpretation does press itself forward: psychical impotence. This Freud discusses as a masculine tendency 'towards Debasement in the Sphere of Love' (*SE* xi, pp. 177–90) such that 'the behaviour in love of men in the civilised world today' bears its stamp (p. 185). It is the case that for all human beings 'the finding of an object is in fact a re-finding of it' (*SE* vii, p. 222) but this affects men and women differently as they pass through the Oedipus complex on the way to adult heterosexual desire (if they do) and can lead to the particular liability of men to sexual overvaluation (see above, p. 69). Whereas the female Oedipal trajectory moves from the mother to the father and so to the re-finding of the mother in the figure of an adult male, the male trajectory moves directly from the mother to another woman. Men are more likely to over-value and more likely to retain the first sexual object, the figure of the mother, so that any love for other women risks recalling that forbidden image. And hence a masculine tendency to separate sacred from profane love, an ideal love based on the mother from the real experience of sexual satisfaction (in some cases a man may be potent with 'bad' women, such as prostitutes, but impotent with 'good', his wife). In consequence there is a tendency, particularly masculine, to regard 'the sexual act basically as something degrading' (*SE* XI, p. 186), an effect compounded, so Freud argues, because of the physical 'position of the genitals *inter urinas et faeces*' (p. 189). Psychical impotence may result for a man to whom thus all sex appears disgusting.

The speaker of *The Waste Land*, looking for a transcendent experience of ideal love, discovered in sexuality only 'the copulation of beasts' and so his eyes turned to pearl like those of drowned Alonso in *The Tempest* (l. 48). He can only see sexuality as death: the woman 'undone' (sexually betrayed) is like one 'undone' by death (see ll. 63, 292, 294); 'White bodies naked on the low damp ground' (l. 193) may be either making love or rotting; he may have seduced the hyacinth girl 'a year ago' (l. 35) but for him she is like a corpse 'planted last year' (l. 71).

In 'A Game of Chess', the speaker fantasises while watching the woman brush her hair, picturing her as Cleopatra, Imogen, Dido, himself entering the roles of Antony, Iachimo, Aeneas. But as the sexual drift becomes overt in the idea of Philomel, 'So rudely forced' (l. 100), it breaks down into thoughts of rape, death, obscenity and filth (' "Jug Jug" to dirty ears', l. 103). When she speaks to him in her jagged questions (ll. 111 ff.) he thinks about 'Nothing again nothing' (l. 120) just as after the hyacinth garden he 'knew nothing'. The cockney voices (ll. 139–72) act out a projection of his own phantasies of meaningless copulation ('. . . if you don't give it him, there's others will . . .', l. 149). At first in 'The Fire Sermon' the speaker is driven backwards and forwards between desire and death. Thoughts of casual seduction (he identifies with the 'heirs' who have 'left no addresses' for the 'nymphs', ll. 180–1) lead to images of the skull beneath the skin ('But at my back . . . I hear / The rattle of the bones . . .', ll. 185–6), yet almost immediately the same antithesis ('But at my back . . .', l. 196) re-introduces desire, Sweeney, Mrs Porter and her daughter, a movement which as in 'A Game of Chess' breaks down at the idea of rape: 'Jug jug jug . . . / So rudely forc'd' (ll. 203–4).

The mythological neutrality of Tiresias, bisexual, victim of senile impotence, is compromised if its initial context is recognised, for the speaker has just been – or thought of being – the object of Mr Eugenides's homosexual proposition (ll. 207–14). But the mask of Tiresias also fits in that the speaker feels himself to be spiritually blinded by his vision after the hyacinth garden and because it provides a rationalised impersonality through which he can re-work and re-live his own experience by observing it projected onto the intercourse between the typist and the clerk. At the moment of sexual climax they are displaced as he interposes himself to say he has 'foresuffered all', as indeed he has, not so much as Tiresias at Thebes but after the hyacinth garden when like Dante at the end of the *Inferno* he 'walked among the lowest of the dead' (ll. 243–7). At Thebes, Tiresias foresaw the discovery that the wife of Oedipus was his mother, and so his name recalls the idea of maternal incest which at the deepest level motivates the 'tendency towards debasement in love' Freud discusses.

Still the speaker's neurotic fixation persists and returns again to be repeated obsessively in the stories of the three Thames-daughters. It is really one story, the same as before, since each is a woman 'undone' in what is felt as an act of mechanical impassivity. The first is seduced not so much by a person as by the city, 'Richmond and Kew / Undid me . . .' (ll. 293–4), lines which again equate love and death for she speaks in the words of La Pia, said to have been done to death by her husband at Maremma (see *Purgatorio* v.133ff.). In the second story he is remorseful while she remains unmoved ('. . . After the event / He wept . . .', ll. 297–8). The third woman appears to have been seduced during a weekend at Margate and sits on the beach totally disabused, like the speaker, knowing nothing,

> I can connect
> Nothing with nothing. (ll. 301–2).

In the idea of arriving at Carthage ('To Carthage then I came', l. 307) the speaker identifies himself once again with Aeneas. When Aeneas left Dido she killed herself after ordering her body to be burned on the shore so that Aeneas in his departing ship might see it, 'Burning burning' (l. 308).

It is crucial for this reading of the text to appreciate that 'the woman' is in no sense actively aggressive. She acquiesces passively to the insistence of male desire and so is seen to act 'with automatic hand' (l. 255). For the speaker her moral indifference, her acceptance of corporality in the act of sexual intercourse, constitutes a positive absence, a denial of spiritual meaning, which turns his eyes to pearl and reduces him to impotence. In this respect he has been the drowned mariner since the moment after the garden consigned him to a living death, and so, in 'Death by Water', as he imagines himself as Phlebas, forgetting and sinking, his obsessive state passes on from one quality to another. The difference between the first three sections of the poem, in which there is a recognisable everyday reality, and the last, 'What the Thunder Said', in which any such reality is dissolved into phantasmagoria, can be understood as the difference between neurosis and psychosis. He can make no other progress.

The voice which addresses us in the final section of *The Waste Land* speaks with the fluency and bland repetitiveness of one for whose ego the distinction between reality and fantasy has broken down: obsessive images (water, rock), hallucination ('Who is the third . . .?'), imaginary noises ('What is that sound . . .?'), imaginary explosions ('Falling towers'). He has crossed a frontier ('He who was living is now dead', l. 329) and sees the landscape through the mineral eyes of Phlebas as stony rubbish, a handful of dust, a desert of rock, stone, sand, mountains. The crowing of the cock (l. 392) which 'stood' on the rooftop brings once again an access of sexual desire linked to its own defeat, though now the same old knot is articulated in a new register of megalomania. Speaking portentously in the person of a Hindu prophet or perhaps Jehovah speaking to Job he utters three pronouncements. The first ('The awful daring of a moment's surrender', l. 403) could refer to the hyacinth garden and the second to 'A Game of Chess' ('each in his prison', l. 413). The third once more unites love and death. It seems to evoke a moment of sexual fulfilment, the boat responding to the sailor as a woman to the touch of her lover, her heart responding

> Gaily, when invited, beating obedient
> To controlling hands   (ll. 421–2)

But the lines say only that she 'would' have responded, not that she did, and possibly, as both Kenner (1964, p. 162) and Pinkney (1984, p. 113) have suggested, the heart responds to 'controlling hands' round the neck. Like Desdemona, like the first Thames-daughter and La Pia, this woman is 'undone' in a double sense with love and death superimposed.

Within the perspective established here the last paragraph, usually read as summing up the poem, can be read either expressively or textually. Read aloud, its mimetic significance is unmistakable: the speaker collapses into incoherence, ending up 'mad againe' (l. 431), his cries ('Datta. Dayadhvam . . .') imitating a fit, a seizure. But we cannot read it only like that for the incoherence also presents itself as writing which is not – and cannot be – fully motivated by personal intention, a series of juxtapositions – from a nursery rhyme in English, a religious poem in Italian, a Latin story about a swallow, a French sonnet, Kyd's Elizabethan play – whose origin is simply textual as much as it is expressive. The speaker's loss of any rational control (in a sour joke the note to the last line refers to a 'Peace which passeth understanding') and the final disintegration of the poem take place together.

In the social phantasy offered to the reader by *The Waste Land* there is an ideology of modernism: the human condition is unchanging, the self is locked in its solitude, the social is beyond comprehension, the subject is in dissolution. And through the text this ideological assertion brings into play pathological forms of phantasy. There is both a contrast with and some continuity from nineteenth-century precedents such as Tennyson's *Maud*. In *Maud* the speaker is presented to the reader mainly as a single voice, a dramatised character in a realistically conceived narrative situation whose state of mind the reader may rationalise or disavow. In contrast the modernist form of *The Waste Land* breaks with realist represen-tation. A state of mind has become pervasive and generalised, extending as though to occupy the whole space of the text and presented to the reader without apparent point of origin in a personal situation so that it hardly seems like a state of mind at all. Such at any rate is the prevailing reading of the text. It must be qualified if we try to think together three features of the poem: its derivation of modernist ideology from a feeling of loss; its positive negation of transcendence; the psychological cohesion of the represented speaker's experience.

The Waste Land founds its articulation of a modernist ideology in a sense of absence which is treated as transcendent absence. The fear that human life is 'a handful of dust' (l. 30), the moment of vision after the hyacinth garden, forms a point of origin both for the ideological connotations of the text and its exploration of patholo-gical phantasy. In this respect, in this negative mode, the presumed transcendence of the ego constitutes a centre for the poem's meanings. The ego is positively *not* master of the world it surveys, for the speaker's drive to scopophilic domination is constantly denied by his feeling of blindness ('My eyes failed'), his incapacity to distinguish reality from fantasy, the perceived from the imagined. Yet while it is said that the 'I' failed, the poem is largely predicated upon this 'I' which 'knew', even though what it knew was 'nothing'. The ego is 'not master in its own house' but that which is not master is the supposedly transcendental ego.

The vision of absence at the heart of love also stands as a centre round which the poem dramatises an individual voice, a 'presence' determined in a consistent psychological disposition. The speaker's idealised overvaluation of 'The Woman' arising from fixation on the mother leads, in the experience of sexual intercourse, to the debasement of love, psychical impotence, *horror feminae*, a wish for death. In the 'Darwinian' texts examined, masculine fear of castration was projected aggressively onto the feminine, particularly in the phantasy figure of the castrating woman. The consistency of the phantasy structure excited by *The Waste Land* can be measured from the way this figure does not appear in the poem. Because generalised *horror feminae* ('all the women are one woman') develops in the form of impotence, it is projected back onto the feminine as her in-difference ('with automatic hand'), her spiritual passivity, while aggression is directed at the speaker's own ego ('we are in rats' alley'). The women are seen as victims rather than aggressors.

Although formally and textually *The Waste Land* tends to disrupt any fixed position for the reader, this effect is not continued fully into its meanings. The transcendental ego denied by the signifier is partly re-introduced by the signified. This contradictory disjunction and the fact that the poem's negative theology establishes a unified patholo-gical phantasy mark the text as modernist and transitional. While *The Waste Land* retains a version of social phantasy joining it back to a poem such as *Maud*, Pound's 'Pisan Cantos' can be seen to advance towards something much more radically postmodernist.

Pound: 'The Pisan Cantos' (1948)

Is Ezra Pound's judgement correct when he says *The Cantos* are 'botched' (1970, p. 375)? They sometimes read like the megalomanic phantasies of Senatspräsident Schreber in Freud's classic case of paranoia. The poem is 'an obstinately difficult work' which, even after receiving considerable critical attention, 'seems hardly less problematic and contradictory than it ever did' (Nicholls 1984, p. 1). Its contradictoriness can be stated in various ways. There is in the first place an unbridgeable distance between the levels of signifier and signified. At the former the poem can be seen as modernist and progressive, foregrounding the work/play of the signifier in a mode that is both pleasurable and promises to deny a position to the ego as transcendental because it makes plain the dependence of its represented speaker on the discourse which constructs him as 'ego scriptor' (p. 458; all page references are to Pound 1975). Yet at the level of the signified the text approaches the condition of a private language, an idiolect. Within the signified, contradictions multiply. While aiming to speak usable truth in concrete *exempla*, the poem's concreteness writes itself into an aestheticised abstractness that defies comprehension. Committed officially to empiricism, indeed to pragmatism and common sense, it relies on a set of metaphysical and essentialist assumptions – about history, the just economy, the hierarchy of civil society, the state, the individual, relations of gender, art, knowledge. Seeking to unfold a great narrative encompassing the whole of human history and ambition, to lead the reader through a Dantean pilgrimage from despair, across the purgatory of human error, to a new-found secular paradise, the text comprehensively deconstructs the possibility of any such linearity. In the face of these difficulties and the length of the complete text, all that will be attempted here is a note on one section.

Despite the contradictions mentioned above, 'The Pisan Cantos' adhere to a materialist ideology: in Pound's paganism the transcendental God of Christianity is not dead but simply not in question. Nor again, despite inconsistency, does the poem obviously reproduce what was earlier described as the ideology of modernism. Instead of a static view of the human condition, the poem's outlook is thoroughly, if waywardly, historical; the individual, though sometimes solitary, is presented usually as a hero (the represented speaker himself, Mussolini) or villain who takes on value in relation to other people and society. Though the self is shown both suffering and enduring it is not apparently threatened with dissolution because it does not claim an origin for itself in a transcendent unity. And the social formation, far from being inexplicable, is submitted to repeated, dogmatic explanation.

Ideological assertion in 'The Pisan Cantos' takes the form of a narrowly conceived version of political economy. In summary, as far as possible in its own words: the fall into usury at the Renaissance results in the corruption of every form of just value, economic, social, cultural, intellectual. The private ownership of banks who 'rob the public for private individual's gain' (p. 437) and set out to make money 'out of nothing' (p. 468) by charging interest on capital without regard to production leads to the oppression of working people (the peasant having 'to pay twice as much grain / to cover his taxes and interest', p. 474), the commodification of art (architectural columns ordered 'by the gross', p. 480) and the rise of a group or sub-class of 'loan swine' (p. 479) and arms dealers who have an interest in starting and continuing wars. In contrast, the right man could nationalise the banks (as did Mussolini, p. 513) and establish a financial system in which production and wages are based 'on work done' (p. 481). From this would follow the building of 'Dioce whose terraces are the colour of stars' (p. 425), not the city of God but an earthly paradise. Avowedly utopian and despite some fascist trimmings, the poem's assertion reveals its class character in its similarity to the agrarian populism of Steinbeck's *The Grapes of Wrath*.

But 'The Pisan Cantos' are set in what Thomas Pynchon's *Gravity's Rainbow* names as 'The Zone', 'the wreckage of Europe' (p. 458) in 1944–5. With the devastating defeat of Italy, the hope that Dioce would be historically reborn through Mussolini's fascism is overthrown. 'The Pisan Cantos' are founded in an attempted recuperation of that defeat:

'The Pisan Cantos' suggests two main reasons for the collapse of the regime. On the one hand, it was the result of defects and weaknesses within the state itself . . . 'the stupidity of the populace' . . . [and] another which attributes the failure of the regime to external causes . . . 'monopolists' . . . 'usurers'. . .
(Nicholls 1984, p. 169)

Against some sentimental readings of the section, Nicholls's work asserts that 'neither "explanation" undermines the *idea statale* . . . nor does it diminish Mussolini's heroic status' (*ibid.*). It is this ideological manoeuvre, admitting failure only to reaffirm resurgence ('I believe in the resurrection of Italy quia impossibile est', because it's impossible, p. 442) that sets in motion the main structure of phantasy in the text. OΫ ΤΙΣ, 'I am no man' (p. 426, see also pp. 425, 430, 499);

'of no fortune and with a name to come' (p. 439, see also p. 446): from
the charged polysemy of 'The Pisan Cantos' it is this chain of ideas in
and around the represented speaker which may be singled out (as it is
in Rabaté's discussion, 1986, p. 145 ff.) to suggest how the ideological
theme becomes worked in with unconscious material to constitute a
social phantasy. Homer's *Odyssey* IX 106–565 gives the story of
Odysseus and Polyphemus, how Odysseus is caught by the giant,
imprisoned in a cave while the Cyclops eats two of his men and how
he blinds the creature in its one eye, telling him 'Οὖ τις ἐμοί γ" ὄνομα,'
'Noman is my name' (l. 366). Allusions to this incident therefore
connote the old familiar Oedipal struggle between father and
rebellious son over castration, kill or be killed, eat or be eaten, blind
or be blinded. For Lacan it is the order of the signifier which institutes
lack, and so, in negotiating the Oedipus complex under patriarchy the
son must surrender his imaginary conception of the father as fully
present and acknowledge instead that the father is a symbol, the
'Name of the Father' (see 1977a, pp. 199–202). According to this
logic, the speaker of these Cantos, like Satan in *Paradise Lost*, will
stay stuck in self-defeating aggression, he will remain 'no man' unless
he can accept castration, acquiesce to the fact that the father is a name
and not a full presence, and accede to adult male identity and
heterosexual desire – in sum, that he is of 'no fortune' but may have,
like the father, 'a name to come'. The ideological movement of
recuperation, defeat and possible rising again is enacted for phantasy
in this process of Oedipal stasis and possible transition.

Aporia, statis, impotence, the fear of being 'no man', regressive
refusal of castration before the father's threat is articulated in the text
through references to 'the tower'. From his prison camp the speaker
can see in Pisa both the famous leaning tower of the Campanile, 'the
tower che pende', which leans (p. 443) and is seen 'through a pair of
breeches' (p. 431, see also pp. 428, 430) and another tower which he
takes as the Torre della Fame in which, according to *Inferno* XXXIII,
Ugolino was imprisoned with his sons until he ate them ('chewed his
son's head', p. 436, see also pp. 438, 447, 514). The tower symbolises
both the speaker's loss of virility and the menace from the father
which he cannot come to terms with. Crucially, it also refers to the
defeat of Italian fascism by the United States:

> the bacon-rind banner alias the Washington arms
> floats over against the Ugolino (p. 486)

Refusing castration as he refuses the conquest of Italy, the speaker is driven back into pre-Oedipal impotence. At the same time, in another movement, the speaker's wish ('the drama is wholly subjective', p. 430) for the founding of his ideal state, Dioce, is expressed at the level of phantasy as identification with the father and accession to male heterosexual desire. One might say that 'no man', οὐ τίς (ou tis), must be replaced by 'Hast 'ou' (pp. 449, 520). But the male Oedipal trajectory is incomplete, constantly *overlaid* by regressive impotence and psychopathology.

To the extent that he rebels against the father's law the speaker inclines towards the feminine position, which, in the complex sequence described already for Tennyson's *Maud*, generates paranoia (there are various anal references in the section: see 'a.h.' = arsehole, p. 437, p. 443; 'the bottom', p. 438; 'the pit', p. 449). Paranoia is expressed in the extremely polarised division between male heroes and villains. Obsessional figures of the castrating father (Ugolino, Churchill, Washington, 'the loan swine') are posed in an equally delusional polarity with the supposedly fully phallic father (Mussolini, 'the Brothers Adams'). Similarly, development towards adult heterosexual desire cannot escape regressive fears of impotence from which ensue hysterical assertions of virility, 'I have been hard as youth sixty years' (p. 513, see also p. 431).

Male heterosexual desire is the overwhelming and endless preoccupation of 'The Pisan Cantos', a profusion which makes page notation almost redundant: *femina, femina*; κύθηρα δεινά (fearful/wonderful Aphrodite); Demeter; Persephone; Artemis; Maya (mother of Hermes); Dirce (wife of the king of Thebes); Circe; Isotta degli Atti (lover of Malatesta); Cunizza da Romano (who had an intrigue with Sordello and whose name suggests 'cunnus', p. 238, glossed delicately by Edwards and Vasse as 'pudendum muliebre', 1971, p. 47); La Nascita (Botticelli's Venus born from the waves); la scalza, the barefoot woman, who is the moon (p. 453); 'little sister who would dance on a sax-pence' (p. 477), La Cara (p. 459), 'la pastorella dei suini' (woman pigkeeper, p. 460). Through imagery and allusion, much in the private language of lovers which has meaning only for them, every single term opens with unexpected pleasure onto others, backwards and forwards across the text (as Nassar shows well, 1975, pp. 71–98). Male desire is both beautifully figured but also profoundly, even pathologically, phallocentric (as argued by Ellman 1979 and Durant 1981). My abbreviated account will attend to the way masculine phantasy here is both reaffirmed and possibly subverted.

For the speaker the expression of desire indicates negotiation of the Oedipus complex and transition towards adult identity – and so it underpins and substantiates the ideological countermand to defeat. But it remains entrammelled in the regression it seeks to elude. A supposedly undivided masculinity encounters a supposedly undivided femininity in a traditional phantasy which imagines difference as unity and all the women as *The* woman ('where the definite article stands for the universal', Lacan 1982, p. 144): 'womankind' (p. 484), lover, wife, sister, mother, daughter. If she is one so is he: 'Priapus' (p. 489), 'a hard man', a male Lynx (pp. 487–92), a leopard, panther, cat. If he represents culture or at any rate the animal, she is seen as nature or a landscape, moon, clouds, light, mist, pool ['bel seno' etc. = beautiful bosom (in rare times, see above); 'Δημήτηρ' = Demeter]:

> bel seno (in rimas escarsas, vide sopra)
> 2 mountains with the Arno, I suppose, flowing between them
> so kissed the earth after sleeping on concrete
>
> bel seno Δημήτηρ copulatrix
>   thy furrow   (pp. 469–70)

But this figuration reproduces patriarchal sexual phantasies for the reader (if it does) only by exceeding them, especially in two respects. Even if *The* woman is one, there are always more than one of them, for the poem 'does not, of course, subscribe to any taboo on adultery' (Dekker 1963, p. 99). The speaker always has 'three ladies' (p. 445), three women on his mind, 'Tre donne intorno alla mia mente' (p. 483), and to this extent the poem challenges the patriarchal law limiting – seeking to limit – desire to monogamy. Secondly, it eschews inwardness. For example, the passage cited above ('bel seno . . .') or the following:

>   Saw but the eyes and stance between the eyes,
> colour, diastasis,
>   careless or unaware it had not the
>   whole tent's room
> nor was place for the full Εἰδὼs
> interpass, penetrate
>   casting but shade beyond the other lights
>   sky's clear
>   night's sea
>   green of the mountain pool
>   shone from the unmasked eyes in half-mask's space
>   (p.520)

('*Εἰδὼs*' =knowing). To be read in the context of allusions to chrysalids, the colour of light, who 'mate in the air' (p. 432) this description of sexual intercourse, comparing a vaginal 'diastasis' (separation) to that of the iris of the eye, resists intention and velleity, halting instead at a vivid rendition of the surfaces of the body. Its portrayal of a diffuse corporeality, tactile and synaesthetic, does not treat sexuality as a version of spiritual truth. For the modernist textuality of the poem, its foregrounding of the work/play of the signifier, precludes the confessional mode, and the represented speaker does not have (nor does he lack) a self which might experience such transcendental inwardness.

In some degree 'The Pisan Cantos' reinstate sexual desire in terms of an *ars amatoris*, which, at least in the history of sexuality covered by the present study, has disappeared since Ovid (see chapter 3). Certainly the poem does not envisage male sexuality according to the mode of scopophilic mastery and narcissistic confidence dominating the poetic tradition since courtly love (see chapter 4).

In comparison with *The Waste Land*, this section of *The Cantos* is a postmodern text. Its textuality, the precedence accorded to the signifier, consistently exhibits the represented speaker as effect rather than origin of discourse, a moving point temporally fixed in the process of enunciation. And this denial of a transcendent position is carried through into the signified. The poem does not assume meaning as an absolute point of origin around which its narrative and social phantasy can be structured, nor does it admit, through negation, the positive lack of such a centre. Although it may seek truth, it is able to uphold only localised and contradictory truths in the necessarily diverse fields of history, political economy, gender, aesthetics. And since it does not presume a point of origin, there is no centre onto which a 'presence', the subjective unity of a represented speaker, can be held. The question of the subject in the poetry of Eliot and Pound and the need to discriminate between *The Waste Land* and 'The Pisan Cantos' can best be referred to the debate over modernism and postmodernism and to Lyotard's argument introduced into the discussion above (p. 35).

Modernism and postmodernism in poetry

Distinguishing, in *The Postmodern Condition*, between scientific knowledge and narrative knowledge, Lyotard claims that it is 'impossible to judge the existence or validity of narrative knowledge on the basis of scientific knowledge and vice versa' (1984, p. 26). This is questionable. However, this epistemological account is much less interesting and has – rightly – gained far less currency than the account he offers (somewhat in the margins of his own argument) of the contemporary cultural situation. Following through the view that cultural and discursive forms generally are based in and derive their force from narrative, Lyotard proposes that the classical period – roughly from the Enlightenment to the close of the nineteenth century – was presided over by two metanarratives, that of the emancipation of the people and that of the triumph of speculative reason or pure knowledge. Now, in the post-war period after the great upheaval of modernism, a postmodern condition has emerged in which 'the grand narrative has lost its credibility' (p. 37). Hierarchisation and metanarrative as legitimation of scientific knowledge have given way to a ' "flat" network of areas of inquiry' (p. 39) to 'islands of determinism' (p. 59), local areas of manoeuvre judged by their capacity to come up with new moves in a system which *The Postmodern Condition* terms 'paralogy' (thus replacing the notion of an overarching Logos with that of a jostling but non-exclusive parallelism). It is Lyotard's willingness to greet this avowedly new cultural situation (non-hierarchic, decentred, postmodern) as an 'increase of being' exciting 'jubilation' (p. 80) which has provided most controversy.

As was considered earlier, Fredric Jameson in *The Political Unconscious* has already underwritten Lyotard's account of the foundational mode of human culture as narrative but developed it crucially in two directions – first by making the post-structuralist assertion that such narrativisation was constituted as a necessary epistemological occlusion of a historical reality working always behind our backs, and then by affirming that Marxism survived ineluctably as the one great narrative through its ability to comprehend and make sense of all the others. In a long essay, 'Postmodernism, or the cultural logic of late capitalism' (1984), Jameson was able to follow through and validate his previous account through a cultural analysis of postmodernism.

This essay inspects a whole range of high and popular cultural forms, including Hollywood film along with Godard, architecture, painting, advertising, as well as a contemporary poem, 'China' by Bob Perelman. Admitting that these do not exhibit entire homogeneity, it argues nevertheless that they conform to the cultural dominant of postmodernism. This, consistent with Lyotard's description of paralogy and illustrated by a contrast between Van Gogh's 'Peasant Shoes' and the postmodernism of Warhol's 'Diamond Dust Shoes', is characterised as 'a new kind of flatness or depthlessness' (1984, p. 60), mere stylistic collocation, one which denies the reader or viewer any critical distance or awareness in relation to the presented text. Whereas, so it is implied, the modernist text works to shock or alienate its reader (often with politically progressive intentions), the postmodern text does not. In consequence postmodernism differs from modernism in that 'the alienation of the subject is displaced by the fragmentation of the subject' (p. 63), a fragmentation arguably schizoid; in postmodern culture 'there is no longer a self to do the feeling' (p. 64). In consequence again, our critical sense of the historical and of alternatives to a hermetically closed present is eroded if not made impossible altogether. To explain the causes of the postmodern condition, Jameson is ready with a great narrative: late capitalism, as analysed by Ernest Mandel, seeks to extend commodification into every area: 'what has happened is that aesthetic production today has become integrated into commodity production generally' (p. 56). In 'the world space of multinational capital' (p. 92) traditional forms of criticism and resistance are blocked as the subject is transformed into an adjunct of localised consumption.

Jameson's argument advances an entirely opposite evaluation of postmodernism to that of Lyotard yet both share a difficulty and a contradiction. In the first place each works through a form of totalising argument, making the assumption that all the different levels and effects of contemporary culture express a single origin or cause, for Lyotard the postmodern condition resulting from the end of metanarrative, for Jameson late capitalism. This presumption is particularly manifest in their willingness to enter judgement for or against postmodernism as though it were a homogeneous unity. If, however, analysis proceeds on another basis altogether, one which accords a specific effectivity to each mode and recognises the social formation as a decentred structure in which each social and discursive practice acts within its own 'time', then such overall assessments become much harder to make. Architecture, film (whether Godard or Hollywood), literature – and within literature, poetry – must be considered in terms of a separated autonomy and qualified in terms of that particularity. In Jameson this difficulty is compounded by the fact that his argument can be viewed as functionalist, not least in its failure to explain at all the mechanism by which late capitalism comes to affect and operate through the diverse cultural forms discussed (for this kind of objection to certain Marxist arguments, see Elster 1985).

Secondly, the tendency of both writers has been to install the concept of postmodernism within the context of a deeply historical perspective. Thus, the very concept of postmodernism, while explicitly denying this in its own constitution, necessarily and contradictorily presumes a historical metanarrative: a classical temporality opposed to postmodernism in Lyotard, a modernism versus postmodern period in Jameson. But if we lived in a postmodern culture as it is described we would no longer know how to say so. Postmodernism would be as invisible to us as water to the fish who breathes it. So long as postmodernism continues to be discussed, it hasn't finally arrived.

Yet in spite of these objections a contrast between modernism and postmodernism can be constructively deployed if it is restricted to a specific discursive form – in this case poetry, especially the poetry of Eliot and Pound – and if it is drawn on as a means to focus attention on the question of the subject and phantasy. Jameson argues that postmodern culture entails 'the disappearance of the individual subject' (1984, p. 64) and his account of a contrast between the modernist and postmodernist subject has been well developed elsewhere. Terry Eagleton has argued that with postmodernism alienation vanishes since 'there is no longer any subject to be alienated' (1986, p. 132), and on this basis has discriminated and defended modernism as a preferred alternative:

old-fashioned modernism . . . is still agonizedly caught up in metaphysical depth and wretchedness, still able to experience psychic fragmentation and social alienation as spiritually wounding, and so embarrassingly enmortgaged to the very bourgeois humanism it otherwise seeks to subject. Postmodernism, confidently post-metaphysical, has outlived all that fantasy of interiority . . .   (p. 143)

The modernist subject, then, is the traditional autonomous subject alienated from itself. In a way that is supported by the previous account of *The Waste Land*, Eagleton's account reveals the close continuity between the traditional dramatisation in poetry of the transcendental or would-be transcendental subject encountered in poetry from Donne to its Victorian crises, and the modernist subject whose transcendence is predicated on a sense of absolute loss according to Eliot's negative theology. Further, this account corresponds well with the distinctions indicated here between texts of Eliot and Pound, between a modernist and postmodernist subject. If the modernist subject of *The Waste Land* is 'agonisedly caught up in metaphysical depth', the subject of *The Cantos* is postmodernist, one whose non-accession to spirituality, transcendence and interior dimension is matched by the realisation of its potential across a more concrete and material exteriority, historical, social, aesthetic, and a corporeal sexuality rendered closely in terms of the body. The break with tradition occurs not with Eliot but with Pound.

Attending to the specificities of poetry, and particularly those specificities represented by the two texts contrasted here, a qualified endorsement of postmodernism can be made. Fears for a postmodernist loss of the individual subject seem to be much exaggerated, in fact to arise from the posing of a doubtful either/or: either the full subject or no subject at all; that is, either the modernist subject whose plentitude is expressed negatively in its alienation and sense of absolute loss or the postmodernist subject, fragmented and psychotic, deprived of all coherent interiority. In an essay of 1938, 'A category of the human mind: the nature of person, the notion of "self"', the anthropologist, Marcel Mauss, notes that there has never been a language in which 'the word "je – moi"' . . . did not exist' and that 'there has never been a human being without the sense not only of his [*sic*] body, but also his simultaneously mental and physical individuality' (1979, p. 61). The entire disappearance of the individual subject seems unlikely, especially if (to shift the terms) the subject is in fact always present as an ego, as what Lacan terms the imaginary. What may be named as the *classical subject*, apparently self-made, a would-be effect only of its ultimately concealed depth and inwardness, the bourgeois subject in other words, is historically determined and does not represent the only form the ego can take or the only way individuals can make choices. Pound's presentation of the postmodern subject is one possible version of a relative stability of an 'I' which claims no transcendence.

At the same time, if the modernist crisis of the classical subject and its postmodernist fading imply that there will be no more (bourgeois) nature, the evidence of these two texts is that this may well be a good thing. In the present narrative, which began by juxtaposing Donne's 'Elegy 19' with a poem from Ovid's *Amores*, then traced the discovery of this self back through the poetry of courtly love and forward through the phallocentric phantasies of Milton and the Augustan period into the Victorian crisis defined as the revelation that the ego was no longer master in its own house, in the continuity of this tradition the emergence and persistence of the classical subject has come to be understood as in every respect aggressive and exploitative: assuming itself to be as self-originating as God, it is constituted in the need to appropriate everything other than itself to its own avowed self-sufficiency as origin of power and knowledge. This feature has been strongly marked in the field of sexuality. Through the interaction of narcissistic and sexual phantasies, in relation to differing ideological matrices, what has been demonstrated is that the transcendent ego is a masculine ego, constantly maintaining its dominance by equating masculinity with knowledge, activity, looking and mastery, and femininity with sexuality, passivity, and being looked at. In sum, the 'I' of this subject depends on a hypostasised idea of The Woman as its subordinate Other. Postmodern culture – at least on the contradictory evidence of Pound's 'Pisan Cantos' – envisages an end to the social phantasy structured around scopophilic male narcissism.

The concept of postmodernism and a reading of Pound's poetry in relation to it thus begins to indicate a positive aspect, an assessment that may be further substantiated if *The Cantos* are examined more generally as a form of phantasy. For if the ego is constituted by a split in the subject between conscious and unconscious and if neither the transcendent ego nor its modernist inversion as loss are at issue in the text, then it may be read as pointing to new possibilities for the psychoanalytic subject. Thus, while phantasy structures are put to work in and around the speaker of 'The Pisan Cantos', they defy analysis in terms of a *consistent* mechanism or related set of mechanisms, whether the Oedipal transition, psychical impotence, paranoia or megalomania (though there are phantasy effects corresponding to each of these). Within psychoanalysis, this loosening or dispersal may be referred to the complex notion of defence, a process in which the ego is both stake and agent, both what is to be defended and what does the defending. For the 'I' must maintain itself against its other, both diachronically by persisting as a continuous identity and synchronically by defining itself against what it is not (a structure whose effect is to catch up the figure of The Woman as its object and its other). An ego aiming to function transcendentally will in defence of itself construe as pathological psychic operations it might count as less of a threat if it did not try to defend itself absolutely. It may be that if less is claimed in and for the ego, less needs to be expelled in order to give it room.

Hence follows a conclusion to be made with some hesitancy. If the categories of neurosis and psychosis do not fully apply to 'The Pisan Cantos', there is a respect in which they may be considered 'post-Freudian'. If the text does not assume a point of transcendence it is because it does not work via a dramatisation of the ego as transcendent. And without this, the lines between sanity and madness, conscious and unconscious, truth and phantasy, 'presence' and the Other, become relativised. Various mechanisms of phantasy, some pathological, are offered to the reader in a dispersal across the poem but there may be no unified development corresponding to the inherited idea of 'the individual'. This poetic text may anticipate a possible re-drawing of the boundaries of consciousness and repression in and across the subject.

So far it has been proposed that – at least in the main poetic tradition – forms of phantasy were imbricated with ideologies in a way linking phantasy to the historical in the form of social phantasy. Now this reading of *The Cantos* points to the idea that the boundaries between conscious and unconscious, the ego and the Other, may themselves be historically variable. Phantasy itself can be read as a historical concept and effect, especially if the contrast between Ovid and Donne is recalled, together with the argument that in ways we can only as yet refer to as rediscovery, Pound's text proclaims the value of the body, pleasure and satisfaction as against the canonical appeal of narcissism, mastery and phantasy. In fact, implicit throughout, this proposal must now become explicit.

If the self, conceived as autonomous and self-originating, cannot be equated with human nature but must rather be understood as a particular historical formation, that is, the form and mode offered to ever-changing human identity in the period starting with the 'discovery of the individual' in (among other things) the poetry of courtly love, then our understanding of psychoanalysis is profoundly altered. Adhering closely as it does to this particular realisation of self, in fact predicated *in part* on a local historical effect, the theoretical problematic of psychoanalysis must be recognised as historically determined. The next section, Postscript, will turn attention to the consequences and effects of recognising that psychoanalysis in its own fashion is itself a version of social phantasy.

9

POSTSCRIPT

. . . one is never in a position to discover the whole truth   Sigmund Freud

The first two chapters of the present study have worked to re-launch psychoanalysis as a necessary discourse for literary studies on the grounds that it was preferable to its immediate competitor, conventional literary criticism. The limitations of psychoanalytic discourse were noted but kept on ice; now the time has come to try to confront some of them. In fact, they can be focused on a single, central assertion: psychoanalysis is itself a discourse, itself a form of text. As Shoshana Felman puts it directly, 'psychoanalysis itself is equally a body of language' (1977, p. 6). From this assertion problems radiate in several directions – to psychoanalysis as historically determined practice and so itself instance of ideology, to its use in literary study as a metalanguage, to psychoanalysis as a covertly moralistic discourse. Responding to these questions will help to make more explicit some assumptions made in the preceding chapters.

Psychoanalysis as ideology

It is not entirely novel to contend that psychoanalytic theory is itself a product of history. In 1940, for example, Lionel Trilling remarked that 'psychoanalysis is one of the culminations of the Romanticist literature of the nineteenth century' (1953, p. 33). A much more far-reaching critique of this kind has been entered by Michel Foucault and subsequently by Fredric Jameson.

When Lacan asserts that 'the beginning of the seventeenth century' is the 'inaugural moment of the emergence of the subject' (1977b, p.

223) he must mean the subject as supposedly self-defining and autonomous. Foucault's *The History of Sexuality* substantiates this view by documenting how the confessional mode of discourse made room for a historical articulation of subjectivity as inwardness. Within this overarching continuity Foucault uncovers the genealogy by which psychoanalysis is cognate with the nineteenth-century construction of sexuality in medical discourse. Although the remarks about psychoanalysis in *The History of Sexuality* are polemic rather than systematic, a clear view emerges: psychoanalysis is 'a rationally formed discourse' like other scientific discourses of the age of positivism (1981, p. 55); it is a *'scientia sexualis'* (p. 70) but also, paradoxically, to a certain extent 'an *ars erotica*' (p. 71) (and the second more effectively because it passes itself off as the first); psychoanalysis functions also as a 'wonderfully effective' practice of moral prohibition, one 'worthy of the greatest spiritual fathers and directors of the classical period – in giving a new impetus to the secular injunction to study sex and transform it into discourse' (p. 159). Though psychoanalysis cannot be accommodated completely to any of these unsympathetic descriptions the main theme of the criticism is plain: psychoanalysis exercises power by claiming a knowledge of truth conceived as inward and subjective, a sexual truth, truth as sexuality. As such psychoanalysis is revealed to be dependent on the history it would analyse and which, through its own discursive and practical effectivity, it helps to produce.

It would only be a very partial response to point out that this hostility is directed mainly at psychoanalysis as a practice and an institution, precisely as therapy (or the hope for it). Disappointed at the obstacles met in the consulting room, particularly in the treatment of psychotics, Freud wrote in *An Autobiographical Study* in 1924: 'By itself this science is seldom able to deal with a problem completely, but it seems destined to give valuable contributory help in the most varied regions of knowledge' (*SE* xx, p. 70). He thus foresaw that the future of psychoanalysis would lie less with therapy than with its exploitable potential as a conceptual system and mode of interpretation. On the evidence of the writing discussed here in chapter 2, he was right.

In its analysis of literature the Machereyan problematic relies heavily on a psychoanalytic conceptualisation, one which is reproduced and reworked by Jameson. And Foucault's own analysis of power as a diffused non-teleological process is modelled partly on

Freud's account of sexuality, just as his description of confessional discourse borrows from the account of narcissism and the super-ego. In this work – even in that undertaken by Foucault from a position antagonistic to psychoanalysis – the hermeneutic vitality of the psychoanalytic framework is implicitly acknowledged, and that has been the primary reason it has been mobilised in this present study.

Yet if Foucault's criticisms have been directed at psychoanalysis rather as a social practice, Jameson has criticised it particularly as a discursive form, precisely as a hermeneutic. In this his avowed aim has been 'to historicize Freudianism itself' (1981, p. 62).

Considered as a theoretical discourse, psychoanalysis, so Jameson argues, is itself a symptom of the privatisation of individuality and the consequent psychic fragmentation which the epoch of the capitalist mode of production introduces into history. Permeated by the structures of reification and abstraction analysed by Lukács in *History and Class Consciousness*, psychoanalysis theorises desire as outside of time, 'always the same', as individual, not social, thus remaining 'locked into the category of the individual subject' (p. 68). Based in a conception of 'the family as private space', psychoanalysis begins from an 'isolation of sexual experience' (p. 64) which construes sexuality as autonomous rather than from the first an effect of relationships. Psychoanalysis, in sum, as a body of language, a discourse, is ideologically determined, permeated by its dependence on the particular conception of individuality dominant in the bourgeois epoch.

There are a number of preliminary ways to respond to this. Psychoanalysis has not been taken here (it is the old accusation of pansexualism) only as a discourse concerned with sexuality – narcissism and phantasies of self-love have been attended to just as much as those exciting sexual desire, and so too though to a much lesser extent has the death drive expressing itself in the pathological phantasies of Victorian poetry, in Eliot, in Pound. Nor has the human subject been regarded as 'always the same' since a historical perspective and principle has been used to argue that the phantasies made available by poetry are always imbricated with social meaning and so, in that respect, always historical. And psychoanalysis has been drawn on as a theoretical discourse directed at 'the category of the individual subject' precisely because it provides terms for the systematic analysis of a general range of fantasy and 'the personal' in literature for which at present there is no reasoned alternative (least of all that practised in traditional literary criticism).

But these are lesser issues. The real point is that response must begin here by *endorsing* the criticism that psychoanalysis is very much what the critique says, as it is advanced in both Foucault and Jameson. It would be entirely inadequate to reply by asserting the objective truth of psychoanalysis, affirming for example that gravity exercised its force before Newton and that there was Oedipus before any Oedipus complex. Ground already covered in the way it's been covered here proves the limits of that kind of argument. The Darwinism examined in chapter 7, for example, shows it is impossible to draw a final line between the truth of a science and the ideological commitments of its discourse in a way that would exclude the latter. Nor would it be consistent for a study of poetry as social phantasy, which throughout has assumed the concept of ideology, to deny that ideology, like power, comes from everywhere and acts everywhere, even in the science psychoanalysis was always meant to be. But, resisting the temptation to go any further into epistemological arguments, one must set a limit to criticism of a scientific discourse, and particularly one in the area of 'the human sciences', made on the grounds that it is ideologically penetrated and complicit. For how could any systematic analysis of 'the unconscious' be produced wholly in separation from practices and discourses historically determined, produced as it were from a position outside and looking on? There can be no such pure, ideologically uncontaminated theoretical discourse and we have no right to expect one.

But the knife cuts both ways. For if history sets people problems only by providing at the same time the means for their resolution, the ideological saturation of psychoanalysis is precisely the condition for its analytic and political effectivity. To the extent that psychoanalysis derives from and depends upon historical conditions – from the twelfth-century Renaissance onwards, the social isolation of the apparently self-made self and the increasing abstraction of sexuality as inner truth – then to that extent it becomes able to criticise what it discovers.

Two modes of theoretical criticism can be contrasted as that of a critique and that of a deconstruction. While a critique aims to stand apart from its object, attacking it from the outside, a deconstruction seeks rather to inhabit its object, as Derrida explains:

The movements of deconstruction do not destroy structures from the outside. They are not possible and effective, nor can they take accurate aim, except by inhabiting those structures. Inhabiting them *in a certain way*, because one always inhabits, and all the more when one does not suspect it.

Operating necessarily from the inside, borrowing all the strategic and economic resources of subversion from the old structure, borrowing them structurally, that is to say without being able to isolate their elements and atoms, the enterprise of deconstruction always in a certain way falls prey to its own work. This is what the person who has begun the same work in another area of the same habitation does not fail to point out with zeal.

(1976, p. 24)

Both critique and deconstruction become possible only because each inhabits a structure, operating necessarily from a point of view which is situated, always contingent, so that both 'fall prey' to partiality and ideological contamination. But, for Derrida, the critique is liable to the error of logocentrism, of conceiving its own activity as originating in entire independence from its object (so that Jameson can follow a Marxist like Raymond Williams in condemning psychoanalysis from the outside for presupposing the universal human subject). In contrast, therefore, to a deconstruction, a critique assumes a mastery which necessarily brings with it misrecognition and self-deception, all the more so 'when one does not suspect it'.

Such dangers are sufficiently clear in Jameson's *The Political Unconscious* but they are no less evident in Foucault, particularly in those areas this present study has contested with *The History of Sexuality*, for Foucault's zeal in critique of psychoanalysis renders him insensitive to difficulties in the alternative account offered. As was noted in the discussion of Ovid and Donne, a Foucauldian account of confessional discourse is limited by its incapacity to deal substantially with the content of such discourse. It cannot deal with content because, though able to analyse the historical construction of those positions for the subject, it has no explanation of the mechanisms by which subjects come to take up that space and identify themselves in those positions: why, in other words, people should come to *want* to confess. And it lacks an account of mechanisms because it denies and seeks to supplant explanations in terms of the operation of the unconscious. In this respect (though it is not certain how exactly we should weight this), the Foucauldian analysis of social relations and the historical formation constitutes a monism whereas that put to work here in the discussion of poetry as social phantasy has ascribed to an admitted dualism by calling on two incommensurate modes of explanation from both historical material-ism and psychoanalysis.

Predicated strongly (but not exclusively) on the bourgeois subject, intimately inhabiting the structures of a particular subjectivity, psychoanalysis can only offer itself as deconstruction rather than critique. As deployed in the present study it has worked on those structures from the inside, by attending especially to two possibilities: one, the textual meanings fulfilling narcissistic wishes for the self, poetic reflections of what Lacan calls 'the mirage that renders modern man so sure of being himself'; the other, poems in which sexual phantasy is aroused and where psychoanalysis exercises a special effectivity if mobilised not as a recommendation for patriarchy but as an analysis of one.

Contestation takes place through engagement rather than at a distance; far from being a dismissal, the status of psychoanalysis as historically determined is a condition for its force as political intervention. That power inheres in psychoanalysis considered as text rather than as truth, and it is to the question of the textuality of psychoanalysis that discussion must now turn.

Psychoanalysis as text and metalanguage

In the first chapter Shoshana Felman's polemical essay was called in evidence to pose the question of psychoanalysis as metalanguage for the discussion of literature. This needs to be understood in terms of the distinction between object language and metalanguage.

Object language and metalanguage, a distinction drawn in the area of formal logic by Alfred Tarski, separates what is said in a sentence of a language – how a language is *used* – from a higher order or metalanguage in which the object language is mentioned or discussed. Thus, if I write in Navajo Indian about the linguistic properties of Modern English, Modern English is the object language and Navajo Indian is the metalanguage, seeming to stand outside and beyond English, and taking it as an object of study. The distinction obtains for this study of poetry since a total of sixteen poems and passages from longer poems have been the object of analysis and, in conjunction with the theory of ideology from historical materialism, psychoanalytic theory has functioned in the place of a metalanguage enabling texts to be discussed as social phantasy.

Poems don't interpret themselves. Initially it was argued that no interpretation of literature, no criticism of poetry, can be written except by means of a metalanguage and that psychoanalysis was a better metalanguage than that of conventional literary criticism. It is now time to consider further the possible benefits and penalties incurred by depending on this metalanguage in what has been in certain evident respects an exercise in applied psychoanalytic criticism.

For Felman the relation between psychoanalysis as metalanguage and literature as text is comparable to the relation between master and slave in the Hegelian account. But in the first place the power or authority of a metadiscourse accrues not only 'internally' from its discursive effectivity but also 'externally' from its position in different social and discursive formations, and so the effect, even of what may seem to be the 'same' ideas, is widely variable (an assertion I have tried to argue through with reference to recent French writing and the diverse significance it takes on in its contrasted reception in Britain and in the United States; see Easthope 1988).

In North American culture, for example, psychoanalysis seems to be able to rely on a conviction it misses in Britain. Given its present institutional status in Britain it is hard to imagine someone reading, for example, the discussion of *Paradise Lost* in terms of the essay by Ernest Jones on *flatus* without thinking that psychoanalysis, far from being a serious authority, had no authority at all. The conventional British academic response to psychoanalysis hardly differs from its 'common sense' reception. Psychoanalysis is taken to be fundamentally comic and in large part this ensues from the impact of a generally rationalist and systematising discourse in a traditionally empiricist culture. Psychoanalysis comes across as a self-deceived excuse for talking about the 'lower' necessities of human experience in highly abstract terminology. So in these cultural conditions the adoption of psychoanalytic discourse, far from risking the closed superiority of a metalanguage, frequently proves to be positively self-detonating. Although not reliable, the effect is deliberate and to be welcomed (especially if it erodes the habitual ideological distinctions between 'serious' and 'silly', between work and play).

Secondly, the suitability of psychoanalysis to perform as a metalanguage, written into its vocabulary and logic, lays on it the obligation – if it is used at all in literary criticism – to fulfil its promise of rigour, comprehensiveness and systematicity. Any temptation to modify the programme in the face of textual difficulties has to be resisted as far as possible. This is because any willing adaptation increases the risk of misreading and partial reading as the critic, finding in the poem what he or she desires, shapes the theory accordingly (the hypothesis of the unconscious means that such desire is in play anyway, an issue which will return here soon enough). At the same time, the aim of thorough and consistent application has its own separate effect in literary criticism. Precisely *because* it presents itself so forcibly as a rigorous and unrelentingly systematic conceptualisation, a psychoanalytic reading puts itself in question, foregrounding and drawing attention to itself as a mode of interpretation and hinting always at its possible status as rationalisation. For this reason I have been glad to avoid the softening of abstractions and liberal hesitations of conventional criticism ('it may be that . . .', 'one might think that . . .', 'it seems . . .') for these always lay covert claim to the self-evident certainties of common sense. Against appearances to the contrary, it is the systematic tone which, by acknowledging itself as a means of constructing the literary text, opens rather than closes off the discourse.

Thirdly, as a metalanguage for literary study, psychoanalysis can be criticised for trying to stand outside the texts it discusses, treating them simply as objects for a discourse whose superiority is shown in its impersonal resistance to being affected by what it analyses. But this one-way relation between psychoanalytic discourse and poetic texts has not been maintained here. Although, as was proposed in the opening chapters, psychoanalytic theory in its account of art, points away from the relatively asocial, narcissistic quality of phantasy and towards the idea of social phantasy, that has been an extension of the theoretical basis. While accepting that there is no prospect of a unified theory to comprehend both psychoanalysis and historical materialism (the burden of chapter 2), psychoanalysis *has* been modified here in response to the tradition of poetry. This has occurred in two ways.

One has been the concept of social phantasy. Because they are public, textual discourse unlike the more private expression of phantasy in dreams, poems are necessarily produced in relation to ideologies. So the proclaimed analysis of texts as the imbrication of phantasy and ideological meaning, represents a reworking of the psychoanalytic metalanguage in response to the pull of the text. To that extent it is no longer properly 'meta' in the sense that it stays unalterably superior to the attraction of the poems. This purpose has been explicit throughout. However, another sense in which the hypothesis of 'phantasy' was revised while being used has not yet been openly declared.

Psychoanalysis has found it difficult to respond to the ways modes

of subjectivity are in part historically determined. In certain passages
Freud broaches just this possibility. One was discussed at the end of
the chapter contrasting Ovid and pagan sexuality with Donne and
Christianised desire – Freud makes a historical distinction between
ancient culture in which there were (supposedly) no obstacles to
sexual satisfaction and the way the Christian era, precisely by
imposing such obstacles, created psychical values for love. Another
such contrast is made between 'Oedipus' and 'Hamlet'. In Sophocles,
Jocasta tells Oedipus not to worry about incest with the mother
because such ideas are common in men's dreams. Citing this, lines
which helped him towards conceptualising the Oedipus complex,
Freud draws on the two literary texts to argue the historical
variability of repression and of the split between conscious and
unconscious:

Another of the great creations of tragic poetry, Shakespeare's 'Hamlet', has
its roots in the same soil as 'Oedipus Rex'. But the changed treatment of the
same material reveals the whole difference in the mental life of those two
widely separated epochs of civilisation: the secular advance of repression in
the emotional life of mankind. In the 'Oedipus' the child's wishful phantasy
that underlines it is brought into the open and realised as it would be in a
dream. In 'Hamlet' it remains repressed; and – just as in the case of a neurosis
– we only learn of its existence from its inhibiting consequences. Strangely
enough, the overwhelming effect produced by the more modern tragedy has
turned out to be compatible with the fact that people have remained
completely in the dark as to the hero's character.   (*SE* IV, p. 264)

Oedipus is taken as symptom of a culture which is relatively
unrepressed, Hamlet of one in which repression and neurosis have
advanced. Without necessarily underwriting the larger cultural
critique indicated by Freud here the present study of a poetic
tradition has worked with the assumption that the 'discovery of the
individual' dramatised in poetry has constituted something very like
an 'advance of repression' for reasons which can be sketched out as
follows.

Although no structure of meaning remains immune to phantasy
and outside its effects, for Freud there is a definite polarisation
between satisfaction and phantasy (one effaced in Lacan's account of
desire): the more of one, the less of the other. This is clear in Freud's
discussion both of neurosis (in which libidinal demands take the form
of phantasies which both express wishes and defend the subject
against them) and of sublimation (a mechanism in which sexual drive

becomes able 'to exchange its originally sexual aim for another one', *SE* IX, p. 187, by being drawn into the orbit of narcissism). The history of poetry traced here has been a history of a subjectivity seeking to render itself unchallengeably self-sufficient, autonomous, transcendental, a history expressing itself at the level of the signifier in confessional discourse and at the level of the signified in phantasies of scopophilic male narcissism. That history, then, as a discovery of the individual is exactly *a history of the subject moving from satisfaction into phantasy.*

Whereas for Foucault the history of the period from the beginnings of courtly love represents sexual expression – the more discourse, the more sexuality – for a psychoanalytic perspective on the other hand, the more discourse, the more phantasy there is in the place of satisfaction. Once again when this juncture in the argument is reached, the very concept of phantasy taken as a foundational hypothesis for the analysis of a poetic tradition begins to undergo transformation. The need for it in order to engage with a specific object is vindicated at the same time and in the same logic by which its metalinguistic status is decisively undermined.

A fourth objection to psychoanalytic discourse as a metalanguage arises specifically from its application to poetry, perhaps the most serious challenge of all. Even if it is granted, as was asserted at the start, that no literary text reads itself and that criticism can only opt between competing metalanguages, it can be argued that the literary analysis must aim at the specificity of a particular text. In the development of criticism after the structuralism of the 'sixties the 'moment' of the text's specificity is signally recognised in Barthes's *S/Z* of 1970 – or rather not so much in that and the way it has generally been received as in his retrospective account, recalled in an interview. Asked about a structuralist analysis 'of the *forms* of literary discourse' Barthes replied:

In *S/Z*, I reversed this perspective: I refused the idea of a model transcendent to several texts (and thus, all the more so, of a model transcendent to every text) in order to postulate, as you said, that each text is in some sort its own model, that each text, in other words, must be treated in its difference, 'difference' being understood there precisely in a Nietzscheian or a Derridean sense. Let me put it another way: the text is ceaselessly and through and through traversed by codes, but it is not the accomplishment of a code (of, for example, the narrative code), it is not the *'parole'* of a narrative *'langue'*.
(1971, p. 44)

However, as Barthes recognises, if there can be no private language, this ideal of textual particularity can never be realised. A text wholly refusing to take place on the grounds of intertextuality, wholly self-referential and 'its own model' could not be read by anyone and would stay, in Jeremy Hawthorn's acute metaphor, like a sardine tin which contained inside the key for opening it. Quite as much as the full text, the fully specific text is an impossible object. No critical account, reading or interpretation, can escape the law of language whereby the particular can only be represented in terms of a universal. So the specificity of a text cannot be written about, interpreted, criticised, thought about or experienced at all except through a betrayal of that unique specificity.

An identical conclusion emerges if the literary text is thought of as phantasy. Theoretically, phantasy expressed as a dream has a similar specificity, which is betrayed if the particularity of the dream-work is analysed separately in terms of a manifest content under which is revealed the truth of a latent meaning (see above, pp. 10–19). But the dream-work remains private and incommunicable unless it is successively revised in translation from dream to inner speech and from there to outward, textual discourse where it acquires meaning for others. As was argued, the literary text considered as phantasy differs from a dream in that it *starts* there, having already lost its unique significance. Since therefore loss of the unique text is ineluctable for criticism, whatever its metalanguage, the question is how much is surrendered and for what purposes. Here the question of psychoanalytic discourse as a metalanguage conducts the argument back towards the purpose and political intention of a critical enterprise.

Psychoanalysis, morality and politics

Psychoanalysis can be seen as a moralising discourse. The accusation is made in Foucault's description of it as 'wonderfully effective' in giving an impetus to 'the secular injunction to study sex and transform it into discourse' but it is an old charge perfectly caught in one of J. V. Cunningham's epigrams from *The Exclusions of Rhyme*:

> The Elders at their services begin
> With paper offerings. They release from sin
> The catechumens on the couches lying
> In visions, testimonies, prophesying:
> Not, 'Are you saved?' they ask, but in informal
> Insistent query, 'Brother, are you normal?'

Cunningham's target is the practice of therapy rather than the quality of psychoanalytic writing but it can be urged, nevertheless, that the terminology of psychoanalysis conceals a morality in its avowedly abstract and scientific language, and conceals it the more insidiously because of that vocabulary.

Such an objection touches on the preceding analysis of the poetic tradition because it has underwritten the thesis that what have been identified as phantasies around masculine narcissism should be criticised and condemned. Thus, someone might argue, a subjective moral judgement has been imported surreptitiously under the guise of an objective and impartial analysis. Instances would be the use of terms such as 'narcissistic', 'regressive', 'fetishistic', and the concepts of masquerade or disguise. The objection would be clearly pointed if the question was asked bluntly: 'What is wrong with scopophilic male narcissism?'

Each of the terms cited has a technical rather than evaluative meaning. Narcissism distinguishes forms of drive which take the self as their object from those which takes others as their object. Regression, referred to frequently in the analysis of Pound's *Cantos*, is used in the temporal sense of a subject's reversion to past phases of development, an instance therefore of the wider principle of psychoanalysis that no one easily surrenders something that has once been a source of pleasure. The notion of disguise, though not formally a technical term, is often used by Freud to describe the relation between the latent and manifest content of dreams and so, in the case of phantasies, to their explicit content as subjected to secondary revision as distinct from the unconscious wishes expressed in the phantasy. The concept of mask or masquerade is more difficult. Introduced by Joan Riviere in her paper 'Womanliness as a masquerade' (1929) and borrowed by Lacan, it is not really a formal term. Lacan's account of the sexual relation as a 'masquerade' (1977a, p. 290) corresponds to the analysis of the ego as always produced in a process of misrecognition and so of 'being in love' as a mutual misrecognition in which both sexes have a role.

Each term can be given a precise definition and codified in a terminological dictionary (such as *The Language of Psycho-analysis* by Laplanche and Pontalis, 1980). Each term is intended to be as scientifically neutral as palaeolithic, femur or cumulo-nimbus. But even so it is undeniable they have moral connotations. In part this is because psychoanalysis has tinted the common sense of our century, its terminology acquiring connotations from currency in everyday discourse. And in part it follows from the close correspondence between a theoretical analysis of the unconscious and much human behaviour. If a pejorative moral meaning attaches to the idea of narcissism we might hold Ovid as much responsible as Freud for the view that excessive concern with the self is morally wrong. Strictly understood, there is nothing inherently *wrong* with regression – or any other operation of the psyche – but it is hard to imagine a society in which childhood is not generally regarded as a preparatory and therefore inferior stage to being grown up. Yet this is only a preliminary answer.

There can be no absolute or final distinction between 'fact' and 'value'. Nor, to put it in rather different terms, between ideology and the theoretical practice of a scientific discourse (which in principle in Althusser's account is a 'process without a subject'). Two examples may be pertinent. One would be the application of chemistry in the debate over 'acid rain' and the likely responsibility of Britain's industry for the destruction of forests in Northern Europe. As a scientific discourse with a precise terminology defined within a set of coherent theoretical concepts the analysis provided by chemistry of the effects of sulphur dioxide as soil acidity is objectively analytic. But it is of course a discourse deployed inevitably in conjunction with other discourses so that its applied consequences become political and not necessarily moralistic (for such reasons Lyotard's opposition between 'scientific knowledge' and 'narrative knowledge' is hard to maintain).

A second and more germane example would be the willingness of some feminist writers to draw on psychoanalysis in an attempt to examine the origins of patriarchy in the unconscious. Freud's own explicit opposition to feminism is well known, indeed notorious (see, for example, the polemic footnote in the essay on 'Female Sexuality' of 1931, *SE* XXI, p. 230). And this attitude certainly infiltrates the work, when, to give only a minor example, Freud entitles an essay 'On the universal tendency to debasement in the sphere of love' even though that debasement is discussed exclusively as a condition of men (an error of prejudice not absolved by the translation of *Allgemeinste* as 'most prevalent' rather than 'universal'). Nevertheless, the analytic rigour and impartiality of psychoanalysis remains sufficient for writers such as Juliet Mitchell and Laura Mulvey to re-read it with a very different intention, and one which has been followed here.

Poetry and Phantasy has been both descriptive and evaluative. The theoretical perspective of psychoanalysis has been deployed in a context which makes the findings of critical analysis inseparable from a judgement of them. That context ensues from the historical perspective adopted, and the evaluation is not so much moralistic as *political*. All literary criticism is inescapably 'political' though, if it is to be literary criticism at all, it is not just political. The political commitment of *Poetry and Phantasy* owes most to the perspective of historical materialism whose narrative has been assumed even if this feature has not always been sufficiently foregrounded.

In some degree this study has tried to compensate for the risk of formalism taken by *Poetry as Discourse* by setting out to explore the categories of the ideological and of phantasy in application to a specific poetic tradition (besides history and 'the personal' – and the extra-discursive – how much else is there?). To test the hypothesis that, in poetry, ideology and phantasy are imbricated as social phantasy has meant reviewing a wide range of poems from different conjunctures. This in turn has led to the problem of defining conjunctural ideologies (a problem not confined to the study of literature). Too often the topic of ideology has been 'frozen' in a provisional account – of courtly love, of Romantic ideologies, of ideology in Darwinian theory, of modernism – in order to get on to the analysis of the phantasy excited alongside them.

Nevertheless, the story told is grounded in the view that what is wrong with scopophilic male narcissism is that, while assuming 'individual' and 'social' as polarised categories, it privileges the idea of the supposedly self-made and isolated individual over the social and typically defines this individuality as a masculine mastering of the feminine. Central texts in the canon of Western poetic tradition from the twelfth century on give content and substance to this expression both in the way they reproduce ideologies and as they become occasions for phantasy. At first the effect seems progressive. The poetry of courtly love anticipates the possibility of an individual inwardness opposed to the confines of feudal order though already the cost of this transcendence is marked in the way sexual desire is sublimated into forms of self-love dependent on the figure of woman as an object fixed in place for idealisation. Poetry of the seventeenth century and Augustan period shows these structures being extended and confirmed as the feminine becomes marginalised by the male bond and a confidently patriarchal version of the father/son relation (though such confidence collapses in later eighteenth-century poetry). Romanticism signals a renewed and would-be exclusive commitment to narcissism while the poetry of Darwinism presages a crisis both for the autonomous self and traditional gender relations that becomes more fully expressed in the modernism of Eliot and Pound. Just as at the level of the signifier the tradition worked to promote the effect of a single voice really speaking, so, correspondingly, its signified content was an expression of a narcissistic individualism.

That, presented in a stark outline for the sake of the summarising argument here, is the narrative. And there are certainly other ways of telling the story. Conventional literary criticism, when it does raise its sights above the level of the individual author and the single text as (invariably) his personal experience to inspect the history of the canonical tradition, cannot but recount the gradual discovery of individual selfhood as the unfolding at last of human nature and civilisation. That version also can only describe by evaluating, by relying on an endorsement of liberal humanism that is ultimately political in implication. And, in order to remain what it is, it must continue hostile to both historical materialism and psychoanalysis, to all accounts of the self as effect of ideological construction or the process of the unconscious. As such it never has to confront the bases of its own project, either as the conscious adherence to a political perspective or as the unconscious effect in which a poetic text becomes charged with desire for readers and critics.

It has been argued here that aesthetic discourse in contrast to a dream takes place intersubjectively both in virtue of being textual discourse itself and through a shared and typical symbolism. This, it has been assumed, provides sufficient public basis on which details can be debated, cited, and called in evidence according to the conventional protocols of literary criticism. However, in using the terms 'phantasy', 'phantasy structure' and 'social phantasy' no claim has been put forward that these are necessarily the phantasies a reader actually *experiences*, and this has been kept in mind throughout by constant mention of phantasies as 'offered' to the reader. In a practice of reading the situation is not so straightforward, as can be understood quickly enough if the psychoanalytic thesis of bisexuality is recalled.

In his essay, '"A Child is Being Beaten"' (*SE* XVII, pp. 175–204), Freud argues that the same phantasy scenario of a child being beaten can provide varied positions its imaginers take up differently according to the oppositions active/passive, masculine/feminine, participant/voyeur, beater/beaten. And a textual phantasy, as John Ellis explains with reference to the cinema, in fact involves for its viewer 'multiple and shifting' points of identification (1982, p. 44). Thus a reader of a poem such as Donne's 'Elegie 19' almost certainly identifies *both* (through their active and their masculine side) with the represented male speaker as a subject *and* (through their passive and their feminine side) with the woman represented as an object for the speaker's gaze. Founded as it is in confessional discourse, the canonical poems discussed here (Pound's *Cantos* transgress the canon) either explicitly or implicitly offer themselves as the imaginings of a single, unified male speaker, a speaker who is both male and whose would-be monosexuality (masculine and only masculine) *itself* conforms to traditional male desire. In both respects, therefore, the canonical poems typically operate to constrain and fix a reader's identification even if they do not finally determine it.

It is as the texts proffer themselves that they have been analysed here, even when the analysis reveals moments at which the official strategy undoes itself, when for example Eve speaks in *Paradise Lost* (IX.820–5). There is no alternative, for who can say exactly what a reader actually comes to desire in the phantasies offered? Unlike the reader, however, the critic, by the act of writing is known to have accepted that offer.

There are three aspects of the critic's desire in the sense that literary texts have held a place as objects of that desire. They have first of all become invested, charged, otherwise they would not have been written about, and this, I would say, is especially the case with poetry. In fact unless the poems become pleasurably invested, they can't be discussed with any sympathy or insight. But the economy of that pleasure needs to be understood by analogy with the concepts of transference and counter-transference. In the therapeutic situation of psychoanalysis the analysand must undergo transference, as his or her unconscious wishes become actualised in relation to the analyst. Even so, the analyst must be aware of and must manage counter-transference, a process in which the analyst's own wishes and desires become projected onto the relation with the analysand. The literary critic, then, is positioned as both analysand and analyst, both experiencing and analysing phantasy: a double bind, therefore. The more the texts excite desire the better (potentially better) the criticism; but the more they do so, the greater the chances of an effect like counter-transference, that is, of a merely personal reading, one for which theory is only a rationalisation to deny more effectively its unconscious motivation. If, as Foucault acutely notes, psychoanalysis performs both as *scientia sexualis* and *ars erotica*, then so does literary criticism.

These reflections converge on a question that might be asked as follows: why has this study of poetry sought out for analysis expressions of scopophilic male narcissism and phantasies of patriarchal domination? There is no full answer to this but there are two replies. One is to remark that it is entirely consistent with the position taken throughout to recall that the critic also is not a source but an effect. If this analysis of poetry enacts the forms of desire it means to criticise this shows only that, no exception to the rule, the critic himself is symptomatic of a historical situation. It is a piece of additional proof that the presently dominant structures of phantasy are what they are claimed to be (for an attempt to open this question in terms of contemporary popular culture, see Easthope 1986). And of course it reveals how literary criticism is itself a form of social phantasy.

But it is social phantasy in a second respect as well. Literary criticism differs from psychoanalytic therapy in being primarily textual discourse and so more like the relation of poem and reader than that of analyst and analysand. Whatever may be the case of the critic's desire for the poem, the critical writing is public and intended for others. *Poetry and Phantasy* operates within the hermeneutic of literary criticism, evidencing its argument through a close reading of fictive texts. Although the book has worked hard to deal openly with the theoretical perspective in which those readings are produced, no full, programmatic justification could be given for the validity of these readings outside the readings themselves. How far they remain arbitrary or personal rather than a means to increase the systematic understanding of poetry can only be judged from the extent to which they become shared, acknowledged, disputed. Whatever closure is imposed on the poetic texts by the readings, these take on value only if they open the texts for reading by others.

TEXTS

'Maiden in the mor lay', in *English Verse 1300–1500*. Ed John Burrow (Longman Annotated Anthologies of English Verse, vol. I). London: Longman, 1965.

Amores 1.5, in *P. Ovidi Nasonis: 'Amores'*. Ed. E. J. Kenney. Oxford: Clarendon Press, 1961.

'Elegy 19', in *The Poems of John Donne*. Ed. Herbert J. C. Grierson. 2 vols. Oxford: Clarendon Press, 1912.

'Elegia 5' (translation of Ovid), in *The Complete Works of Christopher Marlowe*. Ed. Fredson Bowers. 2 vols. Cambridge: Cambridge University Press, 1973.

'Can vei la lauzeta mover', in *Bernard de Ventadour: Chansons d'amour*. Ed. Moshé Lazar. Paris: Libraire C. Klincksieck, 1966.

'Rime 190', in *Petrarch's Lyric Poems: The 'Rime Sparse' and Other Lyrics*. Ed. Robert M. Durling. Cambridge, Mass.: Harvard University Press, 1976.

'Who so list to hounte', in *Collected Poems of Sir Thomas Wyatt*. Ed. Kenneth Muir and Patricia Thomson. Liverpool: Liverpool University Press, 1969.

Paradise Lost, in *The Poetical Works of John Milton*. Ed. Helen Darbishire. London: Oxford University Press, 1958.

Absalom and Achitophel, in *The Poems and Fables of John Dryden*. Ed. James Kinsley. London: Oxford University Press, 1962.

The Rape of the Lock, in *The Poems of Alexander Pope*. Ed. John Butt. London: Methuen, 1963.

'To a Skylark', in *The Complete Works of Percy Bysshe Shelley*. Ed. Thomas Hutchinson. London: Oxford University Press, 1960.

In Memoriam, Maud, in *The Poems of Tennyson*. Ed. Christopher Ricks. 3 vols. 2nd edn. London: Longman, 1987.

'Dover Beach', in *The Poems of Matthew Arnold*. Ed. Kenneth Allott. 2nd edn. Miriam Allott. London: Longman, 1979.

The Waste Land, in *Collected Poems, 1909–1962*. T. S. Eliot. London: Faber, 1963.

'The Pisan Cantos', in *The Cantos of Ezra Pound*. Revised collected edn. London: Faber, 1975.

REFERENCES

Abercrombie, N., Hill, S., and Turner, B.S., 1980. *The Dominant Ideology Thesis*. London: Allen and Unwin.

Allott, Kenneth and Allott, Miriam, 1979. *Arnold: Poems*. London: Longman.

Althusser, Louis, 1977. *Lenin and Philosophy*. Tr. Ben Brewster. London: New Left Books.

Althusser, Louis and Balibar, Etienne, 1975. *Reading Capital*. Tr. Ben Brewster. London: New Left Books.

Appleyard, J. A., 1965. *Coleridge's Philosophy of Literature*. Cambridge, Mass.: Harvard University Press.

Armstrong, Isobel, 1982. *Language as Living Form in Nineteenth-Century Poetry*. Brighton: Harvester.

Arnold, Matthew, 1956. 'The study of poetry' (1880), in *Essays in Criticism*. Second series. London: Macmillan, pp. 1–33.

Bakhtin, Mikhail (V. N. Voloshinov), 1973. *Marxism and the Philosophy of Language* (1929). Tr. Ladislav Matejka and I. R. Titunik. New York: Seminar Press.

   1976. *Freudianism, A Marxist Critique* (1927). Tr. I. R. Titunik. New York: Academic Press.

Barker, Francis, 1984. *The Tremulous Private Body*. London: Methuen.

Barsani, Leo, 1978. *A Future for Astynax*. London: Marion Boyars.

Barsby, John A. (ed.), 1973. *Ovid's Amores, Book One*. London: Oxford University Press.

Barthes, Roland, 1964. *On Racine*. Tr. Richard Howard. New York: Hill and Wang.

   1971. 'A conversation with Roland Barthes', in *Signs of the Times: Introductory Readings in Textual Semiotics*. Ed. S. Heath, C. MacCabe and C. Prendergast. Cambridge: Granta, pp. 41–51.

Bédier, Joseph, 1896. 'Les Fêtes de mai et les commencements de la poésie lyrique au Moyen Age', *Revue des deux mondes*, 135 (May), pp. 146–72.

Beer, Gillian, 1983. *Darwin's Plots*. London: Routledge and Kegan Paul.

Belsey, Catherine, 1985. *The Subject of Tragedy: Identity and Difference in Renaissance Drama*. London: Methuen.

   1988. *John Milton*. Oxford: Basil Blackwell.

214

Bloom, Harold, 1963. *The Visionary Company*. New York: Anchor Books. 1969. *Shelley's Mythmaking*. Ithaca: Cornell University Press.

Boase, Roger, 1977. *The Origin and Meaning of Courtly Love*. Manchester: Manchester University Press.

Brecht, Bertolt, 1977. 'Against Georg Lukács', in *Aesthetics and Politics*. Tr. Stuart Hood. London: New Left Books, pp. 68–85.

Bredvold, Louis I., 1956. *The Intellectual Milieu of John Dryden*. Ann Arbor: University of Michigan Press.

Brenkman, John, 1976, 'Narcissism in the text', *Georgia Review*, 30, 2 (Summer), pp. 293–327.

Broadbent, John, 1964. *Poetic Love*. London: Chatto and Windus.

Brooks, Cleanth, 1968. *The Well-Wrought Urn. Studies in the Structure of Poetry*. Rev. edn. London: Dennis Dobson.

Brown, Nathaniel, 1979. *Sexuality and Feminism in Shelley*. Cambridge, Mass.: Harvard University Press.

Bryson, Norman, 1983. *Vision and Painting: the Logic of the Gaze*. London: Macmillan.

Buckley, J. H., 1960. *Tennyson, The Growth of a Poet*. London: Oxford University Press.

Burrow, John (ed.), 1977. *English Verse, 1300–1500*. London and New York: Longman.

Cameron, K. N., 1974. *Shelley, The Golden Years*. Cambridge, Mass.: Harvard University Press.

Chernaik, Judith, 1972. *The Lyrics of Shelley*. Cleveland: The Press of Case Western University.

Chiòrboli, Ezio (ed.), 1924. *Petrarcha: Le Rime Sparse*. Milan: Trevisini.

Clancier, Anne, 1973. *Psychanalyse et critique littéraire*. Toulouse: Edoard Privat.

Coleridge, Samuel Taylor, 1854. *The Statesman's Manual* (1817), in *Complete Works*. Ed. W. G. T. Shedd. 7 vols. New York: Harper and Bros. 1859. *Aids to Reflection* (1825). London: Edward Moxon.

1949. *Biographia Literaria* (1817). Ed. J. Shawcross. 2 vols. London: Oxford University Press.

1956. *Collected Letters of Samuel Taylor Coleridge*. Ed. Earl Leslie Griggs. 6 vols. London: Oxford University Press.

Cormican, L. A., 1960. 'Milton's religious verse', in Boris Ford (ed.), *Pelican Guide to English Literature*. Harmondsworth: Penguin, vol. 3, pp. 173–92.

Cosslett, T., 1982. *The 'Scientific Movement' and Victorian literature*. Brighton: Harvester.

Craig, David, 1960. 'The defeatism of *The Waste Land*', *Critical Quarterly*, 2, 3 (Autumn), pp. 241–52.

Davie, Donald, 1967. *Purity of Diction in English Verse*. London: Routledge and Kegan Paul.

Dekker, George, 1963. *Sailing After Knowledge: the Cantos of Ezra Pound*. London: Routledge and Kegan Paul.

de Man, Paul, 1983. *Blindness and Insight*. 2nd rev. edn. Manchester: Manchester University Press.

Denomy, A. J., 1947. *The Heresy of Courtly Love*. New York: Declan X. McMullen.

de Rougement, Denis, 1956. *Passion and Society*. Rev. edn. Tr. Montgomery Belgion. London: Faber.

Derrida, Jacques, 1976. *Of Grammatology*. Tr. Gayatri Chakravorty Spivak. Baltimore: Johns Hopkins University Press.

1981a. *Dissemination*. Tr. Barbara Johnson. London. Athlone Press.

1981b. *Positions*. Tr. Alan Bass. London: Athlone Press.

Docherty, Thomas, 1986. *John Donne Undone*. London: Methuen.

Donaldson, E. Talbot, 1970. 'Patristic exegesis in the criticism of medieval literature: the opposition', in *Speaking of Chaucer*. Ed. E. Talbot Donaldson. London: Athlone Press, pp. 134–53.

Dowling, William C., 1984. *Jameson, Althusser, Marx*. London: Methuen.

Dronke, Peter, 1968. *Medieval Latin and the Rise of the European Love-Lyric*. Rev. edn. 2 vols. London: Oxford University Press.

du Quesnay, M. Le M., 1973. 'The Amores', in *Ovid*. Ed. J. W. Binns. London: Routledge and Kegan Paul.

Durant, Alan, 1981. *Ezra Pound, Identity in Crisis*. Brighton: Harvester.

Durling, Robert M., 1976. 'Preface', in *Petrarch's Lyric Poems, The Rime Sparse and Other Lyrics*. Tr. Robert M. Durling. Cambridge, Mass.: Harvard University Press.

Eagleton, Terry, 1970. *Exiles and Émigrés*. London: Chatto and Windus.

1978. 'Tennyson: politics and sexuality in "The Princess" and "In Memoriam"', in *1848: The Sociology of Literature*. Ed. F. Barker *et al.* Colchester: University of Essex, pp. 97–106.

1982. *The Rape of Clarissa*. Oxford: Basil Blackwell.

1983. *Literary Theory. An Introduction*. Oxford: Basil Blackwell.

1984. *The Function of Criticism*. London: Verso.

Easthope, Antony, 1982. 'Poetry and the politics of reading', in *Re-Reading English*. Ed. P. Widdowson. London: Methuen, pp. 136–49.

1983. *Poetry as Discourse*. London: Methuen.

1986. *The Masculine Myth in Popular Culture*. London: Paladin.

1987a. 'Towards the autonomous subject in poetry: Milton "On his Blindness"', in *Post-Structuralist Readings of English Poetry*. Ed. R. Machin and C. Norris. Cambridge: Cambridge University Press, pp. 122–33.

1987b. 'Jokes and ideology: "The Frogs" and "Earnest"', *New Comparison*, 3 (Summer), pp. 117–32.

1988. *British Post-Structuralism: Since 1968* London: Routledge.

Edwards, J. H. and Vasse, W. W., 1971. *Annotated Index to the Cantos of Ezra Pound*. Los Angeles: University of California Press.

Eliade, Mircea (ed.), 1987. *The Encyclopaedia of Religion*. New York: Macmillan, vol. 15.

Eliot, T. S., 1957. *On Poetry and Poets*. London: Faber.

1961. *Selected Essays*. 3rd ed. London: Faber.

1971. *The Waste Land: A Facsimile and Transcript of the Original Drafts*. Ed. Valerie Eliot. London: Faber.

Ellis, John, 1982. *Visible Fictions: Cinema, Television, Video*. London: Routledge and Kegan Paul.

Ellman, Maud., 1979. 'Floating the Pound: the circulation of the subject of "The Cantos" ', *Oxford Literary Review*, 3, 3, pp. 16–27.

Elster, Jon, 1985. *Making Sense of Marx*. Cambridge: Cambridge University Press.

Empson, William, 1961. *Seven Types of Ambiguity* (1930). Harmondsworth: Penguin.

Everett, Barbara, 1975. 'Eliot in and out of *The Waste Land*', *Critical Quarterly*, 17, 1 (Spring), pp. 7–50.

Felman, Shoshana, 1977. 'To open the question', in S. Felman (ed.), *Literature and Psychoanalysis, The Question of Reading: Otherwise, Yale French Studies*, 55/56, pp. 5–10.

Fineman, Joel E., 1986. *Shakespeare's Perjured Eye: The Invention of Poetic Subjectivity in the Sonnets*. Berkeley: University of California Press.

Fish, Stanley E., 1967. *Surprised by Sin: The Reader in Paradise Lost*. London: Macmillan.

Forrester, John, 1980. *Language and the Origins of Psychoanalysis*. London: Macmillan.

Foucault, Michel, 1979. *Discipline and Punish*. Tr. Alan Sheridan. Harmondsworth: Penguin.

1980. *Power/Knowledge, Selected Interviews and Other Writings*. Ed. Colin Gordon. Brighton: Harvester.

1981. *The History of Sexuality. Vol. 1: An Introduction*. Tr. Robert Hurley. Harmondsworth: Penguin.

1984. *Histoire de la sexualité*; vol. 2, *L'Usage des plaisirs*; vol. 3, *Le Souci de soi*. Paris: Gallimard.

Freccero, John, 1975. 'The fig tree and the laurel: Petrarch's poetics', *Diacritics*, 5 (Spring), pp. 34–40.

Freud, Sigmund, 1953–74. *The Standard Edition of the Complete Psychoanalytic Works*. Tr. James Strachey. 24 vols. London: Hogarth Press and the Institute of Psycho-Analysis. (Abbrev.: *SE*).

Froula, Christine, 1983. 'When Eve reads Milton: undoing the canonical economy', *Critical Inquiry*, 10, 2 (December), pp. 321–47.

Gadamer, Hans-George, 1975. *Truth and Method*. Tr. G. Barder and J. Cunningham. New York: Seabury Press.

Gardner, Helen (ed.), 1965. *John Donne: 'The Elegies' and 'The Songs and Sonnets'*. London: Oxford University Press.

1982. *In Defence of the Imagination*. London: Oxford University Press.

Gilbert, Sandra and Gubar, Susan, 1979. *The Madwoman in the Attic: The Woman Writer and the Nineteenth-Century Literary Imagination*. New Haven: Yale University Press.

Gilson, Étienne, 1934. *La théologie mystique de Saint Bernard*. Paris: Liège.

Gliserman, Susan, 1975. 'Early Victorian science writers and Tennyson's "In Memoriam": a study in cultural exchange', *Victorian Studies*, 18, 3 (March), pp. 277–308, and 18, 4 (June), pp. 437–59.

Goldin, Frederick, 1967. *The Mirror of Narcissus in the Courtly Love Lyric*. Ithaca: Cornell University Press.

Green, André, 1979. *The Tragic Effect*. Tr. Alan Sheridan. London: Cambridge University Press.

Greenblatt, Stephen, 1980. *Renaissance Self-Fashioning from More to*

Shakespeare. Chicago: University of Chicago Press.

Hartman, Geoffrey H., 1978. 'Psychoanalysis: the French connection', in Geoffrey H. Hartman (ed.), *Psychoanalysis and the Question of the Text* (Selected Papers for the English Institution, 1976–77, New Series, 2). Baltimore: Johns Hopkins University Press, pp. 86–113.

Heath, Stephen, 1974. 'Lessons from Brecht', *Screen*, 15, 2 (Summer), pp. 103–29.

    1976. *'Anata mo'*, *Screen*, 17, 4 (Winter), pp. 49–66.

    1981. *Questions of Cinema*. London: Macmillan.

    1982. *The Sexual Fix*. London: Macmillan.

Hegel, G. W. F., 1969. *Hegel's Science of Logic*. Tr. A. V. Miller. London: Allen and Unwin.

Hill, T. D., 1979. 'The fool on the bridge: "Can vei la lauzeta mover" Stanza 5', *Medium Aevum*, 48, 2, pp. 198–200.

Hillis Miller, J., 1975. *The Disappearance of God*. Cambridge, Mass.: Harvard University Press.

Hirst, Paul Q., 1979. *Law and Ideology*. London: Macmillan.

Hirst, Paul Q. and Woolley, Penny, 1982. *Social Relations and Human Attributes*. London: Tavistock.

Holland, Norman, 1968. *The Dynamics of Literary Response*. New York: Oxford University Press.

Hough, Graham, 1947. 'The natural theology of *In Memoriam*', *Review of English Studies*, 33, pp. 244–56.

    1960. *Image and Experience*. London: Duckworth.

Huizinga, Johan, 1955. *The Waning of the Middle Ages*. Harmondsworth: Penguin.

Hunter, George, 1980. *Paradise Lost*. London: Allen and Unwin.

Hussain, Athar, 1981. 'Foucault's "History of Sexuality"', *m/f*, 5/6, pp. 169–91.

Jakobson, Roman, 1960. 'Concluding statement: linguistics and poetics', in *Style in Language*. Ed. T. A. Sebeok. Cambridge, Mass.: MIT Press, pp. 350–77.

Jameson, Fredric, 1979. *Fables of Aggression: Wyndham Lewis, the Modernist as Fascist*. Berkeley: University of California Press.

    1981. *The Political Unconscious*. London: Methuen.

    1984. 'Postmodernism, or the cultural logic of late capitalism', *New Left Review*, 146 (July/August), pp. 53–92.

    1986. 'Religion and ideology: a political reading of *Paradise Lost*' in F. Barker *et al.* (eds.), *Literature, Politics and Theory*. London: Methuen, pp. 35–56.

Jones, Ernest, 1951. 'The Madonna's conception through the ear', in *Essays in Applied Psychoanalysis*. London: Hogarth Press, vol. 2, pp. 266–357.

    1953–7. *Sigmund Freud: Life and Works*. 3 vols. London: Hogarth Press.

Kendrick, Christopher, 1986. *Milton: A Study in Ideology and Form*. New York: Methuen.

Kenner, Hugh, 1964. *The Invisible Poet: T. S. Eliot*. New York: Citadel Press.

King-Hele, Desmond, 1960. *Shelley, His Thought and Work*. London: Macmillan.

Klein, Melanie, 1973. 'Some theoretical conclusions regarding the emotional life of the infant', in *Developments in Psycho-Analysis* (1952). Ed. Joan Riviere. London: Hogarth.

Knight, G. Wilson, 1943. *The Starlit Dome*. London: Oxford University Press.

Koëhler, Erich, 1964. 'Observations historiques et sociologiques sur la poésie des troubadours', *Cahiers de civilisation médiévale*, 7, pp. 27–51.

Lacan, Jacques, 1977a. *Ecrits*. Tr. Alan Sheridan. London: Tavistock.

  1977b. *The Four Fundamental Concepts of Psycho-Analysis*. Tr. Alan Sheridan. London: Hogarth Press.

  1977c. 'Desire and interpretation of desire in *Hamlet*', tr. James Hulbert, *Yale French Studies*, 55/56, pp. 11–52.

  1982. *Feminine Sexuality: Jacques Lacan and the 'école freudienne'*. Ed. J. Mitchell and J. Rose. London: Macmillan.

Laplanche, J., and Pontalis, J.-B., 1980. *The Language of Psycho-Analysis*. Tr. D. Nicholson-Smith. London: Hogarth Press and the Institute of Psycho-Analysis.

Lazar, Moshé, 1964. *Amour courtois et 'fin amors' dans la littérature de XIIe siècle*. Paris: Librairie C. Klincksieck.

Leavis, F. R., 1964. *Revaluation, Tradition and Development in English Poetry* (1936). Harmondsworth: Penguin.

  1972. *New Bearings in English Poetry*. Harmondsworth: Penguin.

Lentricchia, Frank, 1980. *After the New Criticism*. London: Athlone Press.

Lever, J. W., 1978. *The Elizabethan Love Sonnet*. London: Methuen.

Lewis, C. S., 1973. *The Allegory of Love* (1936). London: Oxford University Press.

Lukács, Georg, 1963. *The Meaning of Contemporary Realism* (1958). Tr. John and Necke Mander. London: Merlin Press.

  1971. *History and Class Consciousness* (1923). Tr. Rodney Livingstone. London: Lawrence and Wishart.

Lyotard, Jean-François, 1984. *The Postmodern Condition: A Report on Knowledge*. Tr. Geoff Bennington and Brian Massomi. Manchester: Manchester University Press.

MacCabe, Colin, 1981. 'On discourse', in *The Talking Cure*. Ed. C. MacCabe. London: Macmillan, pp. 188–217.

McFadden, George, 1978. *Dryden, The Public Writer 1660–1685*. Princeton: Princeton University Press.

Macherey, Pierre, 1978. *A Theory of Literary Production*. Tr. Geoffrey Wall. London: Routledge and Kegan Paul.

Marcus, Steven, 1984. *Freud and the Culture of Psychoanalysis*. Boston: Allen and Unwin.

Marx, Karl, 1954. *The Eighteenth Brumaire of Louis Bonaparte* (1852). Moscow: Progress.

  1973. *Grundrisse* (1953). Tr. Martin Nicolaus. Harmondsworth: Penguin.

  1974. *Capital*. 3 vols., (1867). Tr. Samuel Moore and Edward Aveling. London: Lawrence and Wishart.

  and Engels, Frederick, 1950. *Selected Works*. 2 vols. London: Lawrence and Wishart.

1970. *The German Ideology* (1846). Ed. and tr. C. J. Arthur. London: Lawrence and Wishart.

Mason, H. A., 1969. *Humanism and Poetry in the Early Tudor Period.* London: Routledge and Kegan Paul.

Matthiessen, F. O., 1968. *The Achievement of T. S. Eliot* (1935). London: Macmillan.

Mauss, Marcel, 1979. 'A category of the human mind: the nature of person, the nature of "self" ', in *Sociology and Psychology.* Tr. Ben Brewster. London: Routledge and Kegan Paul.

Merchant, Carolyn, 1982. *The Death of Nature: Women, Ecology, and the Scientific Revolution.* San Francisco: Harper Row.

Milner, Andrew, 1981. *John Milton and the English Revolution.* London: Macmillan.

Minta, Stephen, 1980. *Petrarch and Petrarchism, The English and French Tradition.* Manchester: Manchester University Press.

Mitchell, Juliet, 1975. *Psychoanalysis and Feminism.* Harmondsworth: Penguin.

Montefiore, Janet, 1983. 'Feminist identity and the poetic truth', *Feminist Review.* 13 (Spring), pp. 69–84.

Morris, Colin, 1972. *The Discovery of the Individual, 1050–1200.* London: SPCK.

Mulvey, Laura, 1975. 'Visual pleasure and narrative cinema', *Screen*, 16, 3 (Autumn), pp. 6–18.

Nassar, Eugene P., 1975. *The Cantos of Ezra Pound, The Lyric Mode.* London: Johns Hopkins University Press.

Nicholls, Peter, 1984. *Ezra Pound: Politics, Economics and Writing.* London: Macmillan.

Pêcheux, Michel, 1982. *Language, Semantics and Ideology.* Tr. Harbans Nagpal. London: Macmillan.

Perrin, Jean, 1973. *Les Structures de l'imaginaire Shelleyan.* Grenoble: Presses Universitaires de Grenoble.

Pinkney, Tony, 1984. *Women in the Poetry of T. S. Eliot.* London: Macmillan.

Pitman, Ruth, 1973. 'On *Dover Beach*', *Essays in Criticism*, 22, 2 (April), pp. 109–36.

Popper, Karl, 1969. *Conjectures and Refutations: The Growth of Scientific Knowledge.* London: Routledge and Kegan Paul.

Pound, Ezra, 1963a. *Ezra Pound: Translations.* New York: New Directions. 1963b. *The Literary Essays of Ezra Pound.* London: Faber. 1970. *Ezra Pound, A Critical Anthology.* Ed. J. P. Sullivan. Harmondsworth: Penguin.

Priestley, F. E. L., 1973. *Language and Structure in Tennyson's Poetry.* London: André Deutsch.

Rabaté, Jean-Michel, 1986. *Language, Sexuality and Ideology in Ezra Pound's 'Cantos'.* Albany: State University of New York Press.

Ramsey, Paul, 1969. *The Art of John Dryden.* Lexington: University of Kentucky Press.

Rapaport, Herman, 1983. *Milton and the Postmodern.* Lincoln: University of Nebraska Press.

Ray, William, 1984. *Literary Meaning: From Phenomenology to Deconstruction*. Oxford: Basil Blackwell.

Reiman, Donald H., 1976. *Percy Bysshe Shelley*. London: Macmillan.

Ricks, Christopher, 1972. *Tennyson*. London: Macmillan.

Riviere, Joan, 1929. 'Womanliness as a masquerade', *International Journal of Psychoanalysis*, 10, pp. 303–13.

Robertson, D. W., Jr., 1950. 'Historical criticism', *English Institute Essays*. Columbia University Press, pp. 3–31.

   1968. 'The concept of courtly love as an impediment to the understanding of medieval texts', in *The Meaning of Courtly Love*. Ed. F. X. Newman. Albany: State University of New York Press, pp. 1–15.

Roper, Alan, 1965. *Dryden's Poetic Kingdoms*. London: Routledge and Kegan Paul.

Roppen, Georg, 1956. *Evolution and Poetic Belief* (Oslo Studies in English 5). Oslo: Oslo University Press.

Rose, Jacqueline, 1981. 'The Imaginary', in *The Talking Cure*. Ed. C. MacCabe. London: Macmillan, pp. 132–61.

Saussure, Ferdinand de, 1959. *Course in General Linguistics* (1915). Tr. Wade Baskin. New York: Philosophical Library.

Schiller, J. C. F. von, 1967. *On the Aesthetic Education of Man*. Tr. E. M. Wilkinson and L. A. Willoughby. Oxford: Clarendon Press.

Schneider, E. S., 1953. *Coleridge, Opium and 'Kubla Khan'*. Chicago: University of Chicago Press.

Shatto, Susan and Shaw, Marion (eds.), 1982. *Tennyson: 'In Memoriam'*. London: Oxford University Press.

Shelley, P. B., 1965. *The Complete Works of Percy Bysshe Shelley*. Ed. R. Ingpen and W. E. Peck. 10 vols. London: Ernest Benn.

Sinfield, Alan, 1971. *The Language of Tennyson's 'In Memoriam'*. Oxford: Basil Blackwell.

   1986. *Alfred Tennyson*. Oxford: Basil Blackwell.

Southall, Raymond, 1973. *Literature and the Rise of Capitalism*. London: Lawrence and Wishart.

Stallybrass, Peter, and White, Allon, 1986. *The Politics and Poetics of Transgression*. London: Methuen.

Stead, C. K., 1964. *The New Poetic*. Harmondsworth: Penguin.

Sulloway, Frank, 1980. *Freud, Biologist of the Mind*. London: Fontana.

Tennyson, Hallam, 1897. *Alfred Lord Tennyson: A Memoir by his Son*. 2 vols. London: Macmillan.

Thomas, W. K., 1978. *The Crafting of 'Absalom and Achitophel'*. Waterloo: Wilfred Laurier University Press.

Thompson, John O., 1980. *Echo and Montana*. Edmonton: Longspoon Press.

Thomson, Patricia, 1964. *Sir Thomas Wyatt and his Background*. Stanford: Stanford University Press.

Timpanaro, Sebastiano, 1976. *The Freudian Slip*. Tr. Kate Soper. London: New Left Books.

Trilling, Lionel, 1953. *The Liberal Imagination*. New York: Anchor Books.

Vickers, Nancy, 1982. 'Diana described: scattered women and scattered rhyme', in *Writing and Sexual Difference*. Ed. Elizabeth Abel. Brighton: Harvester, pp. 95–109.

Vygotsky, L. S., 1962. *Thought and Word*. Tr. E. Hanfmann and G. Vakar. Cambridge, Mass.: MIT Press.

Wasserman, Earl R., 1964. 'The English Romantics: the grounds of knowledge', *Studies in Romanticism*, 4, 1, pp. 17–34.

Webb, Timothy (ed.), 1977. *Percy Bysshe Shelley: Selected Poems*. London: Dent.

Weber, Samuel, 1982. *Legend of Freud*. Minneapolis: University of Minnesota Press.

Wellek, René, 1963. 'Romanticism re-examined', in *Romanticism Reconsidered*. Ed. N. Frye. New York: Columbia University Press, pp. 107–33.

Widdowson, Peter (ed.), 1982. *Re-Reading English*. London: Methuen.

Williams, Raymond, 1958. *Culture and Society*. London: Chatto and Windus.

1973. *The Country and the City*. London: Chatto and Windus.

1979. *Politics and Letters*. London: New Left Books.

Wordsworth, Ann, 1981. 'An art that will not abandon the self to language: Bloom, Tennyson and the blind world of the wish', in *Untying the Text: a Post-Structuralist Reader*. Ed. Robert Young. London: Routledge and Kegan Paul.

Wordsworth, William, 1947. *The Poetic Works*. 5 vols. Ed. E. de Selincourt and Helen Darbishire. London: Oxford University Press.

Wordsworth, W. and Coleridge, S. T., 1959. *The Lyrical Ballads, 1798–1805*. Ed. G. Sampson. London: Methuen.

Wright, Elizabeth, 1984. *Psychoanalytic Criticism*. London: Methuen.

Zingarelli, N. (ed.), 1964. *Le Rime di Francesco Petrarcha*. Bologna: Zanichelli.

INDEX

223